SENTENCE MATTERS

with
Sentence Exercises
Proofreading Passages
Writing Assignments

R. Kent Smith

University of Maine

Pearson
Education

PRENTICE HALL, Englewood Cliffs, New Jersey 07632

Library of Congress Cataloging-in-Publication Data
SMITH, R. KENT.
   Sentence matters : with sentence exercises, proofreading passages,
   writing assignments / R. Kent Smith.
      p. cm
   Includes index.
   ISBN 0-13-319039-0
   1. English language—Sentences—Problems, exercises, etc.
   2. English language—Grammar—Problems, exercises, etc. I. Title.
PE1441.S55 1994
428.2—dc20   93-31526
                                          CIP

Editorial production/supervision
  and interior design: F. Hubert
Prepress buyer: Herb Klein
Manufacturing buyer: Bob Anderson
Cover design: Design Source

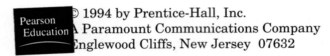

© 1994 by Prentice-Hall, Inc.
A Paramount Communications Company
Englewood Cliffs, New Jersey 07632

Printed in the United States of America

10 9 8 7 6 5 4 3 2

ISBN   0-13-319039-0

PRENTICE-HALL INTERNATIONAL (UK) LIMITED, *London*
PRENTICE-HALL OF AUSTRALIA PTY. LIMITED, *Sydney*
PRENTICE-HALL CANADA INC., *Toronto*
PRENTICE-HALL HISPANOAMERICANA, S.A., *Mexico*
PRENTICE-HALL OF INDIA PRIVATE LIMITED, *New Delhi*
PRENTICE-HALL OF JAPAN, INC., *Tokyo*
SIMON & SCHUSTER PTE. LTD., *Singapore*
EDITORA PRENTICE-HALL DO BRASIL, LTDA., *Rio de Janeiro*

Contents

Preface

TO THE INSTRUCTOR

Each chapter of *Sentence Matters* contains three major sections:

A. **Establishing the Background** clearly presents the essential information about a practical sentence matter.

B. **Gaining the Experience** contains effective exercises to deepen as well as to measure understanding of the sentence matter; an answer key in the back of the text lets students evaluate most of their work.

C. **Applying the Finishing Touch** contains two passages to proofread with the specific sentence matter in mind; this section also contains an engaging writing assignment.

As the **Table of Contents** discloses, *Sentence Matters* addresses issues relating to clarity as well as correctness. The **Instructor's Manual,** in addition to including answers to all of the exercises and proofreading passages, contains teaching suggestions, a comprehensive pretest, chapter tests, mastery tests after every fourth chapter, and a comprehensive posttest.

Writing Assignments. To encourage students to write in creative ways and in authentic voices, imaginative writing assignments are included. These assignments provide students opportunities to engage in all of the writing stages. They also require students to **compare, contrast, relate, interpret, discriminate, define, conclude, imagine, and struggle**—the types of intellectual challenges they will encounter in college and in their careers. The **LONG-RANGE ASSIGNMENTS,** pages 291–292, also provide excellent opportunities for students to learn worthwhile, often intriguing, information, and they lend themselves to both individual and collaborative efforts as they require purposeful, well-done research.

To ensure students have the freedom to develop their **own writing strategies and voices,** introductions, thesis statements, topic sentences, transitions, conclusions, and the like are not emphasized; instead, **clarity, details, and originality** are encouraged. General suggestions, however, are provided for both the chapter and long-range assignments, and, of course, additional advice can be presented during individual conferences.

Students also benefit when they have a clear understanding of the expressions included in the **GLOSSARY OF WRITING TERMS,** pages 345–354, so it is worthwhile to discuss these terms with them when appropriate opportunities arise; the same is true of **WRITING SUGGESTIONS and PROOFREADING TIPS,** pages 293–295. Students also profit from a discussion of the **TO THE STUDENT** remarks in the section immediately following.

However, students benefit the most as writers when they are given sufficient opportunities and freedom to develop their own writing strategies and to discover their own writing voices. The challenging writing assignments in this text can provide students with the opportunities and freedom they need to become effective, confident writers.

TO THE STUDENT

Writing is often described as a process embracing stages of activities like these:

PREWRITING . . . generating and refining ideas through brainstorming, freewriting, interviewing, and researching

WRITING . . . developing a central message, relevant content, and logical organization through the writing of exploratory drafts focused upon audience, purpose, and tone

REWRITING . . . improving the clarity and fluency of the drafts by adding, removing, and rearranging content

EDITING . . . proofreading the final draft for sentence correctness, including spelling, usage, and punctuation

In reality, the stages and activities of the process are not as distinct, exclusive, or orderly as the description suggests. When we write, we blend, reverse, repeat, discard, ignore, and devise elements of the process to fit our purposes and writing style.

Though we are free to manipulate the writing process to fit our needs, putting the editing stage in the final position has this major advantage: **our thoughts remain focused on our topic.** Such concentration permits us to address our chief concerns, particularly that of developing a clear, central message. If, on the other hand, we enter the editing stage too early in the process, our thoughts become distracted from our topic, and our writing becomes inhibited because of a premature concern about correctness.

However, editing's concluding position does not diminish its role in the writing process for this important reason: **a paper's effectiveness is as dependent upon error-free sentences as it is upon appropriate content.** This is true because a paper marred by sentence errors diverts attention from the content, regardless of its impressiveness. In fact, readers may put aside a poorly edited paper after a paragraph or two, assuming writing flawed by errors is probably flawed in content as well.

Despite its importance, proofreading for sentence correctness is often neglected or poorly done. Some writers lack either the will or the patience for this concluding activity; others, however, simply lack the background to proofread well. If the latter is true of you, *Sentence Matters* will provide the knowledge and techniques you need.

Each chapter, featuring three distinct sections, contains information and activities helpful for mastering a specific sentence concern; mastery of each concern will ensure the correctness and clarity of your sentences. Another feature of each chapter is that one of the proofreading exercises is usually about one of the first sixteen U.S. presidents, thus broadening your background of history while developing your proofreading skills. In addition, the unique writing assignments engage you in the entire writing process while permitting you to develop your own writing strategies and point of view. The **LONG-RANGE ASSIGNMENTS,** listed on pages 291–292, will also enable you to gain valuable research experience.

After completing *Sentence Matters,* you will have acquired writing skills and experiences useful not only in your other courses but also in your private life and professional career.

ACKNOWLEDGMENTS

I am most appreciative of the following instructors for their conscientious reviews of and suggestions for this book: Margot Brandes, Bergen Community College; Dr. Donna R. Cheney, Weber State University; Kim Flachmann, California State–Bakersfield; John Alfred White, Jefferson Community College; Gary N. Christensen, Macomb Community College; and Barbara Dicey, Wallace College.

Words of deep gratitude also to the following people associated with Prentice Hall: Edward Francis and Phil Miller for their initial interest and encouragement regarding the text, Carol Wada for her insightful suggestions and skilled editing, and Frank Hubert for his essential contributions during all stages of the text's publication.

Special thanks to the editor of *Clavier Piano Explorer* magazine for permission to adapt "On the Bench with Bob Cousy" (January, 1988), and to Harvey Klinger, Inc., for permission to adapt "The Road," a passage from *Run with the Horsemen* by Ferrol Sams (1985).

I am indebted to Stephanie Graves for her typing and Shawn Smith for his computer assistance, and I am especially grateful to my students, colleagues, and family for their interest, suggestions, encouragement, and patience throughout the development and completion of this text.

CHAPTER ONE
Subjects and Verbs

A. ESTABLISHING THE BACKGROUND

SUBJECTS

To avoid a number of common writing errors, it is essential to understand subjects and verbs, the basic building blocks of sentences.

> The subject is who or what is being talked about in the sentence.

The subject is always a *noun* or *pronoun;* that is, the subject is either a person, place, or thing (*noun*) or a word that stands for one of the preceding (*pronoun*). Common *pronouns* include she, he, her, him, we, us, you, me, they, them, it, who, whom.

The underlined words are subjects in these sentences:

(person—noun)	Jennifer announced her engagement.
(person—pronoun)	She announced her engagement.
(place—noun)	Iowa is a Midwestern state.
(place—pronoun)	It is a Midwestern state.
(things—noun)	The chairs were brought to the stage;
(things—pronoun)	they were arranged in a semicircle.

The subject can be singular, plural, or compound:

(singular)	<u>Reggie</u> was playing basketball in the park.
(plural)	My <u>friends</u> were playing basketball in the park.
(compound)	<u>Reggie</u> and <u>Nathan</u> were playing basketball in the park.
(compound and plural)	My <u>friends</u> and <u>neighbors</u> were playing basketball in the park.

Do Exercises 1 and 2 in Section B before continuing.

SUBJECTS AND PREPOSITIONAL PHRASES

Sentences often contain prepositional phrases, which are groups of words containing helpful information about subjects, verbs, and other important words. These phrases begin with a preposition, which is then followed a word or two later by a noun (a person, place, or thing). Remember this important point: *the noun in a prepositional phrase is* <u>never</u> *the subject of a sentence.*

In the following sentences, the subject is underlined and the prepositional phrase is in parentheses.

<u>People</u> (of this city) have always supported the public schools.

<u>One</u> (of the children) fell off the slide.

(During the talk), <u>Andy</u> took notes.

That large <u>package</u> (on the table) is for Glen.

Remember: The nouns following prepositions are never the subjects of sentences.

These sixteen familiar words are among those that frequently function as prepositions:

above	below	for	on
across	beside	from	over
before	by	in	to
behind	during	of	with

Do Exercise 3 in Section B.

VERBS

> The verb in the sentence tells either what the subject does (action verb)
> or what the subject is or was (being verb).

In the following sentences, the subjects are underlined once and the verbs twice.

(action verb)	The <u>airplane</u> <u><u>cruised</u></u> at 18,000 feet.
(action verb)	After the lightning, <u>thunder</u> <u><u>boomed</u></u>.
(being verb)	Our <u>college</u> <u><u>is</u></u> 150 years old.
(being verb)	Yesterday, <u>Mark</u> <u><u>was</u></u> in the chemistry lab for five hours.

As is true of subjects, verbs can also be plural or compound, as illustrated by these sentences:

(plural)	After four years and countless trips to the dentist, Brian's <u>teeth</u> <u><u>are</u></u> now perfect.
(plural)	<u>Troy</u> and <u>Lois</u> <u><u>practice</u></u> their ice skating routines early every morning.
(compound)	<u>Wanda</u> <u><u>washed</u></u> and <u><u>waxed</u></u> her Sunbird on Saturday.
(compound)	During the day, <u>Zachary</u> <u><u>coughed</u></u> and <u><u>sneezed</u></u> as his cold worsened.

Do Exercises 4 and 5 in Section B. ⟶

HELPING VERBS

The complete verb in some sentences consists of a helping verb as well as a main verb. In each of the examples, the complete verb is underlined twice, with **H** identifying the helping verb and **M** the main verb.

<u>Bob</u> <u><u>must mow</u></u> the lawn before he goes away for the weekend.

My little <u>brother</u> <u><u>has delivered</u></u> the morning paper for six months.

$\overset{H}{\underline{\text{might}}} \overset{H}{\text{have}} \overset{M}{\text{sung}}$

Brenda might have sung a solo earlier in the concert.

$\overset{H}{\underline{\text{will}}} \overset{M}{\text{finish}}$

The plumber will finish his work by this afternoon.

These are among the most commonly used helping verbs:

am	does	ought to, ought to
are	had	have
be, being	has	shall, shall have
been	have, having	should, should have
can	is	was
could, could have	may, may have	were
did	might, might have	will, will have
do	must, must have	would, would have

Do Exercises 6 and 7 in Section B. ⟶

ORDER OF SUBJECTS AND VERBS

English, unlike many languages, depends upon <u>word order</u> to indicate each word's function in the sentence. For example, these two sentences contain the same words but in a different order, resulting in opposite meanings because "horse" is the first sentence's subject and "man" is the second's:

      subject   verb   object
The horse carried the man.

      subject   verb   object
The man carried the horse.

The basic word order of the English sentence is SUBJECT-VERB-OBJECT, as the preceding sentences indicated. Sometimes, instead of an object (a noun or pronoun) a complement (a noun or adjective) is used, but the basic pattern is the same:

      subject verb complement
Della felt happy.

Other words, phrases, and clauses are usually added to the S-V-O or S-V-C framework to modify (describe, clarify, elaborate) one of the three basic elements, but the pattern remains the same:

                  sub   verb   object
In the park, two old men were raking wet leaves.

Occasionally, however, the order is reversed, most commonly in sentences beginning with There, Here, or in sentences asking questions. For example, notice the subject-verb order in the following sentences; the subjects are underlined once and the verbs twice:

There are eggs in the refrigerator.

There still was snow in the mountains in July.

Here comes Katie for her music lesson.

Here is the car of your dreams.

Did you see the movie?

Have Jim and Tony gone to work?

Unless English is your second language, you usually do not have to be concerned with word order as you will naturally use the S-V-O or some other common pattern correctly. Remember this chapter's most important point:

> A sentence must contain a subject and verb.

Do Exercise 8 and the Review Exercise in Section B.

Exercise 5: *Underline the subjects once and the verbs twice; if the sentence contains a preposi-*
tional phrase, put parentheses around it.

1. The beautiful antique dish crashed to the floor.
2. In the darkened bedroom, a sick child tossed and turned.
3. The mail is late.
4. The phone in the kitchen suddenly disturbed the blessed silence.
5. My cat and dog are good buddies.
6. For Jeff, spring and summer were the best seasons.
7. Felix sang and danced in the talent show.
8. The flash of the camera startled the young man.
9. Against all odds, Sam and Joyce planned and built their own house.
10. The restaurant's coffee was lukewarm.

Exercise 6: *Underline the subject once and the complete verb twice, putting* <u>H</u> *above the help-*
ing verb and <u>M</u> *above the main verb.*

1. Roy should have found his car keys by now.
2. Except for Peter, everyone was wearing black sneakers.
3. Haley has bought a used car for less than a thousand dollars.
4. Mildred and Art are searching through the file cabinet.
5. Mike has forgotten her telephone number.

NAME _____   DATE _____

Exercise 7: *Supply logical helping verbs for the main verbs.*

1. Dave and Rhonda _____ coming to dinner this evening.
2. Sylvester, my old cat, _____ gone for three days.
3. If she _____ not twisted her ankle, Terri _____ won the race.
4. _____ you study before supper?
5. Michael, you _____ play on our team any time you like!

Exercise 8: *Underline the subjects once and the verbs twice.*

1. There are some envelopes in the desk.
2. By the way, here is your wallet.
3. How did Joe get the job?
4. Did you ask the gas attendant for directions?
5. There is evidence of dangerous bacteria in this well water.
6. What do you think of our boss?
7. Here are the coupons from today's newspaper.
8. Why are you leaving now?
9. Was Elliot at the party?
10. In the driveway was a shiny new motorcycle.

NAME _____ DATE _____

Chapter 1
Review Exercise: *Underline the subjects once and the verbs twice. Be mindful of prepositional phrases and helping verbs.*

1. Ted and Diane have bought a puppy.
2. Rodney scraped, primed, and painted the front fenders of his car.
3. The members of our club raised money for the Ossinger Community Center.
4. In the afternoon, Dan often took a nap.
5. Did your team win the game?
6. Before morning, snow and sleet blanketed the entire state.
7. Elaine's opinion on that issue is well-known.
8. There are several golf courses and tennis courts open to the general public.
9. Do you really believe in astrology?
10. Martha and Bob operate a crafts store in Flemington, New Jersey.
11. Here is the tape for the package.
12. The police authorities in our city have started a softball league.
13. The logs in the fireplace burned with a hissing sound.
14. We had planned to make the trip to Washington, D. C., by AMTRAK.
15. How did you fix the stove?
16. Georgia and Florida are growing rapidly in population.
17. There is my bus across the street.
18. After lunch, Jessie bicycled for a couple of hours.
19. After gluing the chair's rungs, Marsha applied the clamps.
20. Does anyone know those two guys?
21. Looking embarrassed, Adam apologized to Eve for forgetting to dress.
22. A few passengers got off the plane in Manchester.
23. In the hushed courtroom, a startling story was unfolding.
24. Throughout the game, some obnoxious fans near me screamed at the referees.
25. With a courageous wave to his parents, the young boy stepped aboard the bus.
26. The ill-conceived plan was sharply criticized by the city council.

NAME _____   DATE _____

27. According to eyewitnesses, the driver of the maroon car was driving on the wrong side of the highway.

28. Unfortunately, three players on our team were sick with the flu.

29. Have you ever traveled overseas?

30. There were two phone calls for you during your lunch hour.

31. At the end of intermission, the auditorium's lights flicked off and on three times.

32. On what day of the week is Christmas this year?

33. Except for five people, everyone attended our first class reunion.

34. Hundreds of people called the radio station to ask for the latest weather forecast.

35. By next fall, a shopping center and a motel will be built and opened along this stretch of the highway.

C. APPLYING THE FINISHING TOUCH

(1) Proofreading: *Underline the subjects once and the verbs twice in each sentence. Check your choices with those in the **Answer Key.***

Birth of the Presidency

(1) During the spring and summer of 1787, fifty-five delegates from the thirteen states met in Philadelphia to make some badly needed revisions in the Articles of Confederation. (2) Because of this document's numerous shortcomings, however, the delegates eventually agreed an entirely new proposal was needed. (3) Their efforts led to the development of the remarkable Constitution of the United States.

(4) Among the unique features of the Constitution was the establishment of the presidency. (5) After learning of this feature, many citizens throughout the young nation became alarmed. (6) Would an American president actually differ from a British monarch? (7) They objected, for example, to the president having authority to make treaties, grant pardons, and to appoint public officials. (8) The president also controlled the armed forces, a disturbing prospect for many people.

(9) How were such fears and objections regarding the presidency overcome? (10) The answer lies in the exemplary conduct of the first president. (11) George Washington adhered to the Constitution and respected the rights of the other branches of government. (12) The understandable fears and objections about the presidency quietly disappeared as a result.

NAME _____   DATE _____

(2) Proofreading: *Underline the subjects once and the verbs twice in each sentence. Your instructor will check your work.*

The White House

(1) Unquestionably one of the most popular tourist attractions in the United States, the White House attracts more than one and a half million tourists each year. (2) The White House contains 132 rooms, and (3) it is situated in the middle of eighteen beautifully landscaped acres at 1600 Pennsylvania Avenue, Washington, D. C.

(4) In 1800, John Adams, the second president, and his wife Abigail became the first occupants of the White House. (5) Thomas Jefferson made numerous improvements to the White House and its grounds during his administration. (6) In 1814, during the War of 1812, the British burned the White House, forcing Dolley Madison to flee. (7) The building was rebuilt and finally reoccupied by President James Monroe and his family in December, 1817.

(8) Through the years, numerous additions and improvements have been made to the White House. (9) However, there have also been years of wear and periods of neglect. (10) In fact, in 1948 during President Harry S. Truman's administration, complete restoration of the White House was found to be necessary.

(11) Jacqueline Kennedy, wife of President John F. Kennedy, persuaded Congress to designate the White House a national museum. (12) This led to the restoration of much of the White House's interior. (13) This project was completed in 1962.

NAME _____   DATE _____

(14) A home as well as an office, the White House evokes memories of the many presidents who have lived and worked within its walls. (15) It is no wonder, then, that this historic house attracts thousands of tourists every week of the year.

Writing: Select **one** of the following questions to write about:

- **Who would understand you the best: a ballet dancer, a hockey player, a choir director, or a cattle farmer?**
- **Who do you think will be the next male and female heartthrobs?**

Suggestions: **JOT DOWN** for twenty minutes or so your initial reactions to the question you have selected; at this stage, keep writing as long as you can, accepting <u>what</u> you write as well as <u>how</u> you write.

READ what you have written; see if there are ideas you could develop.

WRITE AGAIN until your central point and main ideas start coming into focus.

WRITE AND REVISE until your central point and main ideas are stated simply and clearly.

CONCENTRATE on supporting your central point and main ideas with specific evidence; your final draft should be <u>dominated</u> by reasons, details, and examples.

COMPLETE your writing over several days; write and rewrite until you are satisfied with what you have written.

REMEMBER, your major challenge is to make sure your central point is supported with <u>specific</u> as well as <u>sufficient</u> evidence.

LIMIT your final draft to two <u>typed</u> and <u>doublespaced</u> pages.

PROVIDE as interesting a title as you can.

PROOFREAD, making certain all sentences contain subjects and verbs and all words are spelled correctly; check **PROOFREADING TIPS,** page 295, for additional suggestions.

Your instructor may have you select
one of the **LONG-RANGE ASSIGNMENTS,** pages 291–292,
to do over the next few weeks;
if so, be sure to look over
the **WRITING SUGGESTIONS,** pages 293–294,
before, while, and after working on this more extensive assignment.

CHAPTER TWO

Fragments

A. ESTABLISHING THE BACKGROUND

> Fragments are word groups lacking subjects or verbs or failing to express complete thoughts.

Speaking in fragments usually doesn't cause problems because our listeners can ask us for clarification if they don't understand. However, when we write fragments, misunderstandings can happen since our readers are unable to ask us questions.

Fragments often occur in the beginning stages of our writing when our attention is rightly focused upon ideas, not upon the "rules" of writing. In fact, attention to fragments and similar matters can wait until we proofread, which is the final step in the writing process for most writers.

When we proofread our sentences for fragments, we need to be alert to these possible omissions:

Missing Subject

Felt the game was lost. (<u>Who</u> felt the game was lost?)

Goes to at least three movies a week. (<u>Who</u> goes to at least three movies a week?)

> *Note:* <u>You</u> can be the implied subject of a sentence:
>
> *Be sure to check the tent for holes.* (<u>You</u> *be sure to check the tent for holes.*)

Also note that phrases and words usually functioning as verbs can be the subject of a sentence:

<u>To play</u> *golf with Ralph is an adventure.*

<u>Painting</u> *is Jennifer's favorite hobby.*

Missing Verb

Our boss friendly to all customers.   (Where's the verb? <u>Friendly</u> is an adjective [descriptive word], not a verb.)

Otis attempting to gain weight for football.

She being snobbish to her old friends.   (Be careful of <u>-ing words</u>; they require **helping verbs:** *Otis* <u>is</u> *attempting to gain weight for football,* and *She* <u>is</u> *being snobbish to her old friends.* A different form of the verb can also be used when appropriate: *Otis* <u>attempted</u> *to gain weight for football.* Also, there are times when *being* can be omitted: *She is snobbish to her old friends.*)

Do Exercise 1 in Section B before continuing.
⟶

DEPENDENT CLAUSE FRAGMENTS

A <u>clause</u> is a group of words containing both a subject and a verb. There are <u>independent</u> clauses, usually called sentences, and <u>dependent</u> clauses, also called <u>subordinating</u> clauses.

Study the differences between the following independent and dependent clauses:

independent clause:	His <u>car</u> <u>was</u> low on gas.
dependent clause:	Although his <u>car</u> <u>was</u> <u>low</u> on gas

Note both clauses have the same subject and verb; however, only the independent clause expresses a complete thought. The word "Although" that begins the dependent clause makes it necessary to have additional information before a full understanding is possible. Therefore, <u>dependent clauses by themselves are fragments.</u>

Dependent clauses, to express complete thoughts, <u>must</u> be attached either before, within, or after independent clauses (sentences) as in these examples:

dependent clause
[Although his car was low on gas], Rick didn't stop at a station.

dependent clause
Rick, [although his car was low on gas], didn't stop at a station.

dependent clause
Rick didn't stop at a station [although his car was low on gas].

dependent clause
The woman [who lives next door] is the owner of a furniture store.

dependent clause
They are renting an apartment [that is two blocks from campus].

When one of these words, called <u>subordinating conjunctions</u>, is followed by a subject and verb, the dependent clause that results must be joined to a sentence to avoid writing a fragment:

after	even if	when
although	if	whenever
as	since	whether
because	that	which
before	unless	while
even though	until	who

Remember: Dependent clauses do not express complete thoughts even though they contain subjects and verbs, so they must be attached either before, within, or after independent clauses (sentences).

Do Exercise 2 in Section B.
→

PHRASE AND CONTEXT FRAGMENTS

A phrase is a word group that adds important or interesting information to a basic sentence, as we have seen in our work with prepositional phrases. Unlike a clause, a phrase <u>never</u> contains both a subject and a verb; therefore,

All phrases not attached to a sentence are fragments.

Here are examples of phrase fragments:

(prepositional phrase)	Frank would like to see you. <u>In the evening.</u>
(infinitive phrase)	Gabe skips lunch every day. <u>To go swimming.</u>
(participial phrase)	<u>Frowning repeatedly.</u> Don was obviously upset.
(gerund phrase)	<u>Running five miles daily.</u> Takes discipline.

As you can readily see, phrase fragments can be corrected by attaching them to a neighboring sentence or to the remainder of the sentence:

Frank would like to see you in the evening.

Gabe skips lunch everyday to go swimming.

Frowning repeatedly, Don was obviously upset.

Running five miles daily takes discipline.

<u>Context fragments</u> result when we assume the subject and verb in a previous sentence provide the meaning needed for the word group we have written:

I still enjoy many of the sports I played in high school. <u>Especially basketball.</u>

My folks have done a lot to our house the past two years. <u>Such as adding a family room and remodeling the kitchen.</u>

I like all seasons of the year. <u>Including winter.</u>

Sharon has a number of interesting collections. <u>For example, Coca-Cola bottles, antique clocks, and turn-of-the-century postcards.</u>

Casey and Kurt are working at the paper mill. <u>Also Martin.</u>

Fragments of this type are easy to write because we unconsciously assume the context of what we have written is adequate for what follows. We need to remember, however, that a word group standing by itself requires a subject and verb and must provide a clear meaning. Context fragments, like phrase fragments, can often be corrected by attaching them to the adjacent sentence:

I still enjoy many of the sports I played in high school, especially basketball.

My folks have done a lot to our house the past two years, such as adding a family room and remodeling the kitchen.

I like all seasons of the year, including winter.

At times, you may prefer to correct context fragments by adding subjects and verbs:

Sharon has a number of interesting collections. For example, she has collections of old Coca-Cola bottles, antique clocks, and turn-of-the-century postcards.

Casey and Kurt are working at the paper mill; Martin is also working there.

Do Exercise 3 and the Review Exercise in Section B.

Chapter 2
Review Exercise: *If the following word groups are sentences, put* **+** *in the space; if they are fragments, put* **O.**

_____ 1. Thinking he should get to work on time for a change, Brad set his alarm for six o'clock.

_____ 2. The Hawkeyes eventually won the game. Tom being surprised by that outcome.

_____ 3. Betty's teeth are in perfect condition. Because she has gone regularly to the dentist.

_____ 4. To stand all day is exhausting.

_____ 5. I thought all the actors did a marvelous job. Especially Anita as the heiress.

_____ 6. Loretta, who I've known for over three years, is a thoughtful friend. For example, she never forgets my birthday.

_____ 7. Taking scenic pictures is David's favorite pastime.

_____ 8. I enjoy owning a car. Although it's expensive.

_____ 9. Olga friendly, cheerful, and considerate. Nevertheless, she seems to lack sincerity.

_____ 10. Throughout the years, the Procters have planted a variety of trees on their property. Such as maple, pine, willow, and ash.

_____ 11. Knocked the lamp over after leaping onto the table.

_____ 12. Gunning the car for all it was worth, Seth reached the emergency room in a matter of minutes. He was greatly relieved to discover his daughter was not seriously injured.

_____ 13. After John prepared the charcoal grill in the backyard.

_____ 14. I believe Norma should be hired. For one thing, she has the proper training.

_____ 15. Then on the third day, reached Salt Lake City.

_____ 16. Doris jumping in the air with joy. Mark was simply smiling from ear to ear.

_____ 17. Leona being the one chosen as captain.

_____ 18. Bill paid all of his bills before leaving in the morning.

_____ 19. If someone calls while I'm gone, please get the person's number. So I can call back.

_____ 20. Feeling alone and homesick, Jason wondered why in the world he had joined the navy.

NAME _____ DATE _____

_____ 21. As time went by, Carrie seldom wrote or called her old high school friends. Except for Samantha.

_____ 22. We soon learned to stand at attention every time our sergeant entered our barracks.

_____ 23. I bought the car on an impulse. Fortunately, no regrets.

_____ 24. Keith enjoyed the biology courses he had taken. But still wasn't sure if he wanted to major in this subject.

_____ 25. Television commentators that seem to think they have all the answers to the world's problems.

_____ 26. Eric's leather jacket, which looks comfortably worn, is brand new.

_____ 27. Turn right on Chapel Hill Road. Right after Alexander Boulevard.

_____ 28. Do you have sunglasses? The sun is really bright today.

_____ 29. Jennifer owns a lot of jewelry. For example, twelve pairs of earrings.

_____ 30. Professor Norton said the test would be postponed until next week. Which we all appreciated, I think.

_____ 31. Yes, I admit it. You were right. I was wrong.

_____ 32. To raise money for college is a challenge for most students.

_____ 33. Fred being the one selected. However, no one complained because he will be a fine representative for our organization.

_____ 34. I'm sorry if you don't believe Rachel, but she told you the truth.

_____ 35. When we heard the good news and the weather improved.

NAME _____   DATE _____

C. APPLYING THE FINISHING TOUCH

(1) Proofreading: *After correcting the eight fragments, rewrite the entire passage on a separate piece of paper. Check your work with that in the* ***Answer Key.***

George Washington: First President, 1789–1797

George Washington was born in 1732 at a Virginia plantation. He apparently received little formal education, but he did learn surveying. At the age of sixteen, joined a surveying group sent to the Shenandoah Valley by Lord Fairfax. For the next few years, Washington conducted surveys in the frontier area. Particularly Virginia and what is now West Virginia.

Washington was commissioned a lieutenant colonel in 1754, and he saw action in the French and Indian War. In one battle, he escaped injury. Although four bullets tore through his coat and two horses were shot from under him.

In 1759, Washington married Martha Dandridge Curtis. A wealthy widow with two children. Until the outbreak of the American Revolution, he managed his lands around Mount Vernon and was involved in Virginia politics.

When the Second Continental Congress met in Philadelphia in May, 1775, Washington was selected as Commander-in-Chief of the Continental Army. After taking command of his poorly trained troops, Washington was confronted with a number of severe problems. Especially supplies.

NAME _____   DATE _____

Eventually, however, Washington fashioned a well-trained army and overcame the other problems as well.

After the Revolutionary War, which lasted six grueling years. Washington returned to his Mount Vernon estate. However, he soon realized the nation was not functioning well under its Articles of Confederation. Therefore, he joined other national leaders in taking steps leading to the Constitutional Convention in Philadelphia in 1787. After the Constitution was ratified by the states, Washington was elected president.

Weary of politics and feeling old, Washington retired. At the end of his second term. He enjoyed less than three years of retirement at Mount Vernon. For he died on December 14, 1799.

NAME _____   DATE _____

(2) Proofreading: *After correcting the fragments, rewrite the entire passage on a separate piece of paper. Your instructor will check your work.*

The Road

Getting to and from school was as much an adventure as learning to read and write. The dirt road was so narrow that there were many places where meeting cars had to take turns. The hills steep, the ditches precipitous and deep. In the valley between two of these steep hills flowed a creek. With a wooden bridge just at water-level.

In rainy spells, the creek rose over the bridge, overflowed its banks, and formed a shallow muddy torrent. Which covered the entire roadbed for approximately two hundred feet. It took a skilled driver indeed to sight between the tops of inundated bushes and roadside weeds accurately enough to maintain an automobile precisely in the center of the road. So the valley could be safely crossed.

It also took shrewd guesswork, dextrous hands. And cold courage. To navigate the invisible bridge. With water swirling above the hubcaps, a driver realized that a slip off the edge would mean submersion in the channel of the creek.

NAME _____   DATE _____

Writing: *Defend or challenge one of these statements:*

- **Macho does not prove mucho.**
- **The important point about sports is that they are unimportant.**

Suggestions: **JOT DOWN** for twenty minutes or so your immediate reactions to the statement you have selected; keep writing as long as you can, accepting <u>what</u> you write as well as <u>how</u> your write.

READ what you've written a number of times; look for statements reflecting your feelings.

WRITE AGAIN, focusing on those statements; keep writing until a central point and some main ideas emerge.

WRITE AND REVISE until you've stated your central point and main ideas clearly.

CONCENTRATE on supplying <u>plenty</u> of specific reasons and concrete examples to back up your views; your reasons and examples will determine whether your opinions are convincing.

BUDGET your time over the next several days so you can read, reflect, and rewrite if necessary.

LIMIT your paper to <u>one complete page</u>, typed and doublespaced.

PROVIDE a short, snappy title.

PROOFREAD for fragments and misspellings, and check **PROOFREADING TIPS,** page 295, for other suggestions.

If you are working on one of the **LONG-RANGE ASSIGNMENTS,**
pages 291–292, be sure to spend some time on it as well.

The **WRITING SUGGESTIONS,** pages 293–294,
should prove helpful to you.

CHAPTER THREE

Run-Ons

A. ESTABLISHING THE BACKGROUND

When two sentences are joined to form a compound sentence, appropriate punctuation must be used; otherwise, a run-on, which blurs clear meaning, is the result.

One type of run-on, a fused sentence, occurs when two sentences are joined with no punctuation:

The table lamp was turned on   the food was served.
Howard planted the bulbs   Virginia covered them with dirt.

A more frequent type of run-on than the fused sentence is the comma splice, a run-on that occurs when two sentences are joined with only a comma:

The table lamp was turned on, the food was served.

Howard planted the bulbs, Virginia covered them with dirt.

Do Exercises 1 and 2 in Section B.

Commas <u>alone</u> are inadequate for joining sentences; instead, sentences should be joined in one of these ways:

● **comma followed by a coordinating conjunction** *(and, but, so, or, for, nor, yet)*:

> *The table lamp was turned on,* **so** *the food was served.*
>
> *Howard planted the bulbs,* **and** *Virginia covered them with dirt.*

● **semicolon (;):**

> *The table lamp was turned on; the food was served.*
>
> *Howard planted the bulbs; Virginia covered them with dirt.*

● **semicolon followed by an adverbial conjunction*** *(such as then, however, therefore, consequently, furthermore)* **which in turn is usually, but not always, followed by a comma:**

> *The table lamp was turned on;* **therefore,** *the food was served.*
>
> *Howard planted the bulbs;* **then** *Virginia covered them with dirt.*

Do Exercises 3, 4, and 5 in Section B. ⟶

There is also the option of expressing the information in a <u>complex</u> sentence rather than in a compound one. A <u>complex sentence</u> is formed by joining an independent clause (sentence) with a dependent clause (fragment). Observe how the information in the preceding compound sentences is presented in complex ones:

>   **dependent clause**   **independent clause**
> **<u>After</u> *the table lamp was turned on, the food was served.*   (Notice a comma alone <u>can</u> be used to join dependent and independent clauses.)

---

*The following are commonly used adverbial conjunctions: *however, therefore, consequently, thus, then, furthermore, also, nevertheless, otherwise, in addition, on the other hand, instead, meanwhile, moreover, as a result.*

**Words used to introduce dependent clauses are known as *subordinating conjunctions;* a list of such words and an explanation of clauses are contained in Chapter Two.

independent clause   *dependent clause*

Howard planted the bulbs <u>while</u> *Virginia covered them with dirt.* (No comma is generally needed between the clauses <u>if</u> the *dependent* clause comes <u>last</u>.)

Do Exercise 6 in Section B.

Finally, of course, there is the option of keeping the sentences separate rather than combining them into a compound sentence:

The table lamp was turned on. The food was served.
Howard planted the bulbs. Virginia covered them with dirt.

Do Exercises 7 and 8 and the Review Exercise in Section B.

B. GAINING THE EXPERIENCE

Exercise 1: *Draw a vertical line between the sentences (independent clauses) in the following run-ons. An example has been done for you.*

Example: Frank won't be coming | he has to work late.

1.   Nancy realized that she had been rude she apologized to the clerk.

2.   The movie is said to be funny surprisingly, even Bob recommends seeing it.

3.   Naturally, we were impressed with the Grand Canyon it's an awesome sight.

4.   Blake loves his old Oldsmobile, he washes and waxes it constantly.

5.   After a spring rain, many birds gather on our large lawn searching for worms they generally stay for hours.

6.   Come if you like we have room.

7.   Karen majored in English her first two years in college her degree is in journalism, however.

8.   I know Ted's proud of you, don't you think he should be?

9.   The boss shouted to get Fred's attention he couldn't hear him, however, because of all the noise at the construction site.

10.   You should always be careful not to tailgate other drivers in front of you may have to stop abruptly.

11.   Everyone asked my parents appreciated each person's concern.

12.   Dennis plans to get in good shape running every day is the way he intends to accomplish this goal.

13.   The Rockets won the key to victory was their unselfish teamwork.

14.   The game was canceled because of the heavy snowfall it has been rescheduled for Saturday.

15.   The flight was assigned the crew selected was elated.

16.   Moving the furniture aggravated Toby's sore back reluctantly, he asked Larry to help him.

17.   Scott called the landlord is coming tomorrow.

18.   Her letter of recommendation was impressive her personality was not that dynamic, however.

19.   We ice-skated for hours the pond's surface was like glass.

20.   No one believed the tale was too incredible.

NAME _____   DATE _____

Exercise 2: *In the space, write C for a correct sentence, FS for a fused sentence, and CS for a comma splice.*

_____ 1. Sheila owns a videocassette, she seldom goes to movies.

_____ 2. My neighbor's flower garden is beautiful; mine, on the other hand, is full of weeds.

_____ 3. The telephone was ringing, and someone was pounding on the door.

_____ 4. The fire glowed, the children began toasting marshmallows.

_____ 5. After the fire glowed, the children began toasting marshmallows.

_____ 6. Rick didn't change the flat tire there was no spare in the trunk.

_____ 7. Mindy was flabbergasted, she hadn't expected a letter from Duncan.

_____ 8. I've loved the Boston Red Sox since I was in the fourth grade.

_____ 9. Rita has a beautiful voice, we heard her sing at church.

_____ 10. When an emergency occurred at work, Wendy was the one who took care of it.

_____ 11. I'm sorry isn't there someone you can call?

_____ 12. Jerry phoned; the news was good.

_____ 13. Jennifer is here for the holidays, but her brother is stationed overseas, so he will be unable to come home.

_____ 14. Everyone sat around the pool the water was too cold for swimming.

_____ 15. A large truck was parked in front of Hudson Hardware; consequently, traffic was delayed on Mills Street.

_____ 16. Rumor has it that Bill is moving a college in Florida has apparently offered him a football scholarship.

_____ 17. The stereo was blaring away, everyone could hear it.

_____ 18. The stereo was blaring away; everyone could hear it.

_____ 19. The stereo was blaring away, so everyone could hear it.

_____ 20. Nothing disturbed Roger, he was the first one to finish the work.

_____ 21. If you'll work for me Friday evening, then I'll work for you Saturday morning.

_____ 22. Brenda thinks she's met him she's not sure, however.

_____ 23. In the morning, Eric begins his enlistment in the marines.

_____ 24. Angela, come here; are you really serious about this matter?

_____ 25. Your decision is wrong, I understand, however, why you made it.

NAME _____ **DATE** _____

6. *(unless—1)*   Bob can improve his defense the coach will bench him.

_____

_____

7. *(when—1)*   The fire whistle blew in the small community volunteer firefighters got to the fire station as quickly as they could.

_____

_____

8. *(since—2)*   Barry has acquired two rare Canadian stamps he attended last month's stamp meeting at the community center.

_____

_____

9. *(because—1)*   Don is easy to get along with I like him as a roommate.

_____

_____

10. *(until—1)*   Stephanie sprained her ankle last week she was jogging two miles a day.

_____

_____

11. *(until-2)*   Stephanie was jogging two miles a day she sprained her ankle last week.

_____

_____

12. *(because—2)*   I took the bus to work my car wouldn't start.

_____

_____

Exercise 7:   *Correct the following run-ons by separating them with either a period or a question mark. Two examples have been done for you.*

Examples: The school's lights were on snow blew across the deserted playground.

The school's lights were on. Snow blew across the deserted playground.

NAME _____   DATE _____

When did Paula and Rick arrive, I haven't seen them since last spring.

<u>When did Paula and Rick arrive? I haven't seen</u>
<u>them since last spring.</u>

1. In the morning, Erica leaves for New Mexico, she has always wanted to visit Santa Fe and Taos.

   _____

   _____

2. Didn't you know that Jepperson's Landscaping was hiring summer help I thought everyone home from college was aware of that fact.

   _____

   _____

3. Mrs. Elliott opened the shutters the brilliant morning sun streamed into the room.

   _____

   _____

4. Mr. Burnell, one of my neighbors, is ninety-years-old he's in remarkably good health.

   _____

   _____

5. Water from the melting snow gushed down the mountainside, there was no immediate danger of flooding in the area, however.

   _____

   _____

6. Megan, what college does your fiancé attend the newspaper would like to include that information in your engagement announcement.

   _____

   _____

7. The bus schedule has been changed for the most part, I still find it convenient to ride the bus to work.

   _____

   _____

NAME _____ **DATE** _____

8. How many states have you been in, I counted up the other day, and I've been in thirty-eight states.

    _____

    _____

9. Doug is extremely considerate to his grandparents, he takes them to their doctor and dentist appointments, does chores around their house, and does most of their grocery shopping.

    _____

    _____

10. Hot dogs, baked beans, and brown bread are a traditional Saturday night meal in New England did you know that?

    _____

    _____

Exercise 8:   *Correct each run-on by using the method indicated in parentheses. Two examples have been done for you.*

Examples: *(semicolon, adverbial conjunction)*   Ralph's videocassette recorder wasn't working properly, we couldn't watch the movies that we had rented for the weekend.

Ralph's videocassette recorder wasn't working properly; therefore, we couldn't watch the movies we had rented for the weekend.

(subordinating conjunction)   John is obviously upset with me I don't know why.

John is obviously upset with me although I don't know why.

1. *(comma, coordinating conjunction)*   I split the cord of wood Josh stacked it against one of the basement's walls.

    _____

    _____

2. *(semicolon)*   It was a hot, humid day Scott couldn't wait to go swimming.

    _____

    _____

NAME _____   DATE _____

3. *(period)*   Dad stopped by Miller's Drugstore to buy a copy of the <u>New York Times</u> he does this every Sunday morning after church.

_____

_____

4. *(subordinating conjunction)*   We played hockey for a couple of hours we went to Karl's Pub for pizzas.

_____

_____

5. *(semicolon, adverbial conjunction)*   Rita's ankle was badly swollen x-rays indicated that it was not broken.

_____

_____

6. *(question mark)*   When was the last time you had a dental check-up, you have a number of cavities.

_____

_____

7. *(subordinating conjunction)*   Stella had her receipt for the merchandise the courteous young clerk promptly refunded her money.

_____

_____

8. *(semicolon)*   David has a bad case of the flu the doctor prescribed antibiotics, fluids, and bedrest.

_____

_____

9. *(semicolon, adverbial conjunction)*   Margaret grew up on a large vegetable farm in New Jersey, she's knowledgeable about gardening.

_____

_____

10. *(comma, coordinating conjunction)*   The Hawks were the favorites to win the regional tournament the Bears upset them in the very first game.

_____

_____

NAME _____   DATE _____

Chapter 3
Review Exercise: A. *In the space, write* C *for a correct sentence,* FS *for a fused sentence, and* CS *for a comma splice.*

_____ 1. Sylvester was meowing at the back door, he wanted to come into the house after it started raining.

_____ 2. Whenever Barbara grows weary from studying, she plays the piano for awhile.

_____ 3. The game starts in twenty minutes we'd better get on our way.

_____ 4. Ted, tell me what the problem is, I'll be glad to help.

_____ 5. As the old saying goes, "If all else fails, then read the directions."

_____ 6. Mother said she won't rest until she hears we've safely arrived at our destination.

_____ 7. Karen didn't apply for the job after all, she doesn't feel that she meets all of the qualifications at this time.

_____ 8. Skiing is a thrilling sport; however, it is expensive.

_____ 9. Our summer cottage doesn't have electricity there is running water.

_____ 10. The dog kept barking, so now I was wide awake.

_____ 11. Hiller is eager for school to end, she has a summer job in Alaska.

_____ 12. Advertisements are often based on psychological principles, such as the desire to be accepted by others.

_____ 13. Phone calls can be a nuisance those from solicitors are the most irritating, don't you think?

_____ 14. It was rush hour, but the traffic didn't seem as heavy as usual.

_____ 15. When my parents got divorced, I was devastated for months.

_____ 16. Their divorce was something I neither accepted nor understood; today I accept it but I still don't understand it.

_____ 17. I'll tell you the truth; I lost my job because I was late to work once too often.

_____ 18. Maturity is accepting responsibility for one's own behavior don't you agree?

_____ 19. Don't you agree that maturity is accepting responsibility for one's own behavior?

_____ 20. Even though Henry was obviously nervous, he gave an excellent presentation to the class.

_____ 21. Kamoa and Mark are making plans for their wedding; it will take place on June 5th in Honolulu, Kamoa's hometown.

NAME _____   DATE _____

_____ 22. A person should wear a helmet anytime he or she rides a bicycle, scooter, or motorcycle it's a sensible rule to follow.

_____ 23. Nate has seen more of the world than most of us, he was in the navy for four years before entering college.

_____ 24. Scores of people were standing in line to buy a ticket even though the cheapest ticket cost thirty dollars.

_____ 25. The temperature was in the nineties and there was little wind no one in the exuberant crowd complained, however, because the featured concert of the summer was about to take place.

B. *Correct each fused sentence or comma splice by using the method indicated in parentheses. Write out the entire sentence.*

1. *(comma, coordinating conjunction)*   I felt I owed Kerry an explanation he wasn't home when I called.

   _____

   _____

2. *(comma, coordinating conjunction)*   Sarah's major requires a foreign language she is beginning French next semester.

   _____

   _____

3. *(semicolon)*   During our camping trip, the men did all of the cooking they also washed all of the dishes.

   _____

   _____

4. *(semicolon)*   Bruce didn't go to work he is ill with the flu.

   _____

   _____

5. *(semicolon, adverbial conjunction)*   I really didn't dress properly for the football game I nearly froze to death.

   _____

   _____

NAME _____   DATE _____

6. *(semicolon, adverbial conjunction)*   Lorraine isn't home I'll have her call when she gets back.

_____

_____

7. *(period or question mark)*   Did you know your headlights are on, you'd better go back outside and turn them off or your car's battery might run down.

_____

_____

8. *(period or question mark)*   We generally do our grocery shopping at Shop and Save where do you do your grocery shopping.

_____

_____

9. *(use the subordinating conjunction* <u>although</u>*)*   Bradley exercises regularly he still must diet carefully to control his weight.

_____

_____

10. *(use the subordinating conjunction* <u>because</u>*)*   She has a beautiful voice, Jennifer is often asked to sing at weddings.

_____

_____

NAME _____   DATE _____

C. APPLYING THE FINISHING TOUCH

(1) Proofreading: *After correcting the six run-ons in this passage, check your work with that in the* ***Answer Key.***

John Adams: Second President, 1797–1801

John Adams was born in the Massachusetts Bay Colony in 1735. Adams was among the earliest members of the Continental Congress in favor of the colonies declaring their independence from Great Britain, during the Revolutionary War and for a number of years afterwards, Adams served his young nation as a diplomat in Europe.

After serving as Washington's vice-president, Adams was elected the second president of the United States he and his wife Abigail were the first couple to live in the White House. During his presidency, France and England were at war, these countries interfered with American shipping. Many Americans urged President Adams to declare war, he was determined to keep his young nation out of such a conflict hostilities did break out between the United States and France at sea.

Although Adams kept the nation out of war, he was unable to keep his party united behind him, and Thomas Jefferson defeated him in the 1800 presidential election. Adams retired to his home in Quincy, Massachusetts, where he lived to be ninety-years-old. On July 4, 1826, the fiftieth anniversary of the Declaration of Independence, John Adams died Thomas Jefferson died on the same day.

NAME _____   DATE _____

(2) Proofreading: *After correcting the run-ons, rewrite the entire passage. Your instructor will check your work.*

Branch Rickey, Baseball's Emancipator

Branch Rickey, a native of Ohio, was born in 1881. He graduated from college in 1906. Rickey, who was a devout Methodist, loved baseball. He became a catcher for the Cincinnati Reds, he was dropped from the team because of frequent injuries and his opposition to playing on Sundays. His playing days ended after short stays with two other major league teams.

Rickey went to the University of Michigan to study law, he graduated in 1911. After practicing law for a short time, Rickey became an assistant to the owner of the St. Louis Browns he also became the manager of the team. He then became manager and president of the St. Louis Cardinals. During his years with the Cardinals, he developed a minor league system for the team and conducted tryout and instructional camps for aspiring players.

After becoming president and general manager of the Brooklyn Dodgers in 1945, Rickey decided to take steps to end race discrimination in baseball. He signed Jackie Robinson, an African-American, to a contract and assigned him to the Montreal Royals, the Royals were the Brooklyn Dodgers' top minor league team. Robinson led the Royals in hitting that year. In 1946, Jackie Robinson joined the Dodgers he became the first African-American to play in the major leagues, and his success opened the door to other talented African-American players.

Four years later, Rickey left the Dodgers to become an executive for the Pittsburgh Pirates, he was associated with the Pirates for five years. Rickey, the "Man Who Emancipated Baseball," was elected to Baseball's Hall of Fame in Cooperstown, New York, he died in 1965.

NAME _____   DATE _____

Writing: With which person would you prefer to have dinner: the person who said the first statement, or the person who said the second?

- **If you want to be a success, rise early, work hard, and strike oil.**
- **If you want a place in the sun, you have to leave the shade of the family tree.**

Suggestions: **READ** the first statement aloud a number of times.

DISCOVER what you think about the statement by jotting down your reactions to it.

VISUALIZE the type of person who would make such a statement; jot down your impressions of him or her.

DO the same in relation to the second statement, then complete this assignment in any way that makes sense to you. Remember your readers will want to know **why** you chose the person you did, so provide them with plenty of **specific reasons** (your reasons can be unusual as long as they are specific!).

ADOPT a tone (for example, formal or informal, serious or humorous, logical or illogical, factual or fanciful) that helps you express your reasons.

LIMIT your paper to one complete page, typed and doublespaced.

PROVIDE an engaging title.

PROOFREAD for fragments, run-ons, misspellings, or any other problem that may have surfaced in your previous papers; check **PROOFREADING TIPS,** page 295, for further suggestions.

Are you working on one of the **LONG-RANGE ASSIGNMENTS,** pages 291–292?

If so, try to devote time to it as well.

CHAPTER FOUR

Subject-Verb Agreement

Read to page 58 —
any question?

A. ESTABLISHING THE BACKGROUND

SUBJECT-VERB ORDER AND AGREEMENT

> Subjects and verbs must correspond in number.

If the subject of a sentence is singular (one person, place, or thing), the verb must also be singular. If the subject of the sentence is plural (more than one person, place, or thing), the verb must also be plural. Notice the subject and verb agreement in these sentences:

(singular subject and verb)   The **dog** **is** obviously hungry.

(plural subject and verb)   The **dogs** **are** obviously hungry.

(singular subject and verb)   **Jim** **was** here about an hour ago.

(plural subject and verb)   **Jim** and **Lori** **were** here about an hour ago.

Note: An <u>s</u> added to a subject generally makes it plural (friend—friend<u>s</u>), but an <u>s</u> added to a verb generally makes it singular (work—work<u>s</u>):

(singular subject and verb)   My **friend** **works** until four o'clock.

(plural subject and verb)   My **friends** **work** until four o'clock.

(singular subject and verb)   My <u>uncle</u> <u>makes</u> beautiful furniture.

(plural subject and verb)   My <u>uncles</u> <u>make</u> beautiful furniture.

    Agreement is not usually a major writing problem as most people naturally match singular subjects with singular verbs and plural subjects with plural verbs. Confusion can sometimes result, though, if there is a word group containing a noun (as in a prepositional phrase) between the subject and verb. However, word groups do <u>not</u> affect the basic subject-verb agreement. Observe, for example, these sentences:

The young <u>man</u> [with the groceries] <u>lives</u> in our apartment house.

The <u>bicycles</u> [in the garage] <u>belong</u> to my brother.

Every Saturday morning, <u>Bob</u>, [as well as a few others in the dorm], <u>takes</u> his dirty clothes to a neighborhood laundromat.

The fuel <u>pump</u>, [not the carburetor], <u>is broken</u>.

**Do Exercise 1 in Section B
before continuing.**

    Chapter One pointed out that the usual subject-verb order is often reversed in sentences starting with <u>There</u>, <u>Here</u>, and in sentences asking questions. Whatever their order, however, subjects and verbs must agree in number. Examine the subject-verb order and agreement in the following sentences:

Six police <u>officers</u> <u>are</u> on duty to handle the coliseum's traffic.

There <u>are</u> six police <u>officers</u> on duty to handle the coliseum's traffic.

The sixty dollar <u>check</u> <u>is</u> here.

Here <u>is</u> the sixty dollar <u>check</u>.

Where <u>are</u> Brian's cassette <u>tapes</u>?

When <u>did</u> <u>Pat</u> <u>join</u> the air force?

Do Exercise 2 in Section B.

INDEFINITE PRONOUNS

As you have learned, the subject of a sentence is either a noun (person, place, or thing) or a pronoun (a word that substitutes for a noun, such as *she, he, you, it*).

The following pronouns, called **indefinite pronouns,** are often subjects in sentences; the essential point to remember about these indefinite pronouns is that they should be used only with **singular verbs.**

each	anybody	anything	anyone
either	everybody	everything	everyone
neither	nobody	nothing	one
somebody	something	someone	none

Study the following sentences to reinforce the fact **indefinite pronouns** are used with **singular verbs.**

1. <u>Each</u> of the carpenters <u>does</u> excellent work.
2. <u>Either</u> of the keys <u>opens</u> the door.
3. <u>Neither</u> of the movies <u>was</u> enjoyable.
4. <u>Anybody</u> <u>is</u> welcome to go with us to the game.
5. <u>Everybody</u> in Marlene's family <u>is</u> sick with the flu.
6. Despite the poor weather, <u>nobody</u> is <u>leaving</u> the game.
7. Fortunately, <u>somebody</u> <u>was willing</u> to help me.
8. <u>Is</u> there <u>anything</u> wrong with your car?
9. <u>Everything</u> in the refrigerator <u>has spoiled</u>.
10. Happily, <u>nothing</u> <u>has happened</u> to cancel our trip to Atlanta.
11. There <u>is</u> <u>something</u> wrong with the furnace.
12. <u>Anybody</u> with lots of money and the right connections <u>is invited</u> to their parties.
13. Evidently, <u>everyone</u> in the city <u>goes</u> to the beach on the weekend.
14. <u>One</u> of the cars obviously <u>has</u> a bad muffler.
15. <u>Someone</u> across the street <u>was trimming</u> a hedge.

Remember: Indefinite pronouns use singular verbs.

Do Exercise 3 in Section B.

WHO, WHICH, THAT CLAUSES

A clause, as you will recall from Chapter Two, is a group of words containing a subject and verb. *Who, which,* and *that* are often the subjects of clauses, and they can refer to either singular or plural subjects, so take particular care your verbs are in agreement with them. Study this example:

(who—singular) The person [who is speaking today] comes from my hometown.

> *The basic sentence,* The person comes from my hometown, *has a singular subject (*person*) so a singular verb (*comes*) is used.*

> *The clause is* who is speaking today; *because* who *is referring to a singular subject (*person*), a singular verb (*is*) is used.*

(who—plural) The people [who are speaking today] come from my hometown.

> *The basic sentence,* The people come from my hometown, *has a plural subject (*people*) so a plural verb (*come*) is used.*

> *The clause is* who are speaking today; *because* who *is referring to a plural subject (*people*) a plural verb (*are*) is used.*

Here is another example:

(that—singular) The camera [that takes the sharpest pictures] is over twenty years old.

> *Because* that *is referring to a singular subject (*camera*), a singular verb (*takes*) is used.*

(that—plural) The cameras [that take the sharpest pictures] are over twenty years old.

> *Now* that *is referring to a plural subject (*cameras*), so a plural verb (*are*) is used.*

Do Exercise 4 in Section B. ⟶

OTHER WORDS TO NOTE

When *both* and *few* function as subjects, they always require plural verbs:

> <u>Both</u> <u>are</u> *experienced sailors.*
> <u>Few</u> *in the choir* <u>seem</u> *able to read music.*

When *some* functions as a subject, it depends upon the noun it relates to whether a singular or plural verb should be used:

> <u>Some</u> *of the cake* <u>is</u> *missing.*   (*Some* is considered singular because *cake* is singular, so the singular verb <u>is</u> is used.)
> <u>Some</u> *of the cakes* <u>are</u> *missing.*   (*Some* is considered plural because *cakes* is plural, so the plural verb <u>are</u> is used.)

When compound subjects are joined by *either–or, neither–nor,* and *not only–but also,* the verb should agree with the closer subject:

> *Either* several <u>cars</u> *or* a <u>bus</u> <u>is needed</u> for the field trip.   (*bus,* a singular subject, is closer to the verb, so the singular verb <u>is</u> is used.)
> *Either* a <u>bus</u> *or* several <u>cars</u> <u>are needed</u> for the field trip.   (*cars,* a plural subject, is closer to the verb, so the plural verb <u>are</u> is used.)
> *Neither* the <u>defendants</u> *nor* the <u>lawyer</u> <u>knows</u> why the judge declared a mistrial.   (*lawyer,* a singular subject, is closer to the verb, so the singular verb <u>knows</u> is used.)
> *Neither* the <u>lawyer</u> *nor* the <u>defendants</u> <u>know</u> why the judge declared a mistrial.   (*defendants,* a plural subject, is closer to the verb, so the plural verb <u>know</u> is used.)
> *Not only* my <u>parents</u> *but also* my <u>sister</u> <u>was</u> able to attend the ceremony. (*sister,* a singular subject, is closer to the verb, so the singular verb <u>was</u> is used.)
> *Not only* my <u>sister</u> *but also* my <u>parents</u> <u>were</u> able to attend the ceremony. (*parents,* a plural subject, is closer to the verb, so the plural verb <u>were</u> is used.)

Do Exercise 5 and the Review Exercise in Section B.

B. GAINING THE EXPERIENCE

Exercise 1: *For each sentence, underline the subject once and the appropriate verb twice.*

1. The paneling (was done, were done) by my father and mother.
2. The paneling in the basement and hallway (was done, were done) by my father and mother.
3. The region's heat and humidity (makes, make) it difficult to do any physical work during the summer months.
4. My cousin, as well as my grandparents, (was, were) at the wedding.
5. Roger's map, as well as Marilyn's well-written directions, (was, were) all we needed to find the isolated lake cottage.
6. French toast (is, are) my favorite breakfast food.
7. French toast, not bacon and eggs, (is, are) my favorite breakfast food.
8. Alcohol and other drugs, in the speaker's opinion, (causes, cause) most of the crimes in our major cities.
9. Although rain is predicted for tomorrow, the moon (is, are) out tonight.
10. Although rain is predicted for tomorrow, the moon, as well as the stars, (is, are) out tonight.
11. Melissa's shoes and pocketbook (matches, match) her new dress.
12. Drake, not Bradley, (seems, seem) to be the tournament favorite.
13. The cost of medical and dental care (has risen, have risen) sharply the past three years.
14. The costs of medical and dental care (has risen, have risen) sharply the past three years.
15. The fruit salad, consisting of strawberries, watermelon, and bananas, (is, are) delicious.

Exercise 2: *For each sentence, underline the subject once and the appropriate verb twice.*

Rewrite these sentences
The price list for the various computer programs are on the self.

1. Here (is, are) the price list for the various computer programs.
2. All week, there (has been, have been) fog and drizzle along the coast.
3. After the holidays, when (does, do) classes begin?
4. In Oregon and Washington, there (is, are) majestic mountains and beautiful forests.
5. Where (is, are) the electric outlet in this room?

Exercise 3:   *In the blanks before each sentence, write the subject and verb.*

    Subject   **Verb**

1. _____ _____ In our neighborhood, nobody (gets, get) up earlier than our paperboy.

2. _____ _____ There (are, is) someone on the phone for you.

3. _____ _____ One of my sisters (enter, enters) the University of Iowa this fall.

4. _____ _____ Neither of these books (contain, contains) the necessary information.

5. _____ _____ (Is, Are) there nothing in the mail for me?

6. _____ _____ Something (need, needs) to be done to prevent water in our basement.

7. _____ _____ Somebody in this company, fortunately, (thinks, think) about our customers.

8. _____ _____ Each of the players (have, has) confidence in Coach Bonelli.

9. _____ _____ Everybody in the Larson family (play, plays) a musical instrument.

10. _____ _____ No kidding, everyone (hopes, hope) for the best for you.

11. _____ _____ (Has, Have) anyone jogged around the track besides Fletcher?

12. _____ _____ Either of the apartments (is, are) fine with me.

13. _____ _____ In Terry's opinion, everything (are going, is going) wrong at the store.

14. _____ _____ Frankly, (do, does) anybody care about him?

15. _____ _____ (Is, Are) anything mentioned in the newspaper about the accident?

Exercise 4:   *Circle the proper verb for each basic sentence and its clause.*

1. In this part of the country, the weather condition that (cause, causes) the most problems (are, is) drought.

2. The people who (impresses, impress) me the most (are, is) concerned about others, not themselves.

3. Flying lessons, which (costs, cost) a lot, (fill, fills) most of Tom's spare time.

4. The telephone, which (seems, seem) to ring constantly, (don't, doesn't) bother the receptionist.

5. Every morning at six o'clock, my neighbor, who (lives, live) in the house north of me, (go, goes) jogging.

6. The stories that (is, are) the most popular with my children (has, have) to do with science fiction.

7. A train that (arrives, arrive) on time around here (are, is) the exception, not the rule.

8. The people who (is, are) waiting by the bus stop (look, looks) cold.

9. My roommates' stereos, which (is, are) in the same room, occasionally (bombards, bombard) the eardrums of everyone within a three-mile distance.

10. Because my roommates ignored a final warning, the dorm adviser, who (lift, lifts) weights, (has, have) locked their stereos in his closet.

Exercise 5:   *Circle the appropriate verb.*

1. No doubt, both youngsters (are, is) exhausted from the long trip.

2. Few in the audience (know, knows) or (care, cares) who wrote the play.

3. Some of the lions (was, were) prowling back and forth in the cage.

4. Either Percy or his sons (are, is) coming to finish the job.

5. Fortunately, neither the committee members nor the chairperson (believe, believes) in long meetings.

6. Not only his wife but also his friends (believe, believes) Greg should consider becoming a coach.

7. Both of my brothers (love, loves) to play practical jokes.

8. Some of Arlene's report (was, were) missing.

9. Either the employees or their representative (are, is) entitled to attend the meeting.

10. Neither the grueling drills or the screaming sergeant (bother, bothers) Felix.

11. Not only the players but also the coach (appreciate, appreciates) your support.

12. Some of the cars in the parking lot (look, looks) brand new.

NAME _____   DATE _____

Chapter 4
Review Exercise: *Circle the appropriate subject and/or verb for each sentence or clause.*

1. (A dog, Dogs) seem to feel sympathy for people who (are, is) sick.

2. The (candle, candles) that is on the mantelpiece (was bought, were bought) in England by my sister.

3. The friendliness and competence of the teachers (is, are) appreciated by each student who (is, are) serious about learning.

4. Basketball, not field hockey, (is, are) actually Vera's best sport.

5. Those people who (was, were) the hungriest moved quickly to the front of the line.

6. The (driver, drivers) that upset me the most (are, is) those who tailgate.

7. Each of my sisters (earn, earns) more money in her job than I do in mine.

8. (Everyone, People) from miles around attends this church.

9. Here in the rack (is, are) the magazines you are looking for.

10. These old earrings, which (was made, were made) in Switzerland, (was sent, were sent) to me by my boyfriend.

11. The fireplace generally (provide, provides) enough heat for the downstairs.

12. My dad, like most people who (live, lives) in the North, (prefer, prefers) to vacation in the South during January instead of July.

13. The vegetables in the casserole (was, were) still crisp.

14. Everybody I've talked to (recommend, recommends) the movie, especially for children who (love, loves) animals.

15. Four kittens (was, were) asleep in the lawnchair, and each one (was, were) purring softly.

16. Surprisingly, the instructor, not the students, (seem, seems) more nervous about the test.

17. Though the holiday break (begin, begins) tomorrow, a few students in my dorm still (has, have) papers to turn in before they leave campus.

18. Either my parents or my girlfriend (plan, plans) to meet me at the airport.

19. Every time I'm about to fall asleep, either a parade of roaring trucks or a screaming motorcycle (seem, seems) to pass by.

NAME _____   DATE _____

20. Not only her parents but also her grandmother (are, is) coming to dinner.

21. Both of my roommates (are, is) from Reno, Nevada.

22. Carol was disappointed when neither her brother nor her parents (was, were) home when she called.

23. Some of the ice (has, have) melted on the pond.

24. Anyone who (visit, visits) our national parks (benefit, benefits) from the numerous services provided by our nation's park rangers.

25. Both of my sisters (play, plays) in the orchestra and (sing, sings) in the choir.

26. Apparently, neither the game nor night classes (has, have) been canceled because of the storm.

27. However, (everybody, students) who commute will probably stay home.

28. The basketball (player, players) Sheila enjoys watching the most is sitting on the bench next to the coach.

29. No one I've ever seen, not even members of the hockey team, (skate, skates) as well as Donna.

30. (A trip, Trips) there seems long to people who (doesn't, don't) like to travel by boat.

31. All of the mail (are, is) still unopened.

32. All of the guests (are, is) beginning to sit down at the table.

33. Jack believes none of the books we need for our report (are, is) in the library.

34. Terri (say, says) either steak or clams (are, is) fine with her.

35. Although both shows (are, is) too long, each (are, is) worth seeing.

NAME _____   DATE _____

C. APPLYING THE FINISHING TOUCH

(1) Proofreading: *After correcting the nine subject-verb agreement errors contained in this passage, check your work with that in the **Answer Key.***

Thomas Jefferson: Third President, 1801–1809

There is many historians who consider Thomas Jefferson the most brilliant person ever to have been president. Among his talents was those of a gifted architect, inventor, musician, lawyer, writer, and farmer. He was also the author of the Declaration of Independence and the founder of the University of Virginia.

Thomas Jefferson was born in Virginia in 1743. He graduated from William and Mary College at age nineteen, became a lawyer at twenty-four, and was elected to the Virginia legislature at twenty-six. In 1772, Jefferson married a young widow named Martha Wayles Skelton. During their ten-year marriage, the Jeffersons became the parents of one son and five daughters. Tragically, neither the son nor three of the daughters was able to survive to adulthood, and Mrs. Jefferson died when she was thirty-three. Jefferson never remarried; however, there is rumors he fell deeply in love with a married woman.

Jefferson was the principal author of the Declaration of Independence, written in Philadelphia in 1776. During the Revolutionary War, Jefferson served as governor of Virginia. After peace came and the government, including the legislative, executive, and judicial branches, were established

NAME _____   DATE _____

under the Constitution of 1787, Jefferson became President Washington's Secretary of State. Then, after serving as John Adams's vice-president, Jefferson was elected president in 1801.

As president, Jefferson kept the nation out of war, ended the raiding of American ships in the Mediterranean Sea, and negotiated the purchase of the Louisiana Territory from France, an acquisition that more than doubled the size of the United States. Each of these impressive achievements were accomplished despite many difficulties and much criticism.

After his two terms as president, Jefferson retired to his beloved Monticello, his handsome home overlooking Charlottesville, Virginia. There he were able to pursue his numerous interests for many years. Everybody who learn the following fact seldom forget it: Presidents Thomas Jefferson and John Adams both died on July 4, 1826, the fiftieth anniversary of the Declaration of Independence.

NAME _____   **DATE** _____

(2) Proofreading: *After correcting the subject and verb agreement errors, have your instructor check your work.*

The Model T Ford

When automobiles first appeared on the American scene in the early 1900s, only wealthy people was able to afford them. Henry Ford, however, wanted anyone, whether he or she were wealthy or not, to be able to own a car. Ford vowed, "I will build a motor car for the great multitude." His development of the Model T, affectionately called the "Tin Lizzie," enabled him to keep that vow.

Although the Model T's motor, transmission, and ignition was technologically advanced, it was Ford's development of assembly lines that were truly revolutionary. Other manufacturers was responsible for the assembly line, but Ford perfected it. In 1913, using his advanced assembly line approach, workers at Ford's new Model T plant was able to produce a new car in a little over an hour and a half; previously, twelve hours had been required. Eventually, the time, because of further production advances, was reduced to an amazing twenty-four *seconds!*

As the years passed, production time went down as did the Model T's price, from nearly $1000 in 1908 to less than $300 in 1927. Henry Ford had indeed succeeded in his goal of making the automobile available to the average person. As a result, Americans' standard of values were forever changed as they came to believe that owning an automobile was no longer a luxury but a necessity.

NAME _____   **DATE** _____

Writing: After selecting **one** of the following statements to write about, explain why the person who said it was either wise, foolish, confused, or confusing:

- **No person is happy without a delusion of some kind. Delusions are as necessary to our happiness as realities.**
- **Leisure is a beautiful garment, but it will not do for constant wear.**

Suggestions: **JOT DOWN** for twenty minutes or so your initial reactions to the statement you have selected; remember, at this stage you are simply exploring your reactions and thoughts, so write down whatever comes to mind, whether it's serious or humorous, brilliant or bizarre, clear or unclear; if you are unsure of any word's meaning in the statement you are responding to, feel free to consult a dictionary or thesaurus.

EXAMINE your writing for promising ideas; concentrate on these ideas as you write again.

READ, WRITE, AND REVISE until your central point and main ideas point are clearly stated.

WORK HARD to develop specific reasons and convincing examples to support your assertions; avoid the superficial or obvious; try not to be predictable; adopt a tone (for example, sincere, sarcastic, serious, humorous, factual, fanciful, sensible, outrageous) that is appropriate for your response.

LIMIT your final draft to one complete page, typed and doublespaced; do your best to make sure every word contributes to your paper's effectiveness.

PROVIDE an unusual title, one you are confident no one else would think of.

PROOFREAD, making sure your subject and verbs agree and all your words are spelled correctly; consult **PROOFREADING TIPS,** for other suggestions; your paper is worth reading so don't allow it to be sabotaged by fragments, run-ons, or other careless mistakes.

If you are working on one of the **LONG-RANGE ASSIGNMENTS,**
keep in mind the date it is due,
and consult **WRITING SUGGESTIONS** from time to time.

After reviewing Chapters 1–4,
take the **MASTERY TEST** provided
by your instructor.

CHAPTER FIVE

Misplaced and Dangling Modifiers

A. ESTABLISHING THE BACKGROUND

Modifiers provide helpful information about other words in a sentence. **Adjectives,** for example are modifiers describing nouns and pronouns, as in this sentence:

A <u>steady cold</u> rain prevented my <u>elderly</u> neighbor from taking his <u>customary daily</u> walk.

Observe how deprived this sentence would be without the adjectives describing the nouns:

A rain prevented my neighbor from taking his walk.

Notice the help provided by the adjectives modifying the pronoun <u>She</u> in this sentence:

She is <u>talented</u> as well as <u>hardworking</u>.

Without the adjective modifiers, the sentence would actually be incomplete:

She is . . . (???)

Adverbs are also modifiers; adverbs provide additional information about verbs, adjectives, and other adverbs, as illustrated in these sentences:

Linda spoke <u>quietly</u> but <u>distinctly</u>. (the adverbs <u>quietly</u> and <u>distinctly</u> modify the verb <u>spoke</u>)

Sam is <u>extremely</u> happy with his new job. (the adverb <u>extremely</u> modifies the adjective <u>happy</u>)

Because of arthritis, my grandfather walks <u>quite</u> slowly. (the adverb <u>quite</u> modifies the adverb <u>slowly</u>)

Frequently, phrases, particularly those beginning with prepositions, function as adjective or adverb modifiers, as illustrated in these sentences:

The dog <u>on our lawn</u> belongs to the Neffs. (the prepositional phrase <u>on our lawn</u> is an adjective modifying the noun <u>dog</u>)

The little boy hid <u>behind the huge couch</u>. (the prepositional phrase <u>behind the huge couch</u> is an adverb phrase modifying the verb <u>hid</u>)

Using modifiers occurs naturally when you write, so it is unlikely you have had to devote much attention to modifiers. Nevertheless, when you do the final proofreading of your writing, make sure you have followed this writing principle:

> Modifiers should be placed as closely as possible to the words they modify.

MISPLACED MODIFIERS

As the following sentences illustrate, <u>misplaced modifiers</u> can interfere, as least momentarily, with clarity:

Misplaced: Mr. Gall was planting the garden [with his children.]
(. . . <u>planting</u> the garden <u>with his children</u>?)

Clear: Mr. Gall and his children were planting the garden.

or

Mr. Gall, with his children's help, was planting the garden.

Misplaced: Sharon brought the sweater to her roommate [with light blue stripes.]   (. . . <u>roommate</u> with light blue <u>stripes</u>?)

Clear: Sharon brought the sweater with light blue stripes to her roommate.

Misplaced: Yesterday, my brother [almost] rode his bike sixty miles.
(. . . <u>almost</u> rode? Did he ride his bike at all?)

Clear: Yesterday, my brother rode almost sixty miles on his bike.

Misplaced: Rick [nearly] washed and waxed his car for five hours. (Does this sentence mean that Rich <u>considered</u> washing and waxing his car for five hours?)

Clear: Rick washed and waxed his car for nearly five hours.

Reading a sentence with a misplaced modifier is somewhat like watching a television set with a distorted picture; both activities require more effort than necessary. Fortunately, however, simply placing modifiers in their logical position can result in ease of reading, just as fine-tuning the television set can result in ease of viewing.

Do Exercises 1 and 2 in Section B. →

DANGLING MODIFIERS

As you have seen, a <u>misplaced modifier</u> interferes with clarity because of its illogical position in the sentence. A <u>dangling modifier</u>, on the other hand, interferes with clarity because there is no word in the sentence with which the modifier can be associated. Examine the following sentences.

Dangling: <u>Tripping on a tree root</u>, my attention quickly turned to my painful ankle.   (. . . my attention tripped on a tree root?)

Correct: Tripping on a tree root, I quickly turned my attention to my painful ankle.

or

After I tripped on a tree root, my attention was quickly turned to my painful ankle.

Dangling: Swimming back to the raft, a log struck Roy's head. (. . . a log was swimming back to the raft?)

Correct: Swimming back to the raft, Roy struck his head on a log.

or

Roy, while swimming back to the raft, struck his head on a log.

Dangling: At the age of four, my father returned to college. (. . . father returned to college when he was four?)

Correct: When I was four, my father returned to college.

or

My father returned to college when I was four-years-old.

Keep in mind, then, these two basic principles when you proofread your writing:

ONE: Modifiers need the words they modify to be present in the sentence.

TWO: Modifiers need to be placed as closely as possible to the words they modify.

Do Exercises 3 and 4 and the Review Exercise in Section B.

B. GAINING THE EXPERIENCE

Exercise 1:   *Write C in the space if the sentence is correct, M if it contains a misplaced modifier.*

_____   1.   With a scowl, the batter returned to the dugout after striking out.

_____   2.   The batter returned to the dugout with a scowl after striking out.

_____   3.   I loaned my sweater to my roommate that has a v-neck.

_____   4.   I loaned my sweater that has a v-neck to my roommate.

_____   5.   Sleeping in a lawn chair, a sonic boom startled my father.

_____   6.   Sleeping in a lawn chair, my father was startled by a sonic boom.

_____   7.   My father, sleeping in a lawn chair, was startled by a sonic boom.

_____   8.   Burt caught the bus on time barely.

_____   9.   Barely, Burt caught the bus on time.

_____   10.   Burt barely caught the bus on time.

_____   11.   Ralph angrily threw the golf club to the ground.

_____   12.   The golf club was thrown angrily to the ground by Ralph.

_____   13.   Angrily, the golf club was thrown to the ground by Ralph.

_____   14.   John wrapped his ankle that was swollen with an elastic bandage.

_____   15.   John wrapped his ankle with an elastic bandage that was swollen.

_____   16.   He almost needed to paint every room.

_____   17.   He needed to paint almost every room.

_____   18.   Ashley covered the sofa hole that embarrassed her with a pillow before her guests arrived.

_____   19.   Before her guests arrived, Ashley covered with a pillow the sofa hole that embarrassed her.

_____   20.   Ashley, before her guests arrived, covered the sofa hole that embarrassed her with a pillow.

Exercise 2:   *Rewrite the entire sentence after deciding where the modifier given in parentheses should be located. In some cases, you may need to add commas. Circle the word that is modified. An example has been done for you.*

Example: *(with a reassuring smile)*   The dentist comforted the nervous patient.

The (dentist,) with a reassuring smile, comforted the nervous patient.

or

With a reassuring smile, the (dentist) comforted the nervous patient.

NAME _____   DATE _____

1. *(in the maroon sweater)*   The young man plays the saxophone in the college band.

   _____

   _____

2. *(with two large packages)*   A funny looking man struggled into the taxi.

   _____

   _____

3. *(working in the flower garden)*   Mom was stung by a bee.

   _____

   _____

4. *(in jogging clothes)*   The girl watched the squirrel escape from the scolding birds.

   _____

   _____

5. *(that had become cold)*   Amy reheated the casserole in the warm oven.

   _____

   _____

6. *(driving a yellow convertible)*   A woman turned around in our driveway.

   _____

   _____

7. *(on the way to work)*   Whitney saw a bad accident.

   _____

   _____

8. *(with a tiny kitchen)*   Susan rented an apartment during the school year.

   _____

   _____

9. *(with regret)*   Rick remembered that he had forgotten to send his grandparents an anniversary card.

   _____

   _____

10. *(nearly)*   Because he knew most of the answers, Bob won five hundred dollars.

   _____

   _____

NAME _____   DATE _____

Exercise 3:   *Write a <u>C</u> in the space if the sentence is correct, <u>D</u> if it is flawed by a dangling modifier.*

_____   1.   While eating dinner, the lights suddenly went out.

_____   2.   While we were eating dinner, the lights suddenly went out.

_____   3.   As I was driving home from work, the grocery bags in the back seat fell to the floor.

_____   4.   Driving home from work, the grocery bags in the back seat fell to the floor.

_____   5.   After chasing his dog around the neighborhood, Mr. Russell was exhausted.

_____   6.   Mr. Russell, after chasing his dog around the neighborhood, was exhausted.

_____   7.   Listening to music in my room, a mosquito bit me on the arm.

_____   8.   A mosquito, listening to music in my room, bit me on the arm.

_____   9.   While I was listening to music in my room, a mosquito bit me on the arm.

_____ 10.   Working in the garden all morning, Madeline's forehead became sunburned.

_____ 11.   Working in the garden all morning, Madeline sunburned her forehead.

_____ 12.   I needed my toothbrush after eating lots of popcorn.

_____ 13.   After eating lots of popcorn, my toothbrush was needed.

_____ 14.   To receive financial aid, a form must be completed.

_____ 15.   To receive financial aid, you must complete this form.

_____ 16.   To visit the park, people must make a long hike.

_____ 17.   To visit the park, a long hike must be made.

_____ 18.   On hearing about Justin and Sandra's engagement, Ann shrieked, startling everyone in the restaurant.

_____ 19.   On hearing about Justin and Sandra's engagement, Ann's shriek startled everyone in the restaurant.

_____ 20.   On hearing about Justin and Sandra's engagement, everyone in the restaurant was startled by Ann's shriek.

NAME _____   **DATE** _____

Exercise 4: *Write sentences using the modifiers indicated. Circle the word that is modified. An example has been done for you.*

Example: *(Lifting the heavy weight)*

Lifting the heavy weight, (Chuck) grunted and groaned.

1. *(After receiving the gift)*

_____

_____

2. *(While shopping at the mall)*

_____

_____

3. *(Since living in San Diego)*

_____

_____

4. *(On hearing the news)*

_____

_____

5. *(Waiting for the mail to arrive)*

_____

_____

6. *(Stepping carefully)*

_____

_____

7. *(Answering the phone)*

_____

_____

8. *(By beginning immediately)*

_____

_____

NAME _____   DATE _____

Exercise 5: *Rewrite the entire sentence after deciding where the modifier given in parentheses should be located; in some cases, you may need to add commas. Circle the word that is modified. An example has been done for you.*

Example: *(disgustedly)* Colby remarked that he would walk the dog.

Colby (remarked) disgustedly that he would walk the dog.

or

Colby disgustedly (remarked) that he would walk the dog.

1. *(with three drawers)* Andy bought a desk for his room.

_____

_____

2. *(dozing on the couch)* Meredith skimmed through a pile of magazines.

_____

_____

3. *(with the long beard)* Frowning at Heidi, the clerk in the jewelry department asked for her receipt.

_____

_____

4. *(almost)* The small boy wanted every toy in the store.

_____

_____

5. *(which was spotless)* Baxter drove his 1957 Chevrolet down the busy highway towards San Diego.

_____

_____

NAME _____   DATE _____

Exercise 6:   *Each of the following sentences is marred by a dangling modifier; that is, each sentence lacks the word the modifier is supposed to modify. Therefore, revise each sentence so that this error is corrected. Circle the modified word or words. An example has been done for you.*

Example: Eating pizza, playing games, and watching old movies, the evening was enjoyable at the Carlson's home.

Eating pizza, playing games, and watching old movies, (Helen and Don) spent an enjoyable evening at the Carlson's home.

1.   Before going to bed, the cat should be put outdoors.

_____

_____

2.   Listening to the constant roar of the highway traffic, the motel room provided little rest.

_____

_____

3.   Even though wondering what would happen next in the comedy, the eventual outcome was always predictable.

_____

_____

4.   Just finishing the last wall, the paint ran out.

_____

_____

5.   Having never run that great a distance before, his legs became stiff and sore.

_____

_____

Chapter 5
Review Exercise: *Write* <u>C</u> *in the space if the sentence is correct,* <u>X</u> *if it contains either a misplaced or dangling modifier.*

_____ 1. The little girl was teasing our dog in a Halloween mask.

_____ 2. Lionel loaned his typewriter to his girlfriend that is self-correcting.

_____ 3. Movies of the 1940s are popular with thousands of college kids.

_____ 4. With his uncle's financial backing, Duffy was able to open his own store.

_____ 5. Feeling elated, we congratulated one another.

_____ 6. Finally, Rory studied the map with a frown.

_____ 7. Listening intently, Tracy learned how to solve the problem.

_____ 8. Martin finished painting the entire house almost.

_____ 9. George was talking on the telephone in an excited tone.

_____ 10. My brother bought a sweatshirt with an attached hood at Dixon's Sports Shop.

_____ 11. While cooking dinner, Jerry decided to call Carol.

_____ 12. Brian almost needed help with every project.

_____ 13. Anita, with a pleasant smile, answered the customer's question.

_____ 14. My folks bought a boat engine from our neighbors with forty horsepower.

_____ 15. After checking the lights, testing the brakes, and inspecting the exhaust system, Vicky's car was given a new safety sticker.

_____ 16. Before applying the paint remover, Otis opened the windows.

_____ 17. Feeling tense, the exercise was relaxing.

_____ 18. After reading the magazine, Betty felt sleepy.

_____ 19. On the way to the game, the rain started to fall more heavily.

_____ 20. After finishing the concert, a party was given at the hotel by the musicians.

_____ 21. While working in the basement, the telephone rang.

_____ 22. Squinting because of the bright sunshine, Barbara wished she would have remembered to bring her sunglasses.

_____ 23. With an automatic transmission, Seth finds it easier to drive in the downtown traffic.

_____ 24. Smothering a giggle, Holly excused herself and left the table.

_____ 25. During his long career, Coach Watson nearly won four-hundred games.

_____ 26. Quentin bought a large desk for his small room that cost only forty-five dollars.

NAME _____   DATE _____

_____ 27. Evelyn finally returned the book to the library that was three months overdue.

_____ 28. If mashed or fried, my children will eat potatoes.

_____ 29. Abby was ready for a snack and stretch after almost driving for four hours.

_____ 30. Kendall finally agreed yesterday to work on the project.

Rewrite Sentences 31–35 so their intended meanings are clear.

31. Neil must have looked at over twenty used cars shopping on the weekend.

_____

_____

32. After being soaked by the unexpected rain, the warm fireplace felt wonderful.

_____

_____

33. Scattered throughout the apartment, Cindy quickly gathered her books, papers, pens, and purse, stuffed the items into her backpack, then dashed to campus for her first class.

_____

_____

_____

34. Stuart was relieved to see a restaurant driving down the highway at one in the morning.

_____

_____

35. The receptionist only asked the patient to wait for five more minutes, but he stormed out the door.

_____

_____

C. APPLYING THE FINISHING TOUCH

(1) Proofreading: *Correct the six mistakes having to do with misplaced and dangling modifiers; compare your corrections with those in the **Answer Key.***

Johns Hopkins Medical School

One of the most esteemed universities in the world, the citizens of Baltimore are understandably proud of Johns Hopkins University. Its various schools and departments are generally ranked among the best in the nation, but it is its medical school that often receives the highest acclaim.

The medical school, founded in 1893, became the first one associated with a university to admit men and women based solely upon objective qualifications. The Baltimore Women's Committee of that day was responsible for this distinction. After raising the funds to establish the medical school, two conditions were proposed by the committee. First, the committee insisted that men and women be admitted to the medical school "on the same terms." Dismayed, this condition was objected to by the president of Johns Hopkins. He believed women simply were not endowed with the same capacities for medical study as men; therefore, he maintained, lower standards would have to be applied if women were to be admitted. However, the women on the committee would not accept the president's contentions on this matter. Reluctantly, the "on the same terms" policy was finally agreed to by the president.

In addition, the Baltimore Women's Committee insisted that only applicants with appropriate preparation in sciences and foreign languages be admitted to the medical school. Convinced few applicants would be capable of meeting these entrance requirements, opposition to this second condition was voiced by the Johns Hopkins faculty. Standing firm once again, however, the requirements, the most stringent of any medical school at that time, were pushed through by the determined Baltimore Women's Committee.

As a result of the enlightened policies insisted upon by the Baltimore Women's Committee, Johns Hopkins Medical School soon attracted some of the nation's most capable students, leading to the school's early credibility. As time passed, the school's credibility continued to increase for a variety of reasons. Now, as has been the case for many years, Johns Hopkins Medical School is considered one of the finest institutions of its kind in the world.

(2) Proofreading: *After correcting the misplaced and dangling modifiers, rewrite the entire passage on a separate piece of paper. Have your instructor check your work.*

James Madison: Fourth President, 1809–1817

Standing just five feet four inches and weighing only 100 pounds, the smallest person to have served as president is James Madison. Despite his frailty, however, James Madison lived to be an old man.

Madison was born in 1751 in Virginia of prosperous parents. The first-born of twelve children, his early education came from his parents, tutors, and instructors at a private school. Madison then attended the College of New Jersey, now known as Princeton University. His major academic interests were government, law, and theology. Madison eventually abandoned his plan, possessing a weak voice and a fear of public speaking, to enter the ministry.

After completing college, politics became Madison's major concern. Because his ideas about government were the ones incorporated into the Constitution drafted at the Constitutional Convention in 1787, the "Father of the Constitution" is the title given to Madison.

Elected president in 1808, war erupted with Great Britain in 1812. The United States was poorly prepared for the conflict, and the British captured Washington, D.C., burning the White House and other federal buildings spitefully. The United States, however, won some key naval engagements,

NAME _____   DATE _____

and Andrew Jackson led his troops to victory at New Orleans, although this victory actually occurred after the peace treaty had been signed.

After completing his second term as president, Madison and his wife Dolley retired to Montpelier, their Virginia estate, with relief and gratitude. During nineteen years of retirement, an interest in local, state, and national affairs was maintained by Madison; he even served for a time as president of the University of Virginia. Madison died in 1836 at the age of eighty-five.

NAME _____   DATE _____

Writing:　Read the two passages below, then write a paper based upon **one** of these questions:

- **Is one of these discoveries more important than the other?**
- **Is one of these discoveries more interesting than the other?**
- **What do these discoveries tell us about humankind?**
- **What do these discoveries tell us about historians and archeologists?**

Passage One:　Archeologists recently found a stone ax in a prehistoric lake bed in Greece that indicates Europe may have been settled 400,000 years sooner than previously thought. The ax is similar to a type found in Africa dating back 1.6 million years.

Passage Two:　The ancient Greek historian Plutarch recorded details of a battle that took place in 86 B.C. in which Roman soldiers killed over 3,000 invaders from Pontus, a city near the Black Sea. Sulla, the Roman general, erected two monuments to commemorate the victory. In 1991, an American archeologist and his students unearthed one of these monuments.

Suggestions:　**JOT DOWN** rapidly and for as long as you can your first reactions to the question you are responding to; accept <u>what</u> you write as well as <u>how</u> you write.

SCAN your writing to see which remarks best reflect your reactions; concentrate on these remarks when you write again.

RESERVE time over several days to work on this assignment; to be convincing, your reply will need the backing of specific reasons, so don't let rambling explanations find a home in your final draft.

LIMIT your final draft to <u>one complete page</u>, typed and doublespaced.

PROVIDE a "grabber" of a title.

PROOFREAD, paying particular attention to your modifiers and to the type of errors you may have made in previous papers; refer to **PROOFREADING TIPS** for further suggestions.

Are you working on one of the **LONG-RANGE ASSIGNMENTS?**
If you are, be sure to take advantage of the **WRITING SUGGESTIONS.**

CHAPTER SIX

Parallel Structure

A. ESTABLISHING THE BACKGROUND

Parallel structure is the presentation of related information in a sentence in a consistent, balanced manner, thereby contributing to writing clarity. Parallel structure is particularly important in sentences containing conjunctions, such as *and, but, or, either . . . or, neither . . . nor, not only . . . but also.*

Observe the sharper focus of the following sentences after the related information has been balanced grammatically, that is, after it has been presented in the same part of speech and word order:

Balancing Items in a Series

Not Parallel: Don enjoys swimming, tennis, and to work in his garden.

Parallel: Don enjoys <u>swimming</u>, <u>tennis</u>, and <u>working</u> in his garden.

or

Don enjoys <u>swimming</u>, <u>tennis</u>, and <u>gardening</u>.

Comment: The parallel sentences are clearer than the non-parallel one because the items in the series are balanced grammatically; that is, they are all nouns.

Not Parallel: Jason had to vacuum the carpets, to wash the windows, and emptying the wastepaper baskets before he leaves work.

Parallel: Jason has <u>to vacuum</u> the carpets, <u>to wash</u> the windows, and <u>to empty</u> the wastepaper baskets before he goes home.

Comment: The parallel sentence is clearer than the non-parallel one because the items in the series all begin with an infinitive phrase. (An infinitive phrase is <u>to</u> followed by a verb; this combination forms a noun.)

Balancing Similar Information

Not Parallel: My sister's dog is frisky but obeys well.

Parallel: My sister's dog is <u>frisky</u> but <u>obedient</u>.

Comment: The parallel sentence is clearer than the non-parallel one because the related information has been balanced grammatically; that is, <u>frisky</u> and <u>obedient</u> are both adjectives.

Not Parallel: Howard promised to attend the party and he would bring refreshments.

Parallel: Howard promised <u>to attend</u> the party and <u>to bring</u> refreshments.

   or

   Howard promised <u>that he would</u> attend the party and <u>that he would</u> bring refreshments.

Comment: The parallel sentences are clearer than the non-parallel one because of their grammatical consistency, that is, through infinitive phrases (the first parallel sentence) and dependent clauses (the second parallel sentence).

Balancing Contrasting Information

Not Parallel: Lindsay likes small discussion classes better.

Parallel: Lindsay likes small discussion classes better <u>than huge lecture courses</u>.

Comment: The parallel sentence is clearer than the non-parallel one because it indicates what is being contrasted with small discussion classes.

Not Parallel: Not only is Dr. Libby a fine dentist but also an outstanding guitarist.

Parallel: Dr. Libby is not only <u>a fine dentist</u> but also <u>an outstanding guitarist</u>.

Comment: The parallel sentence is clearer than the non-parallel one because the information following the correlative conjunctions (<u>not only</u>, <u>but also</u>) is balanced grammatically, that is, by two adjectives and one noun.

Do all the Exercises in Section B.

Remember: Present related information in a balanced way.

B. GAINING THE EXPERIENCE

Exercise 1: *Complete the parallel structure for each sentence by circling the letter before the appropriate word, phrases, or clause.*

1. My aerobics class is enjoyable, challenging, and

    A. it inspires me.

    B. inspirational.

2. Steve strolled into the kitchen, turned on the radio, and

    A. prepared dinner.

    B. dinner was prepared by him.

3. We were finally able to save money by working extra hours and

    A. eliminating unnecessary purchases.

    B. our unnecessary purchases were eliminated.

4. Art was busy in his garage repairing an old table's legs and

    A. the table's top was also being refinished by him.

    B. refinishing the table's top.

5. I don't know whether Phil is qualified or

    A. interested in the position.

    B. that the position would be of interest to him.

6. During the winter months, I enjoy skating, skiing, and

    A. to use the snowmobile.

    B. snowmobiling.

7. Kenny is upset not only with Betty but also

    A. Charlie has upset him.

    B. with Charlie.

8. Full of energy, Roxanne fed the cat, washed the dishes, and even

    A. the furniture was dusted by her.

    B. dusted the furniture.

9. Whatever your income, whatever your education, and

    A. whatever your age, you need to exercise.

    B. though you may be old, exercise is what you need.

10. Rain is more frequent along the coast than

    A. inland.

    B. it is inland.

NAME _____   DATE _____

Exercise 2:   *In the following set of sentences, one or both of the sentences may present its information in a balanced manner. Circle the letter that appears before those balanced sentences; then underline key words in the parallel structure. An example has been done for you.*

Example: A.   I don't mind changing a car's oil but dislike to fix a flat tire.

               (B.)   I don't mind <u>changing</u> a car's oil, but I dislike <u>fixing</u> a flat tire.

1.   A.   By taking government courses and by working for candidates, Kaye became knowledgeable about politics.

    B.   By taking government courses and because she worked for candidates, Kaye became knowledgeable about politics.

2.   A.   My little brother promised to mow the lawn and that he would weed the garden.

    B.   My little brother promised to mow the lawn and to weed the garden.

3.   A.   Martha is a charming young lady with an outstanding singing voice and who wants to become an actress.

    B.   Martha is a charming young lady who has an outstanding singing voice and who wants to become an actress.

4.   A.   Bob's dormitory is near the library, the student union, and the fieldhouse.

    B.   The library, student union, and fieldhouse are near Bob's dormitory.

5.   A.   Mr. Merritt asked Rodney whether he was afraid of heights and his painting experience.

    B.   Mr. Merritt asked Rodney whether he was afraid of heights and whether he had painting experience.

6.   A.   Jake's car burned oil and needed a new exhaust system.

    B.   Jake's car burned oil and was needing a new exhaust system.

7.   A.   Mark reluctantly agreed to wait for me but refused helping me finish the job.

    B.   Mark reluctantly agreed to wait for me, but he refused to help me finish the job.

8.   A.   The Nichols went to Florida to enjoy Disneyland and to visit friends in St. Augustine.

    B.   The Nichols went to Florida to enjoy Disneyland and for visiting friends in St. Augustine.

9.   A.   Reading detective stories and sports on television are my grandfather's favorite pastimes.

    B.   Reading detective stories and watching sports on television are my grandfather's favorite pastimes.

NAME _____   DATE _____

10. A. Veronica's goal is to become a doctor and to live in Oregon.

    B. Veronica's goal is to become a doctor and living in Oregon.

11. A. While Brian spends time mowing the lawn, his brother spends time weeding the garden.

    B. Brian spends his time mowing the lawn while time weeding the garden is spent by his brother.

12. A. Tim's favorite activities are shooting baskets and playing tennis.

    B. Tim's favorite activities are to shoot baskets and to play tennis.

Exercise 3: *Write* yes *in the blank if the word has proper parallelism,* no *if it does not.*

_____ 1. Coach Barker said our next game not only determines our final league standings but also determines whether or not we are selected for the tournament.

_____ 2. Coach Barker said not only does our next game determine our final league standing but it also determines whether or not we are selected for the tournament.

_____ 3. Either we play our best game of the year or our season is over.

_____ 4. Either we play our best game of the year or we realize our season is over.

_____ 5. Neither our fans believe we can win the game nor the newspaper reporters.

_____ 6. Neither our fans nor the newspaper reporters believe we can win the game.

_____ 7. Not only is Mr. Hughes a rich man, but he is also charitable.

_____ 8. Mr. Hughes is not only a rich man but also a charitable person.

_____ 9. Either Scott will continue teaching or go to graduate school.

_____ 10. Either Scott will continue teaching or he will go to graduate school.

_____ 11. Neither Fred nor John want to be reminded of that unpleasant incident.

_____ 12. Neither Fred wants to be reminded of that unpleasant incident nor does John.

NAME _____ DATE _____

Exercise 4:   *Rewrite the underlined part of each sentence so that the information in the series is in a parallel form. An example has been done for you.*

Example: Bob loves buying, fishing, and to <u>sell</u> old cars.

   selling

1.   Paul is considerate, <u>you can depend on him</u>, and honest.

   _____

2.   Mrs. Bryson's flower garden is spacious, unique, and <u>has beauty</u>.

   _____

3.   My swimming instructor said that I needed to improve my breathing, <u>how to float</u>, and kicking.

   _____

4.   The movie was crude, dull, and <u>lacked logic</u>.

   _____

5.   Before Rita leaves for work, she checks the thermostat, turns off the lights, feeds the cat, and <u>then the doors are locked by her</u>.

   _____

6.   Our community college has excellent programs in dental hygiene, <u>training law enforcement officers</u>, and hotel management.

   _____

7.   I admire my elderly neighbor because he is friendly, <u>has intelligence</u>, and humorous.

   _____

8.   Ashley is pleased with her new car's driving ease, riding comfort, and <u>the mileage she gets per gallon of gasoline</u>.

   _____

9.   The wind commenced to blow, the temperature started to plunge, and the sky <u>was darkening</u>.

   _____

10.   On the Fourth of July in the small community were I live, a parade is held, <u>there is the conducting of contests</u>, and fireworks are exploded.

   _____

NAME _____   DATE _____

Exercise 5:   *Complete each of the following sentences so that it is balanced grammatically. An example has been done for you.*

Example: Sophisticated machines washed, sorted, and

_packed the apples_____.

1. The paint on our house is fading, cracking, and

    _____.

2. Our instructor emphasized that either we did the work assigned or

    _____.

3. Mark is a good student as well as _____.

4. By painting the rooms and _____, we made
    the apartment quite attractive.

5. Cindy likes to shop at the Bickford Mall more than she likes

    _____.

6. Vernon promised the doctor that he would eat more sensibly and

    _____.

7. Blaine had a feeling of accomplishment after reading his assignments,

    studying his notes, and _____.

8. The movie is neither entertaining nor

    _____.

9. Exercise not only helps you to feel better but also

    _____.

10. I was shocked when my friend said that I was insensitive, intolerant, and

    _____.

Chapter 6
Review Exercise: *Write* <u>C</u> *in the space if the sentence has proper parallelism,* <u>X</u> *if it does not.*

_____ 1. The weather was pleasant in the morning, but in the afternoon it became cold, windy, and rainy.

_____ 2. Melba's speech, although short, was inspiring, challenging, and contained humor.

_____ 3. I discovered I could avoid most of the rush hour traffic by leaving thirty minutes earlier and by taking Pawlett Avenue.

_____ 4. Not only Whitney but Yolanda also made the varsity team.

_____ 5. The postal clerk told me to retape the package and that I should add the zip code to the address.

_____ 6. Rosa is happy she will be able to take optional as well as required courses this semester.

_____ 7. Carpentry requires manual dexterity, artistic abilities, and visual skills.

_____ 8. Apparently, Victor loves clothes that are old, bulky, and grungy.

_____ 9. The workers were unhappy with the proposal because it cut health benefits and because of fewer overtime opportunities.

_____ 10. Do you prefer to watch an old movie on a VCR or going to a theater to see a new one?

_____ 11. Though the camera was used, it came with a telephoto lens, a carrying bag, and a price that was affordable.

_____ 12. Erika says she is majoring in chemistry because she would like a career in either pharmacy, medicine, or engineering.

_____ 13. Jim researched the topic by examining articles, reading books, and interviewing experts.

_____ 14. As a result, his report was comprehensive, engrossing, and it had originality.

_____ 15. We hunted for Don's contact lens on the kitchen floor, in the sink, and behind the refrigerator.

_____ 16. If you take the job in the bakery, be prepared to rise early, to breathe flour, and to gain weight.

_____ 17. The symptoms of the disease include a high fever, a nagging cough, an upset stomach, and a neck that is stiff.

_____ 18. Molly is proud of her fame, fortune, and what she has achieved.

_____ 19. Dad plays tennis with an old wooden racket but golf with new clubs made of graphite.

_____ 20. The flooding caused damage in the downtown section as well as in the residential areas.

NAME _____   DATE _____

_____ 21. Lois said a perfect day for her would be shopping at the mall in the morning, swimming at the beach in the afternoon, and dining at a fancy restaurant in the evening.

_____ 22. His temper tantrums shocked, disappointed, and made people disgusted.

_____ 23. To win the game, our team must either make every shot or the referees must be bribed.

_____ 24. Neither Paula nor Lamar seem disturbed about what happened.

_____ 25. Wyoming is not only beautiful but also awesome.

_____ 26. Nurses at our small hospital have to feed and bathe patients, administer shots and other medications, and assist in the surgery and emergency rooms.

_____ 27. Amy is attractive, talented, and has charm.

_____ 28. Karen will either come here, or I will go there.

_____ 29. On Sunday afternoons, Mom read the paper, Dad dozed on the sofa, and I washed and wiped the dishes.

_____ 30. Neither Veronica knows where the car keys are nor does Jeff.

Rewrite Sentences 31–35 so each one has parallelism.

31. Since retiring two years ago, my grandparents have not only completed a number of college courses but they have traveled to Hawaii and Alaska also.

_____

_____

_____

32. My wife and I enjoy a flower garden more.

_____

_____

_____

33. Sidney lost weight by sensible dieting and because he exercised regularly.

_____

_____

_____

NAME _____   DATE _____

34. I quickly learned not to do three things around my temperamental roommate: to talk about sports, to snack on potato chips, and his girlfriend was never to be criticized.

_____

_____

_____

35. My adviser recommends I take either a foreign language course this semester or one in a science.

_____

_____

_____

NAME _____   DATE _____

C. APPLYING THE FINISHING TOUCH

(1) Proofreading: *Correct the eight errors having to do with parallel structure. Check your corrections with those in the **Answer Key.***

Mary Baker Eddy

Mary Baker Eddy, founder of the Christian Science Church, was born in Concord, New Hampshire, in 1821. For the first forty years of her life, Eddy was often frail, sickly, and her emotions varied. In 1862, she regained her health after a doctor convinced her that illness was often caused by the mind. After linking this and other beliefs, Eddy began publishing Science and Health, a handbook that was widely criticized as well as receiving praise.

Eddy was an inspiring teacher and an organizer that was effective. She maintained not only was illness unreal but death also was. To further spread her teachings, Eddy established the Christian Science Association and the Church of Christ Scientist was chartered by her. Her disciples were loyal, committed, and had devotion.

Though often criticized and given ridicule, Eddy was admired more. By the time of her death in 1910, Mary Baker Eddy and the church she had founded were well-known throughout America. She left most of her $2.5 million estate to her church, which numbered nearly 100,000 members.

NAME _____   DATE _____

(2) Proofreading: *After correcting the ten parallel structure mistakes, rewrite the entire passage on a separate piece of paper. Have your instructor check your work.*

James Monroe: Fifth President, 1817–1825

James Monroe, son of a planter and of five children the oldest, was born in Virginia in 1758. He received his basic education at a private school, then entering the College of William and Mary. When the Revolutionary War erupted, Monroe dropped out of college to join the army. During the war, he was wounded twice, given a promotion to major, and cited for bravery.

After his discharge from the army, Monroe studied law under the guidance of Thomas Jefferson, who became his lifelong friend and gave him advice. Monroe entered politics, eventually serving in the Virginia Legislature, the Continental Congress, and the United States Senate. He was also appointed to a number of diplomatic posts and serving as one of President Jefferson's principal negotiators for the Louisiana Purchase. In addition, not only was Monroe appointed secretary of state by President Madison, but twice he was also elected governor of Virginia.

Monroe was elected president in 1816. His presidency is often referred to as the "Era of Good Feelings" because the nation prospered economically and in world influence it grew. Monroe achieved diplomatic success through his Monroe Doctrine, a doctrine that warned foreign nations against further colonization in the Western Hemisphere. In addition, five new states were added to the Union and Florida was acquired from Spain. However, the nation did experience turmoil over the slavery issue when Missouri sought admission to the Union as a slave state. Finally, after two years of heated

NAME _____ DATE _____

debate, Congress agreed to the Missouri Compromise, which admitted Missouri as a slave state and a free state was how Maine was admitted. Nevertheless, from this time on, slavery became an increasingly divisive issue in the country.

After completing his second term as president, Monroe retired with his wife to Virginia, the place they liked better. When his wife died five years later, Monroe moved to New York City to live with one of his daughters. He died there on July 4, 1831, at age seventy-three. Monroe became the third president to have died on a July 4th; both John Adams and Thomas Jefferson had died on July 4, 1826.

NAME _____   DATE _____

Writing: **Would a bowler, gardener, or skydiver be most likely to go around muttering, "Energy and persistence can conquer all things"?**

State your choice and the reasons for it in writing.

Suggestions: **WRITE AND REWRITE** until you come up with convincing reasons for your choice; be imaginative so your writing will be fresh, original, and entertaining.

KEEP WRITING AND REVISING until you are pleased with what you have written; make sure your reasons are supported with numerous <u>particulars</u>.

TYPE AND DOUBLESPACE your final draft, which can be any length.

PROVIDE an intriguing title.

PROOFREAD for misspellings, fragments, subject-verb agreement errors, run-ons, modifier mistakes, and non-parallel structure; see **PROOFREADING TIPS** for further suggestions.

If you are also working on a **LONG-RANGE ASSIGNMENT,**
remember to budget your time wisely
and to keep in mind the **WRITING SUGGESTIONS.**

CHAPTER SEVEN

Verb Tense, Voice, and Person

A. ESTABLISHING THE BACKGROUND

VERB TENSE

Consistency is a characteristic of effective writing; it is a major indication that the writer is familiar with the topic and that he or she has presented information about it in a logical, clear manner. Therefore, you should proofread your writing with consistency in mind. In particular, you should examine your writing to see whether you have

- **stayed focused on your topic and purpose for writing;**
- **maintained a consistent attitude and approach;**
- **provided supporting evidence each time you made an assertion.**

You should also proofread your writing for consistent verb tense; <u>verb tense</u> refers to the time of action expressed by the verb. The basic verb tenses are *present, past* and *future:*

Present:	I <u>walk</u>.
Past:	I <u>walked</u>.
Future:	I <u>will walk</u>.

These three verb tenses have additional time references, referred to as *perfect* and *progressive,* which involve helping verbs and the suffix *-ing:*

Present Perfect:	I have walked.
Present Progressive:	I am walking.
Past Perfect:	I had walked.
Past Progressive:	I was walking.
Future Perfect:	I will have walked.
Future Progressive:	I will be walking.

For writing purposes, knowing the distinction between the various verb tenses is relatively unimportant; maintaining a consistent verb tense, however, is important. You can see this is so by drawing some conclusions about inconsistent verb tense after comparing the following paragraphs on the same subject:

Inconsistent Verb Tense:

In the War of 1812, many of the battles take place on the sea. The United States does well in these naval battles even though it had only sixteen ships compared to Britain's 800. The United States' ships, however, are faster and more maneuverable than the British vessels. In addition, most of the sea battles in this war were duels between single ships. The ships fire their guns at point-blank range, and the sailors often fought in hand-to-hand combat. The ships that fought in this long-ago war, and the officers who command them, should be remember.

Consistent Verb Tense:

In the War of 1812, many of the battles took place on the sea. The United States did well in these naval battles even though it had only sixteen ships compared to Great Britain's 800. The United States' ships, however, were much faster and more maneuverable than the British vessels. In addition, most of the sea battles in this war were duels between single ships. The ships fired their guns at point-blank range, and the sailors often fought in hand-to-hand combat. The ships that fought in this long-ago war, and the officers who commanded them, should be remembered.

Your conclusions about inconsistent verb tense are valid if they are similar to these:

- **Inconsistent verb tense blurs clarity, at least momentarily;**
- **Shifts in verb tense occur most frequently between present and past forms;**
- **A common error involving verb tense is carelessly omitting -ed.**

As an additional check for clarity, be sure to proofread your writing for inconsistent verb tense.

Do Exercise 1 in Section B.

IRREGULAR VERBS

Most verbs form their past tenses by adding either *-ed* or *-d:* walk, walk<u>ed</u>, walk<u>ed</u>; purchase, purchas<u>ed</u>, purchas<u>ed</u>. However, some verbs, called *irregular verbs,* form their past tenses either by changing internally or by using a different word as these numerous examples illustrate:

Present	Past	Past Participle	Present	Past	Past Participle
become	became	become	feel	felt	felt
begin	began	begun	fight	fought	fought
bite	bit	bitten	fly	flew	flown
blow	blew	blown	forget	forgot	forgotten
break	broke	broken	forgive	forgave	forgiven
bring	brought	brought	freeze	froze	frozen
build	built	built	get	got	got, gotten
buy	bought	bought	give	gave	given
come	came	come	go	went	gone
do	did	done	grow	grew	grown
dig	dug	dug	hear	heard	heard
draw	drew	drawn	hold	held	held
drink	drank	drunk	keep	kept	kept
drive	drove	driven	know	knew	known
eat	ate	eaten	lay	laid	laid
fall	fell	fallen	lead	led	led
feed	fed	fed	leave	left	left

Present	Past	Past Participle	Present	Past	Past Participle
lie	lay	lain	stand	stood	stood
lend	lent	lent	steal	stole	stolen
meet	met	met	strike	struck	struck
pay	paid	paid	swear	swore	sworn
ride	rode	ridden	swim	swam	swum
ring	rang	rung	swing	swung	swung
rise	rose	risen	take	took	taken
run	ran	run	teach	taught	taught
say	said	said	tear	tore	torn
see	saw	seen	tell	told	told
shake	shook	shaken	think	thought	thought
shine	shone	shone	throw	threw	thrown
shoot	shot	shot	understand	understood	understood
shrink	shrank	shrunk	wake	woke,	woken
sit	sat	sat		waked	waked
sing	sang	sung	wear	wore	worn
sink	sank	sunk	win	won	won
speak	spoke	spoken	wind	wound	wound
spin	spun	spun	wring	wrung	wrung
spring	sprang	sprung	write	wrote	written

These irregular verbs do not change regardless of tense:

Present	Past	Past Participle
burst	burst	burst
cut	cut	cut
read	read	read
set	set	set

COMMON IRREGULAR VERB ERRORS

Irregular verb errors occur when the past and past participle tenses are used incorrectly. The irregular verbs of *do, did, done* and *go, went, gone* are particularly troublesome for many people; however, if you remember *done* and *gone* require helping verbs (see page 3) as all past participles do, you will avoid making mistakes.

Present	Past	Past Participle (requires a helping verb)
do	did	done
go	went	gone

Incorrect: We <u>done</u> the work last night. (done requires a helping verb, so use did)

Correct: We <u>did</u> the work last night.

Incorrect: My brother has <u>did</u> that stunt many times. (has is a helping verb, so use done)

Correct: My brother has <u>done</u> that stunt many times.

Incorrect: We <u>gone</u> to the movies last night with Buddy and Evelyn. (gone requires a helping verb, so use went)

Correct: We <u>went</u> to the movies last night with Buddy and Evelyn.

Incorrect: Have you <u>went</u> to the new shopping mall? (have is a helping verb, so use gone)

Correct: Have you <u>gone</u> to the new shopping mall?

In addition, the irregular verbs *lie, lay, lain* (to rest, recline; no action shown) and *lay, laid, laid* (to place or set something down; action shown) are often confused:

Incorrect: The cat is <u>laying</u> on the bed. (the cat is resting and there is no action shown, so use lying)

Correct: The cat is <u>lying</u> on the bed.

Incorrect: We need to <u>lie</u> some more logs on the fire. (logs are placed and there is action shown, so use lay)

Correct: We need to <u>lay</u> some more logs on the fire.

Also, be careful not to use nonstandard verbs:

Incorrect: Sheila <u>brang</u> her best friend to the party. (brang is nonstandard, so use brought)

Correct: Sheila <u>brought</u> her best friend to the party.

Incorrect: Sam <u>wrang</u> out his swimming suit before hanging it on the line. (wrang is nonstandard, so use wrung)

Correct: Sam <u>wrung</u> out his swimming suit before hanging it on the line.

Incorrect: I <u>knowed</u> Garth was a good basketball player because I played against him a couple of weeks ago. (knowed is nonstandard, so use knew)

Correct: I <u>knew</u> Garth was a good basketball player because I played against him a couple of weeks ago.

Do Exercises 2 and 3 in Section B.

VOICE

In writing, <u>voice</u> determines whether the subject does the acting or is acted upon. If the subject does the acting, then the verb is in <u>active voice</u>; if the subject is acted upon, then the verb is in <u>passive voice</u>. The identical information can be written in either voice, but notice that the <u>active voice</u> produces a more vigorous and concise sentence:

Passive Voice: The baseball dugout was built by the maintenance crew.
Active Voice: The maintenance crew built the baseball dugout.

Passive Voice: The shopping mall was crowded with people of all ages.
Active Voice: People of all ages crowded the shopping mall.

Although it is not wrong to write in the passive voice, the preceding examples illustrate that sentences in the active voice are more direct and forceful. There may be times when it is necessary or advisable to write in the passive voice, but for most subjects and purposes, you will find that the active voice adds vigor to your writing.

PERSON

Person, as a writing term, refers to the view from which you are writing, which can be one of the following:

First Person: I, we
Second Person: you
Third Person;   he, she, they, one

You should consider your topic, purpose, and audience in deciding whether to write in the first, second, or third person. When you adopt the appropriate point of view as to person, stay with it; otherwise, your sentences will likely be awkward and confusing.

See the value of adopting a consistent person point of view by studying the following versions of the same passage:

Shift in Point of View of Person:

I recently read an interesting book about Dolley Madison, the wife of the fourth president of the United States. <u>One</u> learns, for instance, that she was a young widow living in Philadelphia when she was introduced by Aaron Burr to the well-known James Madison. <u>You</u> discover that her first husband had died during a malaria outbreak. <u>I</u> also found out that Dolley was a head taller and twenty-one years younger than James and that she was much more friendly and outgoing than he was. But despite their physical, age, and personality differences, <u>one</u> learns that the Madisons had a very happy marriage.

Consistent Point of View of Person:

<u>I</u> recently read an interesting book about Dolley Madison, the wife of the fourth President of the United States. <u>I</u> learned, for instance, that she was a young widow living in Philadelphia when she was introduced by Aaron Burr to the well-known James Madison. <u>I</u> discovered that her first husband had died during a malaria outbreak. <u>I</u> also found out that Dolley was a head taller and twenty-one years younger than James and that she was much more friendly and outgoing than he was. But despite their physical, age, and personality differences, <u>I</u> learned that the Madisons had a very happy marriage.

A consistent point of view of person, as the last version demonstrates, contributes to writing clarity. Therefore, add this item to your proofreading checklist.

> Maintain a consistent point of view of person.

Do Exercise 3 and the Review Exercises in Section B.

B. GAINING THE EXPERIENCE

Exercise 1: *Inconsistent verb tense causes lack of clarity in the following passage. Rewrite the passage on the lines that follow; in the first version, put all of the verbs in the present tense. In the second version, put all of the verbs into the past tense. Underline your verbs in both versions.*

Millard Fillmore, who became president after the death of Zachary Taylor, was the second vice president to assume the highest office in the nation after the death of his predecessor; John Tyler was the first vice president to do so. Fillmore assumes the office on July 10, 1850. Fillmore is from the state of New York, and he was fifty-years-old at the time of his inauguration; his father is alive at this time. Fillmore has once been a lawyer, and he had served in the House of Representatives. He is married and the father of two daughters.

Rewritten version with all verbs in the present tense:

_____

_____

_____

_____

_____

_____

_____

_____

_____

_____

NAME _____   DATE _____

Rewritten version with all verbs in the past tense:

_____

_____

_____

_____

_____

_____

_____

_____

_____

_____

Exercise 2: *Underline the correct form of the verb; remember, some tenses require helping verbs, so you may want to review pages 3 and 4 of Chapter One and the first page of this chapter before doing the exercise.*

1. Dodd had never (drove, driven) a truck until he rented one.

2. The snow (begin, began, begun) to fall early this morning.

3. I must have (drank, drunk) a gallon of water after I had (ate, eaten) a bowl of Valerie's chilli.

4. The Wildcats have (blew, blown) a lead, but I still believe they'll (win, won) the game.

5. Fortunately, Aaron (forgive, forgave, forgiven) me, just as he's (forgive, forgave, forgiven) me so many times before.

6. Don has (took, taken) a plane to Minneapolis for a job interview.

7. Melba is calling her parents tonight because she hasn't (wrote, written) to them since she (come, came, come) to school.

8. The meteorologist (say, said) the temperature will drop so low tonight that the river will (freeze, froze, frozen).

9. Reggie (tear, tore) out of his room about an hour ago.

10. Giles was obviously (shook, shaken) by the news that Kris is dating someone else.

11. Security in our dorm needs to be tightened because someone (steal, stole) Jim's computer, and that's the second one that's been (stole, stolen) in less than a month.

NAME _____   DATE _____

12. Serena (spring, sprang, sprung) out of bed this morning to go jogging with her new boyfriend.

13. Jessie didn't feel well this morning, so he has (laid, lain) in bed all day.

14. Professor Lopez, my favorite teacher, (tell, told) me she (teach, taught) at a college in New Jersey before coming here.

15. All witnesses must (swear, swore, sworn) to tell the truth.

16. We (saw, seen) the movie last week, so we're going bowling.

17. Tom (do, did, done) well at the audition, so Mr. Civelli offered him a role in the play.

18. Karla (knew, knowed) you might be late, so she (leave, left) without you.

19. Marty (swang, swung) the bat with all his might, but the ball just dribbled back to the pitcher.

20. Willie (brang, brought) along his guitar, so we (sing, sang, sung) some songs.

Exercise 3: *Write an original sentence for each verb tense.*

1. lie, lay, lain

(lie) _____

_____

(lay) _____

_____

(lain) _____

_____

2. lay, laid, laid

(lay) _____

_____

(laid) _____

_____

(laid) _____

_____

NAME _____   DATE _____

3. go, went, gone

(go) _____

_____

(went) _____

_____

(gone) _____

_____

4. do, did, done

(do) _____

_____

(did) _____

_____

(done) _____

_____

Exercise 4: *Convert the following sentences from the passive to the active voice. An example has been done for you.*

Example: The money for the project was donated by Mr. and Mrs. Murphy.

Active: *Mr. and Mrs. Murphy donated the money for the project.*

1. The garage and basement were cleaned by Steve and Shawn.

Active: _____

_____

2. Appreciation was expressed by the judge to the jury.

Active: _____

_____

3. The coffee was spilled all over the counter by the nervous waitress.

Active: _____

_____

4. The peace and quiet was suddenly interrupted by a roaring lawnmower.

Active: _____

_____

5. The vending machines in the lobby were filled by a young man in a blue uniform.

Active: _____

_____

6. All of the electrical work was done by Mr. Richards.

Active: _____

_____

7. The puzzling murder case was finally solved by Miss Marple, Agatha Christie's most beloved detective.

Active: _____

_____

8. The impressive photographs hanging in the hallway were taken and developed by Frank.

Active: _____

_____

9. The final remodeling decisions were made by my parents.

Active: _____

_____

10. When Ann and Gene announced their engagement, approval was expressed by everyone.

Active: _____

_____

NAME _____ DATE _____

Exercise 5: *The following passage fails to maintain a consistent point of view of person, so after crossing out the inconsistencies, write in the correct words. The first correction has been done for you.*

Thank you, Lesley

Although I grew up in a state where skiing is popular, I never learned to ski as a youngster because I was convinced this sport required more skill and daring than I possessed. However, during my first year in college, my friend Lesley kept urging me to go skiing with her. I made one lame excuse after another about why I couldn't go before I finally admitted to her that I didn't know how to ski. Lesley said "no problem" as she would be glad to teach me, and I knew by the way she said it ~~you~~ I couldn't make any more excuses.

But when the day arrived when I had agreed to go skiing with her, I actually drove over to Lesley's dormitory to tell her I had changed my mind. However, she was already waiting for me, standing in the dorm's parking lot with a big smile and ski equipment sprawled all around her. You couldn't chicken out now, so with fear and trembling, I was soon on my way to the slopes.

I never felt so awkward or as embarrassed in my life as the first few times I tried to stand wearing skis; I quickly concluded there was no way I would ever be able to maintain my balance, health, or dignity on skis. However, within an hour, Lesley not only had me standing but also had me snowplowing down a short beginners' slope. As the day progressed, my skill

NAME _____   DATE _____

and confidence slowly grew, and one could tell I was becoming hooked on skiing.

Lesley deserves the credit for my early progress on skis as she was a patient, understanding, and encouraging teacher. She didn't laugh at one's fears or falls, and her comments were always helpful and reassuring. By the end of the day, I was confidently skiing down the longest beginners' slope, and I was already looking forward to going skiing again.

Since that fateful day three winters ago, I have gone skiing many times. Although I have never become as accomplished a skier as Lesley or some of my other friends, I am able to ski most trails, a feat you would never have dreamed possible when one thinks back to my first day on skis. I will always be grateful to Lesley, for skiing has increased my self-confidence and brought me more pleasure than anyone could ever have imagined.

NAME _____   DATE _____

Chapter 7
Review Exercise: *A.   Underline the correct verb or verbs in each sentence.*

1. Yesterday, I had a difficult time getting my dog to (lay, lie) down so Dr. McIntosh could examine him.

2. Today, however, Rover has (laid, lain) in front of the fireplace for hours.

3. I believe you (laid, lie) your coat on the sofa when you came in.

4. Art believes he should have (gone, went) with Jane to see the realtor.

5. However, if he would have (gone, went), he would have (became, become) irritated with the realtor's high-pressured sales tactics.

6. Instead of pizza, Willie (bring, brang, brought) Chinese food home for supper.

7. I (knew, knowed) he was a talented actor, but I never (knew, knowed) he (sang, sung) so well.

8. After washing the dishes, Marc (did, done) the vacuuming.

9. He even (wrang, wrung) out the tablecloth in the sink.

10. Someone must have (teached, taught) him to do his part when he lives with another person.

11. Louise (see, saw, seen) the movie a couple of weeks ago.

12. Believe me, I have (rode, ridden) that subway more times than I can count.

13. Although we had a good time hunting, we were about (froze, frozen) when we got home.

14. When you hear the bell (ring, rang, rung), the time will be six o'clock.

15. The wind (blowed, blew) so hard last night I thought the roof was going to be (blowed, blown) away.

B.   In the following passage, nine verbs need to be changed to the past tense, and one correction needs to be made in person. In addition, four underlined sentences need to be changed from passive to active voice. Rewrite the passage on the lines that follow.

Texas History

People living in Texas soon learn of their state's colorful history. You

learn, for example, that by the early 1830s many Americans had settled in

Texas, then owned by Mexico. The Mexican government expects the American settlers to become Mexican citizens and to adopt the Catholic religion, steps most of the Americans refuse to take. In addition, Mexican authorities wish to abolish slavery, an action also oppose by the Americans.

In 1836, a revolt erupts. To put down the uprising, a large army was led into Texas by Mexican President Santa Anna. At a mission-fortress in San Antonio called the Alamo, all 183 defenders were killed by Santa Anna's troops. "Remember the Alamo" then becomes the rallying cry of the Americans remaining in Texas, and they become even more determined to achieve independence.

Eventually, the Texas army, commanded by Sam Houston, win a decisive battle at San Jacinto. An independent government was soon formed by the Texans. A few years later, Texas was annexed by the United States.

NAME _____   DATE _____

C. APPLYING THE FINISHING TOUCH

(1) Proofreading: *Correct the two verb tense errors and the eight errors having to do with point of view of person. In addition, change the four underlined sentences from the passive to the active voice. Check your corrections with those in **Answer Key**.*

Handling Criticism

Criticism is brushed off by some people. However, criticism is taken personally by me. I used to respond to faultfinding with either anger or sulkiness. Recently, however, I concluded that criticism is something one will encounter throughout life, so you should learn to deal with it as constructively as possible.

One way I have learned to cope with criticism is really to listen to what my critic is saying. Rather than interrupting with "You don't know what you're talking about" as I previously did, I now acknowledge the person's criticism with "I understand what you're saying." This response, one learns, leads to a positive exchange of viewpoints rather than to an escalation of bitter remarks. In addition, you often discover the person's criticism is justified or at least understandable, so the necessary steps leading to personal improvement or better communications can be taken.

Furthermore, the fine line between criticism and praise is now recognized by me. For example, when someone recently criticized me for making hasty decisions, I remembered the day before another person had complimented me for my decisiveness. Thus, my ability to accept criticism more objectively has improved since recognizing people sometimes reach vastly different conclusions about your behavior.

NAME _____   DATE _____

Finally, criticism is handled more effectively by me today because of a more sensible reaction to it. By focusing on the possible merits of the criticism rather than on the potential damage to my self-esteem, you put yourself in a "no-lose" position: either the criticism prompts me to improve in some way, or it provides me with reassurance that my conduct in this particular matter is appropriate despite the criticism.

Dealing with criticism is not easy for us, but the preceding approaches have certainly helped.

NAME _____   DATE _____

(2) Proofreading: *After changing the underlined sentences from the passive to the active voice and correcting the verb tense and point of view errors, rewrite the entire passage on a separate piece of paper. Have your instructor check your work.*

John Quincy Adams: Sixth President, 1825–1829

I have recently learned some interesting facts about John Quincy Adams, the sixth president of the United States. I learned, for example, that he is the only president whose father also held that office; his father was John Adams, the second president. One discovers also that the lives of John and John Quincy Adams are alike in other respects as well: both graduate from Harvard University, trained as lawyers, entered diplomatic service, and served as peace commissioners; the treaty ending the Revolutionary War was negotiated by John Adams, and the treaty ending the War of 1812 was negotiated by John Quincy Adams. In addition, both Adamses serve only one term as president. Finally, you learn that they were buried side by side in a cemetery in Quincy, Massachusetts.

John Quincy Adams, born in 1767 in Massachusetts, spend his youth in Europe where his father served as a diplomat for the United States. As a result, John Quincy becomes fluent in several languages and learns the customs of various European nations. One can see how this background served him well later when he himself become a diplomat to Holland, Germany, Russia, and England.

After serving as President Monroe's Secretary of State, John Quincy Adams became president in 1825. A number of bold and farsighted proposals were made by Adams during his presidency. He suggests, for example,

NAME _____   DATE _____

that a national university be established and that a comprehensive network of highways and canals be constructed. You learn, however, that none of Adams's proposals received the backing of either the Congress or the general public, and he was soundly defeated for reelection in 1828. However, his public life is not over. In 1831, he was elected to the House of Representatives where he served for eighteen years; he is the only president to have been a congressman after having been president.

In 1848, John Quincy Adams dies at age eighty, two days after collapsing on the floor of the House of Representatives. Truly, no president ever serve his nation so long or in so many capacities as John Quincy Adams.

NAME _____   DATE _____

Writing: Explain in writing the differences in meaning between the two words in either **A, B,** or **C:**

    A. unhappiness / misery

    B. pride / chauvinism

    C. impudence / boldness

Suggestions: **JOT DOWN** for as long as you can anything coming to mind when you concentrate on the first word; do the same for the second word; then look up their precise meanings in a dictionary.

CONCENTRATE on providing illustrations and examples to clarify the distinctions between the two words you have selected; put your imagination to work.

LET A DAY OR TWO PASS after completing your first draft.

READ your first draft a number of times; make any additions, deletions, or other changes you feel are needed; your paper's effectiveness depends mainly upon the quality of your examples and illustrations you use to clarify the distinctions between the two words.

WRITE AND REWRITE until you are pleased with what you have produced.

LIMIT the final draft to <u>one complete page</u>, typewritten and doublespaced.

PROVIDE a title.

PROOFREAD, paying special attention to verb tense, point of view, voice, and the type of errors you may have made in previous papers; also consult **PROOFREADING TIPS.**

If you are working on a **LONG-RANGE ASSIGNMENT,**
be sure to ask a librarian for assistance
if you need help finding adequate information sources.

CHAPTER EIGHT

Punctuation — 1

A. ESTABLISHING THE BACKGROUND

END MARKS

We know from our own proofreading experiences that many of our writing errors are caused by carelessness, not ignorance. Sometimes we simply omit a word: *Last night, the President   *   his State of the Union message.* (* *delivered*)

Carelessness, not ignorance, is often responsible for our punctuation mistakes. For example, we may neglect to punctuate at the end of a sentence, or we may use a period when we should have used a question mark, as in this sentence: *Where did you park the car.*

We may make other simple errors with end marks even though we know the following about periods, question marks, and exclamation points:

● PERIODS follow statements, commands, and abbreviations:

Statement	The sunny weather boosted everyone's morale.
Command	Marc, practice your piano lesson before going out to play.

Abbreviations		
	Dr. Cooper	Rev. Sturdevant
	Lillian Rogers, Ph.D.	10:00 p.m.
	U.S.A.	Ms. White

● **QUESTION MARKS are used after direct questions. Periods are used after indirect ones:**

Direct Question	When is your brother arriving?
Indirect Question	Sharon asked when your brother is arriving.
Direct Question	Darlene, why did you quit your job?
Indirect Question	I asked Darlene why she quit her job.

● **EXCLAMATION POINTS are used after words or sentences expressing strong emotions:**

Good grief!	Look out!
Ouch!	Our team won the game!

To review your competency in using end marks, do Exercise 1 in Section B.

COMMAS

Although we use the versatile comma frequently in our writing, we may sometimes be uncertain about its use and placement in specific sentences. For example, in writing "When you travel by car you should always use your seatbelt," we may initially feel that a comma is needed somewhere in the sentence for clarity, but after further reflection, we may decide a comma is probably unnecessary. However, if we do decide a comma is needed, then we may be unsure as to its proper location in the sentence. (The comma belongs after car.)

— If you sometimes experience such uncertainties with commas, then the background information that follows should prove helpful to you.

1. Items in a Series

Commas are used to separate three or more items in a series:
Travis left his billfold, wristwatch, and ring on the dresser.

We scraped, primed, and painted the garage in one week's time.

Notice that a comma is <u>not</u> used after the last item in the series; in fact, it is incorrect to do so:

Incorrect: Betty turned on the air conditioning, drank a tall glass of ice tea, and finally went swimming, in an effort to escape the blistering heat.

Correct: Betty turned on the air conditioning, drank a tall glass of ice tea, and finally went swimming in an effort to escape the blistering heat.

Note: To avoid possible confusion when listing items in a series, use a comma before the <u>and</u>: We enjoyed swimming, sailing, and hiking on our recent vacation.

2. Descriptive Words in a Series

A comma is used between descriptive words only if (1) the words could be reversed and (2) the word <u>and</u> inserted between them would sound natural, as in the following examples:

The police officer kept calm despite the suspect's <u>belligerent, disrespectful</u> manner.

The descriptive words could be reversed and <u>and</u> inserted between them sounds natural:

The police officer kept calm despite the suspect's <u>disrespectful and belligerent</u> manner.

A comma is <u>not</u> used between descriptive words if the two preceding requirements are not met, as in the following examples:

The <u>old wooden</u> floor groaned every time we stepped on it.   (A comma is not used because "the <u>wooden and old</u> floor sounds unnatural.)

Mindy bought the <u>pale green</u> dress.   (A comma is not used because "<u>green and pale</u> dress" sounds unnatural.)

3. Sentences Connected with Coordinating Conjunctions

As was pointed out in Chapter Four, a comma is used between sentences connected by <u>and</u>, <u>but</u>, <u>or</u>, <u>nor</u>, <u>for</u>, <u>so</u>, <u>yet</u>; the comma should be placed <u>before</u> the conjunction:

Matthew works as a carpenter during the day, <u>and</u> he attends college in the evening.

Brigitte searched everywhere for the car keys, <u>but</u> she couldn't find them.

Juanita will meet us at the restaurant, <u>or</u> she will catch up with us later at the mall.

I didn't know where I was, <u>nor</u> could I read the street signs because of the driving snow.

Emily bought the old school desk, <u>for</u> she loves antiques.

The rain continued all day, <u>so</u> the baseball game was canceled.

There are not any westerns on television any more, <u>yet</u> I think many people miss this type of show.

4. Sentences Connected with Conjunctive Adverbs

When a semicolon and conjunctive adverb are used to join sentences, place a comma after the conjunctive adverb:

Cynthia is taking an overload this semester; <u>furthermore,</u> she plans to go to summer school.

Marc didn't attend school last semester; <u>therefore,</u> he will not graduate this spring.

Harper has a lab class on Thursday afternoons; <u>consequently,</u> he's late to practice.

Fawn lives over forty miles from campus; <u>nevertheless,</u> she never misses a class.

Before continuing this review of commas, do Exercise 2 in Section B.

5. Introductory Material

Use a comma after <u>introductory words</u> like the following:

No, I have never met a movie star.

Yes, the train should arrive on time.

Alas, I failed to take advantage of my opportunity.

However, we became close friends despite our numerous differences.

Dodging and weaving, Jack made it to the four-yard line before being tackled.

Slowly but steadily, the climbers worked their way up the mountain.

A phrase, you will recall from Chapter Two, is a word group that adds important or interesting information to a basic sentence. (A phrase never contains <u>both</u> a subject and verb.) You should use a comma after <u>introductory phrases</u> like the following:

After breakfast at our grandparents, we left for Chicago.

During the game, someone blew a whistle.

Walking rapidly, Regina got to church on time.

Having recovered from his operation, Paul was soon back to work.

A clause, you will also recall from Chapter Two, is a group of words containing both a subject and verb. Dependent clauses begin with a subordinating conjunction like <u>although</u>, <u>because</u>, and <u>if</u>. A comma should be used when a sentence <u>begins with a dependent clause</u>; a comma is unnecessary if the dependent clause comes later.

Comma: Because he was tired, Fred didn't go jogging with us.

No Comma: Fred didn't go jogging with us because he was tired.

Comma: Although she had studied the correct material, Amy wasn't confident that she had done well on the test.

No Comma: Amy wasn't confident that she had done well on the test although she had studied the correct material.

6. Extra Information

Carefully examine these two sentences:

Marlene Hall, who is a neighbor of mine, was recently elected to the city council.

A woman who is a neighbor of mine was recently elected to the city council.

In the first sentence, <u>who is a neighbor of mine</u> is extra information because this clause is not needed to identify the subject of the sentence; therefore, commas are placed around such nonessential information.

In the second sentence, however, <u>who is a neighbor of mine</u> is essential to identify the subject; therefore, commas are <u>not</u> placed around such essential information.

Here are additional examples:

David Jackson, an old friend from college, is president of the company.
An old friend from college is president of the company.

In the first sentence, commas are placed around <u>an old friend</u> because it is extra (nonessential) information. However, in the second sentence, <u>an old friend</u> is necessary to identify the subject, so commas are not used. The same reasoning applies to these examples:

<u>I Confess</u>, an Alfred Hitchcock film, is one of my favorite movies.
An Alfred Hitchcock film <u>I Confess</u> is one of my favorite movies.

Commas are placed around interrupting information such as the following:

Brenda, of course, was delighted by the news.
My dog's blanket, tattered and torn, should be replaced with a new one.
Tom's parents believe, therefore, that he shouldn't buy a car.
Joyce's boyfriend, I think, graduated from college last year.

An *appositive* is a noun or noun phrase that renames or further identifies an immediately preceding noun; appositives are usually set off by commas:

David Fernandez, a *lawyer,* is chairing the committee.
Dr. Sabrina Meadows, *president of the college,* will be the speaker.

Occasionally, an appositive appears before the noun it is referring to:

A *registered German shepherd,* Colonel is training to be a guide dog.

If an appositive is essential for clear identification, commas are not used.

The country singer *Ricky Skaggs* is a talented guitarist.

**Do Exercise 3 in Section B
before continuing.**

7. Commas—Other Uses

A comma should be used to set off a <u>direct quotation</u> from the rest of the sentence.

The hostess asked, "Do you have a reservation?"

"When I was in high school," Chuck remarked, "I decided I wanted to become a basketball coach."

"Diane's an excellent pianist," Mr. Copley responded.

A comma should be used when a <u>person is spoken to directly</u>:

Harold, what kind of car are you driving now?

I believe, Debra, that you will enjoy college.

Why are you so angry, Frank?

Commas should be used in the opening and closing of letters:

Dear Roger,   Sincerely yours,

Dear Susan,   As ever,

Commas should be used in <u>addresses</u>, <u>dates</u>, and <u>numbers</u>:

Bangor, Maine	February 20, 1865	34,127
New Orleans, Louisiana	June 15, 1963	1,083,249

My folks were married on October 8, 1974, in Santa Fe, New Mexico.

Atlanta, Georgia, has been selected as the site for the convention.

Do Exercise 4 in Section B.

SEMICOLONS

If you prefer, you can use a semicolon (;) rather than a period to separate closely related sentences:

Daylight was almost gone; Fred would have to hurry to finish the job.

Rain continued to fall; flooding became a real danger.

Norma is an excellent student; she has been accepted into medical school.

My brother is quite shy; I was surprised he asked her for a date.

As the preceding examples demonstrate, a semicolon follows a complete sentence, and it does not require an accompanying coordinating conjunction (and, or, but, for, nor, yet, so) as a comma does when it links sentences. Also notice that although the semicolon is used like a period, the word that follows a semicolon is not capitalized unless it is a proper noun or the pronoun I.

As mentioned, semicolons are not used with coordinating conjunctions, but they are often used with adverbial conjunctions such as however, therefore, consequently, and furthermore:

Bob intended to go hiking with us; however, he has a sprained ankle.

I thought Paul was asking too much for his car; therefore, I didn't buy it.

Gretta is an excellent boss; consequently, her employees are very loyal to her.

We plan to visit Williamsburg, Virginia; furthermore, we hope to see Monticello, Thomas Jefferson's home, and Mount Vernon, George Washington's home.

Note: A comma rather than a semicolon is used before and after an adverbial conjunction if the adverbial conjunction is not located between sentences: You will, however, have to work every other Saturday.

Semicolons, then are used to separate closely related sentences. Another proper, but more infrequent, use of semicolons is to clarify a sentence that contains numerous commas:

Attending the meeting were Travis Claypool, the mayor, Richard Jacobi, the city engineer, and Sandra McCloud, the architect.

Did six or three people attend the meeting? Semicolons eliminate such confusion:

Attending the meeting were Travis Claypool, the mayor; Richard Jacobi, the city engineer; and Sandra McCloud, the architect.

COLONS

Colons (:), like semicolons, should be used after complete sentences. The information that follows a colon should illustrate or explain the sentence that precedes it. Colons are properly used after sentences that introduce

a list	I have three favorite sports: fishing, bowling, and softball.
a long quotation	My older brother says that the following remarks by Arnold Bennett have been a motivating factor in his adult life: "Having once decided to achieve a certain task, achieve it at all costs of tedium and distaste. The gain in self-confidence of having accomplished a tiresome labor is immense."
an explanation	I know why Brian is hanging around you so much: he hopes you will introduce him to your sister.
an example	Glen is an excellent gourmet chef: he is famous for his veal cordon bleu.

Other proper uses of the colon include the following:

Subdivisions of time	10:30 a.m.
Greeting in a formal letter	Dear Madam:
Separating a book title from its subtitle	*Citizen Soldiers: A History of the National Guard*

Do Exercise 5 in Section B.

QUOTATION MARKS

Use quotation marks when you write the exact words of a speaker or author. At the end of a quote, the quotation marks are placed <u>outside</u> the comma, period, or question mark:

"Margaret, I appreciate your willingness to help me," Mr. Simon responded.

Ryan answered, "I should be home within the hour."

"Is it still raining?" Uncle Orville asked.

"Effective time management must begin with a thorough inventory of how you are currently using your time," according to the author of this book.

Bertrand Russell wrote the following: "Thinking you know when in fact you don't is a fatal mistake to which we are all prone."

An *indirect quotation* does not require quotation marks as it is a rewording of what someone said rather than the exact words; the words <u>that</u> and <u>if</u> often indicate an indirect quotation:

Mr. Simon said <u>that</u> he appreciated Margaret's willingness to help him.

Ryan said <u>that</u> he should be home within the hour.

Uncle Orville asked <u>if</u> it was still raining.

The author of this book maintains <u>that</u> effective time management must begin with a complete assessment of how you are currently using your time.

Bertrand Russell said <u>that</u> thinking we know something when we actually don't is a common <u>but</u> serious mistake.

Quotation marks are also used with the titles of songs, poems, short stories, articles, and chapter titles, <u>but</u> the titles of books, magazines, newspapers, movies, and television shows are <u>underlined</u>:

Quotation Marks	**Underlined**
the song "Wheel of Fortune"	the book <u>The Day Lincoln Was Shot</u>
the poem "Death of the Hired Man"	the magazine <u>Newsweek</u>
the short story "Young Goodman Brown"	the newspaper <u>Des Moines Register</u>
an article "What Does Your Name Mean?"	the movie <u>Gone With the Wind</u>
a chapter title "A New Role in World Affairs"	the television show <u>St. Elsewhere</u>

Do Exercise 6 and the Review Exercise in Section B.

B. GAINING THE EXPERIENCE

Exercise 1:   *If a sentence or an abbreviation lacks punctuation or is punctuated improperly, then make the appropriate correction. If a sentence is punctuated correctly, then write C after it. A couple of examples have been done for you.*

Examples: Why can't you go to the game ✗ **?**

The bus driver was friendly and courteous. **C**

1. Are you sure the store is open.
2. My goodness! Have you ever seen such a messy room?
3. My folks just love to watch old movies on their videocassette
4. When did Lt. Means get transferred to Fort Ord?
5. Look out there's a child in the road
6. Kurt asked how much the job paid?
7. I understand that Larry Dennius, MD, will be the luncheon speaker.
8. Gracious. You look terrible.
9. We asked the instructor when the test would be?
10. Charles, turn off your radio and get that paper written immediately.

Exercise 2:   *Insert commas if needed in the following sentences.*

1. The first four presidents of the United States were George Washington, John Adams, Thomas Jefferson, and James Madison.
2. My neighbors are camping at a beautiful provincial park, on Prince Edward Island.
3. The doctor quickly reassured the parents, for he could see how worried they were.
4. David fell asleep watching television, but Roger and Keith played ping-pong until after midnight.
5. Art is one of the most versatile and intelligent, workers we have in our business.
6. Shelly will pick us up at the airport, or she will have a taxi waiting for us.
7. The Ortons raise, corn soybeans and pigs on their Iowa farm.

NAME   *Chantha Chea*   DATE _____

8. Carol's folks operate a small general store, in our bustling little community.

9. I didn't give the begging man any money, yet I felt sorry for him.

10. Marilyn was impressed by his sensitive, insightful reply.

11. The snow continued most of the night; nevertheless the main streets had been plowed before I left for work.

12. I went to the drugstore intending to buy only a newspaper, but I ended up buying toothpaste, shampoo, vitamins, batteries, a magazine and a newspaper.

13. They labored all day in the suffocating sticky heat.

14. Jordan was a math major his first two years in college but he switched his major to economics when he was a junior.

15. Lyman and his pals drove all night; thus they got to Florida before we did.

Exercise 3: *Insert commas if needed in the following sentences.*

1. Bates College, which is located in Maine, is where my mother went to school.

2. Yes, I would like to have dessert.

3. Although he had promised to come, Ryan missed the meeting.

4. Ryan missed the meeting, although he had promised to come.

5. The bus parked behind the Student Union, is the one that goes to the shopping mall.

6. The Cranston bus, which is parked behind the Student Union, is the one that goes to the shopping mall.

7. However, I would be glad to drive you there.

8. Until Vanessa called me, I was uncertain about the outcome of the election.

9. Sidney, believe it, or not was elected our representative.

10. E. B. White's, Charlotte's Web is a popular children's book.

11. Charlotte's Web written by E. B. White, is a popular children's book.

12. Karen, a chemistry major works part-time at a medical laboratory.

13. Slipping and sliding, the giggling couple clung to each other as they gingerly made their way across the icy parking lot.

14. My neighbor, the one who lives to the left of me is a retired police officer.

15. Slowly and quietly, Tex made his way toward the refrigerator.

NAME _____   DATE _____

Exercise 4: *Insert commas as needed in the sentences that follow.*

1. Bert, did you know the boss is looking for you?
2. The company's headquarters is in Los Angeles California.
3. My folks were married on October 12 1966, in Cheyenne Wyoming.
4. The population of Zanesville Ohio is 28655.
5. Professor Goodman said, "The final test for this course is next Friday."
6. Blaine, how about going bowling with me?
7. "The choir practices," Mrs. Folsom informed us "on Tuesdays and Thursdays."
8. Dear Butch,

   Our class will hold its tenth reunion at the Sheraton Hotel in Minneapolis Minnesota on June 18 1993. Rodney said, "I want to see Butch's face at that place!" We've already raised $16432, (just kidding) so we should have quite a bash. Send your reservation Butch to Nora Wilson.

   Yours truly,
   Cappy Patterson

Exercise 5: *Insert semicolons and colons as needed in the sentences that follow.*

1. The business consultant's message can be summarized by these words pro-vide better service to your customers than your competitors.
2. The heavy snowfall made travel difficult consequently, we arrived late for the basketball game.
3. Jennifer sang a solo at the concert I didn't realize she had such a lovely voice.
4. In addition to a tent and sleeping bag, be sure to include these items when you go camping a compass, matches, and first aid kit.
5. I think Jay looks attractive in glasses what's your opinion?
6. My closest friends are majoring in the following subjects Felicia, biology, Allan, elementary education, Scott, philosophy, Terri, psychology.
7. Wayne doesn't know Professor Stillman well he's had only one course from her.
8. Thelma couldn't remember where she had left her pocketbook however, she eventually found it on the hall table.

9. I am reading a fascinating book called A Night to Remember the Sinking of
    the Titanic.

10. Insight into the character of Winston Churchill is provided by the remarks he
    made, including these "One ought never to turn one's back on a threatened
    danger and try to run away from it. If you do that, you will double the
    danger. But if you meet it promptly and without flinching, you will reduce
    the danger by half. Never run away from anything. Never!"

Exercise 6: *Insert quotation marks and underlines as needed in the sentences that follow. At*
the end of a quote, be sure that your quotation marks are placed outside the
comma, period, or question mark. Remember also that indirect quotes do not
require quotation marks.

1. James Morrow said, Curiosity may have killed the cat, but lack of curiosity
    would have killed thousands.

2. Did you read the article Reforming our Schools in Parade magazine?

3. Yes, Tom, I know that you have a job, Ellen responded, but don't you think
    you could ask for tomorrow off?

4. Mr. Pelletier said that his store would be closed next week because of remod-
    eling.

5. My favorite restaurant is the Blue Lion, said Mrs. Archer.

6. The movie The Hoosiers has nothing to do with the book Season on the
    Brink.

7. Our instructor assigned the short story The Secret Life of Walter Mitty and
    the poem Make Believe.

8. Why aren't you going with us? Scott asked.

9. Richard Llewellyn, in his book How Green Was My Valley, stated, There is no
    fence or hedge round time that has gone. You can go back and have what
    you like if you remember it well.

10. Karen said that she doesn't like hot weather.

11. I used to watch the television show Rockford Files, Linda explained, because
    I've always admired the acting of James Garner.

12. Brook read and took notes on the chapter The Birth of Rock and Roll in the
    book Tracing Our Musical Heritage.

Chapter 8
Review Exercise: A. *END MARKS: If a sentence or an abbreviation lacks punctuation or is punctu-*
ated improperly, make the appropriate correction. If a sentence is punctuated cor-
rectly, write C after it.

1. Did you know Rev Mc Hugh came from Scotland.

2. My sister is working on a M A degree in history

3. Good grief Who spilled the paint all over the kitchen floor.

4. How late does the Green Door Cafe stay open.

5. Mr and Mrs Hastings are directing the musical.

6. Look out The ladder is slipping

7. Carol asked me if I knew what time you got off work?

8. When you finish mowing the lawn, Chuck, will you mail these letters for me?

9. Dr Morrison's office is located on Sunset Blvd in Beverly Hills

10. Please tell me why you quit your job.

B. *COMMAS: Insert commas as needed in the following sentences.*

1. I didn't know Helen that you had previously met Troy.

2. After showering shaving and dressing Roland polished his shoes.

3. Mrs. Gillespie gave a moving inspirational talk.

4. The Wilsons who moved to our community from Pennsylvania have many beautiful antiques in their home.

5. Marjorie and Ron visited the old castle and a nearby museum but the others on the tour decided to stay at the hotel to rest.

6. Mr. Fitch said "Where else did you go in England?"

7. According to the newspaper there were over 39500 fans at the game.

8. Yes I read about your engagement in today's paper and I want to express my heartiest congratulations to you.

9. Because it was after midnight Ellen decided she would wait until later that morning to call home to tell her folks the good news.

10. Ivan an outstanding student and athlete was selected to represent the sophomore class at the Salt Lake City Utah conference.

11. Quickly but deftly the chef managed to keep up with the many different orders.

NAME _____   DATE _____

12. Meredith Tim would have asked you to go with him but he knew you wanted to study this evening.

13. I can understand why you're disappointed; however I'm sure he'll call you when he gets back.

14. The Mustangs according to the newspaper are scheduled to play the Horned Frogs this Saturday.

15. Terry arrived late so Joyce who was on time got the job.

C. SEMICOLONS, COLONS, QUOTATION MARKS: Insert semicolons, colons, underlines, and quotation marks as needed in the following sentences.

1. I'll be surprised, Kirby remarked, if my car will start on such a cold morning as this.

2. The following basketball players were selected for the college all-star team Jim Kyper, Providence Hubie Lowell, Syracuse Fred MacDonald, Boston College Dan Elliott, Connecticut and Tyrone Cabot, Villanova.

3. It is a wonderful movie did you see it, Brook? Martha asked.

4. I just read the chapter Plumbing Made Easy in the book Do It Yourself How to Build Your Own Home.

5. Owen said his brother is joining the navy he hopes to serve on a submarine.

6. Virginia is an expert at doing the crossword puzzles in The Boston Globe.

7. If you're late, the instructor warned, you won't be allowed to take the test.

8. The asking price was reasonable therefore, I agreed to buy Tracy's pickup.

9. We will need the following items for the meeting one large table, eight chairs, paper and pens, and a telephone.

10. She felt, however, he would change his mind unfortunately, he never did.

11. In the movie Casablanca, Humphrey Bogart uttered this classic line to Ingrid Bergman Here's looking at you, Kid.

12. The reporter asked the coach, Do you know why Reggie quit the team? Is he going to transfer?

13. Reggie loves one thing above all else basketball.

14. My folks live in Elgin, Illinois my brother lives in St. Paul, Minnesota my grandparents have retired to Sun City, Arizona and I've decided to move to Ogden, Utah.

15. Louise is a pharmacist her husband is an accountant.

NAME _____   DATE _____

C. APPLYING THE FINISHING TOUCH

(1) Proofreading: *Proofread this passage to discover where the following punctuation is needed: three sentences requiring end punctuation; two sentences requiring semicolons; three places where quotation marks are needed; ten places where commas are needed. Compare your work with that in the **Answer Key**.*

On the Bench with Bob Cousy*

Bob Cousy has gone from player to coach and back to player again. However this time he's not playing basketball he's playing the piano. As captain of the Boston Celtics Cousy rarely sat on the bench but these days he's often sitting on a piano bench

What prompted the retired Boston Celtics basketball star to begin piano lessons He replies, An unfulfilled ambition. My mother could never understand why I turned into a jock. His mother loved classical music but the family couldn't even consider piano lessons for Cousy, who was born two months after his parents immigrated to the United States from France. Despite the fact that his family didn't own a piano Cousy cultivated a love for music.

Four years ago, Bob Cousy started studying piano as a beginner with Madelyn Levenson, a Worcester Massachusetts, teacher. Levenson hasn't had to make many concessions to Cousy other than working around his

---

* © 1987 by Accent Pub. Co. Article changed and punctuation deleted from original published form.

NAME _____   DATE _____

schedule, but teaching someone over six feet tall has had its challenges. For example Cousy needed to be taught how to position his long legs carefully under the keyboard as well as how to keep his huge fingers on one key at a time.

Although relaxation and enjoyment are among his reasons for taking lessons Cousy wants to be prepared for and to do well at his lessons. He is currently working on a Bach minuet which is Cousy's first attempt at playing a sonatina and Beethoven's Fur Elise, which has been a particular challenge for him. He exclaims, I've been working on it for at least two months. Cousy says that he has not set specific goals for pianistic achievement he just wants to be comfortable at the keyboard. In the meantime, he is fulfilling a dream while receiving a great deal of personal satisfaction from his playing.

NAME _____   DATE _____

(2) Proofreading: *After correcting the punctuation errors having to do with periods, commas, semi-colons, and quotation marks, rewrite the entire passage on a separate piece of paper. Have your instructor check your work.*

Andrew Jackson: Seventh President, 1829–1837

Andrew Jackson was born in a log cabin on the Carolina frontier in 1767. He was orphaned at an early age and grew up rough tough and headstrong. He received a meager education, and he much preferred action to deliberation nevertheless he eventually became a lawyer. After being admitted to the North Carolina bar, Jackson moved to Tennessee where he experienced a number of financial ups and downs while working as a lawyer storekeeper and landowner.

In 1791, Jackson married Mrs. Rachel Robards. Two years later, they were shocked to learn that Rachel's divorce from her first husband had never been finalized. The Jacksons remarried after the divorce from her first husband but the scandal that resulted haunted them the rest of their lives In 1806, Jackson who possessed an explosive temperament killed a man in a duel after the man made a derogatory remark about Rachel. A friend later remarked, For the man who dared breathe her name except in honor, he kept pistols in perfect condition for thirty-seven years.

When Tennessee became a state Jackson was elected its first representative During the War of 1812, he was given a command of troops, and he led them to victory in the Battle of New Orleans, making him a national hero. In 1828, Jackson defeated John Quincy Adams in a bitterly fought contest for

NAME _____   DATE _____

the presidency. Jackson's victory was marred however when his beloved Rachel died before he was inaugurated.

The United States experienced remarkable changes during Jackson's presidency, including the development of railroads and canals the modernization of farming and the expansion of the Union. Jackson was a forceful decisive president, but he was often controversial. After his two terms as president, he retired to The Hermitage, his beautiful home in Tennessee, where he died in 1845.

NAME _____   **DATE** _____

Writing: Write something worth reading about **one** of the following quotes:

- **Great works are performed not by strength but by perseverance.**
- **Many people die at twenty-five but aren't buried until they are seventy-five.**
- **Without music, life would be a mistake.**

Suggestions: **READ** the first statement several times; jot down your immediate reactions to it: is the statement clear or confusing? inspiring or boring? accurate or inaccurate? foolish or wise? unforgettable or forgettable?

DO the same for the other two statements.

READ through all of your reactions a number of times; decide on the <u>one</u> statement provoking the most promising responses from you.

WORK HARD to develop clear explanations, convincing examples, and specific reasons to support your responses to the statement; do your best to be <u>genuine</u>, <u>insightful</u>, and <u>original</u> (in other words, make sure your explanations, examples, and reasons aren't insincere, shallow, or predictable).

DECIDE what tone would work best for you in this paper: serious? light-hearted? agreeable? critical? dignified? informal? praising? ridiculing?

WRITE, READ, AND REWRITE until you are satisfied your paper accurately reflects your thoughts and feelings.

LIMIT your final draft to <u>one complete page</u>, typewritten and doublespaced.

PROVIDE a thoughtful title.

PROOFREAD, paying particular attention to punctuation and to the type of errors that may have marred your other papers; see **PROOFREADING TIPS,** page 295.

Be sure to budget your writing time wisely
and to consult the **WRITING SUGGESTIONS** (pages 293–294)
if you are doing
one of the **LONG-RANGE ASSIGNMENTS** (pages 291–292).

After reviewing Chapters 5–8,
take the **MASTERY TEST** provided by your instructor.

CHAPTER NINE

Punctuation — 2

A. ESTABLISHING THE BACKGROUND

APOSTROPHES

Apostrophes are used with <u>contractions</u>, which occur when two words are condensed into one word.

they are	they're
should not	shouldn't
were not	weren't

Notice that the apostrophe is placed where a letter or letters have been omitted, not where the words are joined. Here are some additional examples:

had not	hadn't	(NOT had'nt)
does not	doesn't	(NOT does'nt)
would not	wouldn't	(NOT would'nt)

Do Exercises 1 and 2 in Section B. ⟶

Apostrophes are used with <u>possessives</u>, which are nouns and indefinite pronouns that exercise control over or ownership of something. <u>Singular possessives</u> use an apostrophe plus <u>s</u>:

Warren's coat is hanging in the closet.

Safety is everyone's concern.

When a singular noun ends in s, it is considered correct to add an apostrophe only OR to add an apostrophe plus s:

Kansas' history is extremely eventful.

   or

Kansas's history is extremely eventful.

However, for consistency and pronunciation purposes, it is recommended that an apostrophe plus s be used:

We were impressed with Charles's accomplishments.

The Jones's garden needs watering.

Most plural nouns end in s, so just add an apostrophe for the possessive form:

Plural	Plural Possessive	
boys	boys'	The boys' laughter could be heard throughout the gym.
friends	friends'	Her friends' expressions of concern were no doubt sincere.

However, when a plural noun does not end in s, add an apostrophe plus s:

Plural	Plural Possessive	
children	children's	The children's disappointment was understandable.
women	women's	We applauded the women's decision.

When two or more people own or control the same object, the possessive form is used with the last name only:

Jay and Rhoda's cat is named Trixie.   (Jay and Rhoda possess the same cat.)

However, when two or more people possess something individually, the possessive form is used with each name:

Jay's and Rhoda's jobs are in opposite parts of the city.   (Jay and Rhoda possess different jobs.)

SUMMARY—POSSESSIVES

● **Add an apostrophe plus s to all singular nouns including those ending in s.**

  Examples:

  Jeff's parents are coming for a visit
  Phyllis's apartment is quite small.

● **Add an apostrophe plus s to plural nouns not ending in s.**

  Examples:

  The women's efforts were appreciated by everyone.
  A variety of activities occupied the children's time.

● **Add an apostrophe only to plural nouns ending in s.**

  Examples:

  The lawyers' convention will be held in April.
  Did you consider your relatives' opinions?

● **Add an apostrophe to only the last name when there is joint possession.**

  Example:

  Heather and Tom's business is doing well.

● **Add an apostrophe to all names when there is individual possession.**

  Example:

  Rodger's and Ellen's solos followed one another.

Do Exercises 3, 4, and 5 in Section B.

● **Apostrophes are used when numerals and letters are omitted.**

Examples:

My folks bought their house in '86.

Ronald Reagan was elected President in '80.

Carolyn is <u>workin'</u> nights at the hospital.

What makes you think he was <u>braggin'</u> about how much money he makes?

● **Apostrophes are used when numerals and single letters are made plural.**

Examples:

My little brother has a unique way of making <u>9's</u>.

My telephone number ends in four <u>7's</u>.

Your <u>i's</u> should be dotted.

How many <u>s's</u> are there in your last name?

When NOT to Use Apostrophes:

● **Do <u>not</u> use apostrophes with nouns simply because they end in <u>s</u>:**

We received a telephone call from Dori<u>s</u>.   (Doris is not possessing anything, so no apostrophe is needed.)

Car<u>s</u>, truck<u>s</u>, camper<u>s</u>, and motorcycle<u>s</u> jammed the parking lot.   (No apostrophes are needed as the nouns are simply plural; they are not possessing anything.)

● **Do <u>not</u> use apostrophes with possessive pronouns, such as <u>her</u>, <u>hers</u>, <u>his</u>, <u>my</u>, <u>our</u>, <u>ours</u>, <u>your</u>, <u>yours</u>, <u>their</u>, <u>theirs</u>, <u>its</u>:**

The car parked across the street is ours.   (<u>not</u> ours')

The team ended <u>its</u> losing streak last night.   (When <u>its</u> is used with an apostrophe, it means <u>it is</u>: I believe <u>it's</u>, or <u>it is</u>, going to rain.)

Do Exercises 6 and 7 in Section B.

HYPHENS

A hyphen (-) is used in these ways:

- **when fractions and numbers from 21 to 99 are written:**

  one-third   twenty-four
  one-half   eighty-nine

- **in certain compound words:**

  self-control
  ex-minister
  mother-in-law

- **between two or more words serving as a compound adjective:**

  the Texas-Oklahoma state line
  a well-known musician
  a well-to-do couple

- **to join a prefix to a capitalized word:**

  post-Civil War era
  mid-April

- **to divide a word at the end of a line:**

  The National Education Association will hold its year-
  ly convention in Chicago this summer.

PARENTHESES

The most common ways parentheses ( ) are used include the following:

- **to set off extra or clarifying material that interrupts the flow of the sentence:**

Franklin D. Roosevelt (1882–1945) was born at Hyde Park, New York. In 1921, Roosevelt was stricken with infantile paralysis (poliomyelitis). He served as President during World War II. (Incidentally, President Theodore Roosevelt was a cousin.)

● **to enclose numbers or letters used in sentences:**

Donna said that she had to (1) mail some letters, (2) buy some groceries, and (3) check out a book at the library.

To get that information from the computer, you must type (A) ENTER, (B) CODE UC06, (C) FILE HIS 101, and (D) PRINT.

DASHES

A dash — (- - when typed) has these principal uses:

● **to introduce summarizing or clarifying information:**

Jason plays soccer, basketball, and baseball—he loves team sports.

He was obviously a hedonist—he believed that having a good time was the most important thing in life.

● **to create a dramatic effect:**

Fred asked—actually, he demanded—that I give him your telephone number.

I said that I would be happy to—if he had a million dollars.

I'm switching my major—this will surprise you—to music.

● **to indicate an unfinished remark:**

Beverly replied, "Of course, I would love to, but—"

"You don't mean that he's—," Tom gasped.

Do Exercise 8 and Review Exercises in Section B.

B. GAINING THE EXPERIENCE

Exercise 1: *Change the following words into contractions; be sure that your apostrophe is in the correct location.*

Contraction

1. do not   _____
2. can not   _____
3. I am   _____
4. let us   _____
5. we are   _____
6. you are   _____
7. should not   _____
8. who is   _____
9. it is   _____
10. they are   _____

Exercise 2: *Write the proper contraction in each space; be sure that your apostrophe is in the correct location.*

1. Have you been able to find out (what is) _____ wrong with my car?
2. Mark (has not) _____ finished washing the windows.
3. (We are) _____ going shopping at the mall later on.
4. Do you know (who is) _____ coming to the party?
5. Apparently, John (did not) _____ have time to telephone.
6. I (can not) _____ make out his writing, can you?
7. We (should not) _____ park in that space.
8. Grace (was not) _____ happy to hear the news.
9. His friends think that (he will) _____ change his mind about the matter.
10. Why (are not) _____ the stores open today?

NAME _____   DATE _____

Exercise 3:   *Write the correct possessive form for the following nouns and indefinite pronouns. Use an apostrophe plus s for singular nouns ending in s. A couple of examples have been done for you.*

Examples: Edward _____ Edward's _____ sister

Jones _____ Jones's _____ business

1. cheerleaders _____ efforts

2. car _____ motor

3. gentlemen _____ agreement

4. Ross _____ musical ability

5. workers _____ complaints

6. Marlene _____ voice

7. Pamela and Dino _____ apartments (individually owned)

8. somebody _____ billfold

9. friends _____ help

10. Paul _____ sickness

11. dogs _____ barking

12. coach _____ strategy

13. children _____ playground

14. Tyrone and Juanita _____ property (jointly owned)

15. horses _____ pasture

16. Roger Maris _____ homerun record

17. storm _____ damage

18. photographer _____ meeting

19. anyone _____ responsibility

20. cities _____ housing problems

Exercise 4:   *Write the correct possessive form in the space. (Use an apostrophe plus s for singular nouns ending in s.)*

1. All of the (reporter's, reporters') _____ offices are located in the second floor.

2. (Evelyn's, Evelyns') _____ mail is on the table.

3. We can borrow (Don's and Anita's, Don and Anita's) _____ truck.

4. The (men's, mens') _____ clothing department is expanding.

5. Many of the (student's, students') _____ parents attended homecoming.

6. The federal (government's, governments') _____ investigation led to a number of arrests.

7. I appreciated both of my (parent's, parents') _____ encouragement.

8. The (sun's, suns') _____ warmth felt good.

9. (Lois', Lois's) _____ remarks surprised me.

10. The (show's, shows') _____ cancellation was disappointing to my children.

Exercise 5: *Write original sentences for the following nouns and indefinite pronouns after changing them to their possessive form. (Use an apostrophe plus s for singular nouns ending in s.) An example has been done for you.*

Example: basketball

_I can understand basketball's popularity._____

1. clock

_____

2. woman

_____

3. motorcycle

_____

4. stores

_____

5. someone

_____

6. United States

_____

7. players

_____

8. anybody

_____

9. boss

_____

10. professors

_____

Exercise 6: *After reading each sentence, correctly write in the space provided any numeral, letter, or word needing an apostrophe. An example has been done for you.*

Example: ___wishin'___   I was wishin I could go to California with you.

1. _____ Martha graduated from high school in 89.

2. _____ There are three cs and two rs in occurrence.

3. _____ Do you like playin cards?

4. _____ A tornado struck our town in April of 86.

5. _____ I realize that my as and es often look alike.

6. _____ The Civil War took place from 61 to 65.

7. _____ Your 7s look like 2s.

8. _____ The sun is shinin, thank goodness.

9. _____ Her grandparents have lived in New Mexico since 79.

10. _____ The first graders were learning how to make 3s.

Exercise 7: *After reading the sentence, write in the space any words in which an apostrophe is used improperly; write the words as they should be. If a sentence is correct, write* correct. *An example has been done for you.*

Example: ___Her paintings___   Her' paintings' are rather modern.

1. _____ Ralph picked up the papers' and magazines' that were scattered on the floor.

2. _____ The brightness hurts my eyes'.

3. _____ Is this book yours'?

NAME _____ DATE _____

4. _____ I was disappointed with the film's ending.

5. _____ Our' final exams' are in three weeks.

6. _____ Rita's explanation helped me to understand her' problem.

7. _____ How many pets did you have when you were growing up?

8. _____ While my husband was watching the children, I bought some groceries.

9. _____ The kitten rubbed its chin against the fence post.

10. _____ Natalie bought her books' and other school supplies' yesterday.

Exercise 8:   *Place the punctuation mark shown in the margin in its proper location in the sentence. An example has been done for you.*

( )   Example: Nehemiah Grew (1641–1712) was an English anatomist and physiologist.

  -   1.   My wife says that it is un American not to like baseball.

  - -   2.   I was surprised no, shocked to hear that Rosemary and Stuart had eloped.

( )   3.   We finished the season undefeated. By the way, it is rumored that our coach has resigned.

  - -   4.   When asked about his future plans, Coach Barker replied, "I'm really not at liberty to "

( )   5.   We lived in California 1984–1990 before moving to Nevada.

  -   6.   Stan said that he would arrive by mid afternoon.

  - -   7.   Shirley is an excellent student, athlete, and musician she's a gifted person.

  -   8.   Professor Grey, a well known economist, predicts a drop in the unemployment rate during the next eighteen months.

  -   9.   My husband will be thirty three years old next Monday.

( )   10.   Marsha said that I should 1 apologize, 2 buy him a new record, and 3 take him to dinner.

NAME _____   DATE _____

Chapter 9
Review Exercise: A. *CONTRACTIONS: Write the proper contraction in the space; be sure to place the apostrophe in the proper location.*

1. Our neighbors (were not) _____ moving after all.

2. (What is) _____ wrong with Fred today?

3. She (does not) _____ understand why you are so upset with her.

4. My relatives (would not) _____ let me pay for a thing when I visited them last summer.

5. The weather (is not) _____ perfect, but so what?

B. *POSSESSIVES: Write the correct possessive form in each space; study the context of the sentence to determine whether the possessive should be singular or plural. Use an apostrophe plus s for any singular noun ending in s.*

6. The (boy's, boys') _____ celebration ended when they realized how late it was.

7. The (animal's, animals') _____ intelligence was obvious to me.

8. As Lola soon discovered, the (store's, stores') _____ busiest time was on Friday evenings.

9. (Mark's, Marks') _____ anger was completely unjustified.

10. The police will ticket (anyone's, anyones') _____ car parked in the alley.

11. Do you happen to know (Charles', Charles's) _____ telephone number?

12. Dr. Berkman is attending a (doctor's, doctors') _____ convention in San Diego.

13. We were impressed with (Kathy's, Kathys') _____ poise and maturity.

14. The mayor acknowledged that it was the (women's, womens')

_____ efforts that ensured the success of the fund drive.

15. The (bus', bus's) _____ schedule is posted in the lobby.

C. OTHER USES OF APOSTROPHES: On the line before each sentence, correctly write any number, letter or word that either needs an apostrophe added, dropped, or its position changed.

16. _____ My mother was born in 1947 and my dad in 45.

17. _____ Bobs knees' are sore from standing on a ladder all day.

18. _____ The boss was shoutin instructions at us, but we couldn't make out what he was saying.

19. _____ Who owns the ice skates' and skis'?

20. _____ I sometimes forget to cross my ts, so they often look like ls or es.

21. _____ Cindy's friends' will be joining her for lunch.

22. _____ Students' with 4s on their papers earned As.

23. _____ Mr. Jenkins relatives' live in South Carolina.

24. _____ Rodneys' talents include singin and dancin.

25. _____ Doris recovery occurred quickly once the doctor's diagnosis' was made.

D. HYPHENS, PARENTHESES, DASHES: Place the punctuation mark shown in the margin in its proper location in the sentence.

‒ 1. Has life expectancy increased significantly during the past seventy five years?

( ) 2. There were a number of prodigies Mozart was composing music at the age of five in Europe in the eighteenth century.

‒‒ 3. My father I can't believe it is taking saxophone lessons.

‒ 4. Quinn has a lot of self discipline, so I'm sure he'll be able to quit smoking.

‒‒ 5. She fluttered her eyes, smiled seductively, and kissed him lightly on the cheek what a flirt!

( ) 6. He wasn't prepared who is? for such sudden fame.

NAME _____   DATE _____

C. APPLYING THE FINISHING TOUCH

(1) Proofreading: *Correct the nineteen apostrophe errors in the following passage. (Some words need apostrophes, some words should not be punctuated with apostrophes, while other words need the apostrophe changed to its correct location.) In addition, seven hyphens should be used in this passage as well as two sets of dashes and five sets of parentheses. Compare your corrections with those in the **Answer Key**.*

William Henry Harrison: Ninth President, 1841

William Henry Harrison 1773 1841 was born of well to do parents in Berkeley, Virginia. Harrisons father was one of the signers of the Declaration of Independence, and his mother came from one of Virginias most distinguished families.

After attending college in his home state, Harrison went to Philadelphia in 1790 to study medicine; however, after his fathers death in the following year, Harrison quit his medical studies' to accept a commission in the army.

Harrison was assigned by the army to the Ohio Indiana area, which was then called the Northwest Territory. Harrisons commander was the well known General Anthony "Mad" Wayne. Harrison fought in the Indian campaigns that ended in success at least in the white mans point of view in 1794.

The year 1798 was a momentous one for Harrison because he 1 resigned from the army, 2 married Judge John Symmes's daughter, and 3 received a federal land grant to homestead in Ohio. Probably due to his'

NAME _____   DATE _____

father in law influence, Harrison was appointed the following year to be the Northwest Territorys first delegate to Congress.

In the early 1800s, Harrison served as Governor of the Indiana Territory. Harrisons responsibilities this shouldn't surprise you were to defend the settlements against the Indians' and to obtain even more title to Indian lands. Under the leadership of Tecumseh, the Indians' formed a confederation to halt the whites advancement. In 1811, Harrison led a surprise attack on an Indian village at Tippecanoe. Incidentally, this is the source of Harrisons' nickname "Tippecanoe." Harrisons troops suffered heavy casualties, and the outcome was indecisive; nevertheless, the battle was celebrated as a great victory for Harrisons' troops.

After serving in the War of 1812, Harrison entered politics. In 1840, he became the Whigs candidate for President. In the election, Harrison defeated Van Buren, who was'nt successful in his' bid for a second term.

William Henry Harrison was sworn in as president on March 4, 1841. A month later, however, he died of pneumonia, becoming the first president to die in office.

NAME _____   DATE _____

(2) Proofreading: *Correct the twenty-three apostrophe errors; some words need apostrophes while others should have them removed. In addition, some words need the apostrophe changed to its correct location. Also, four hyphens should be used in this passage, as well as one set of dashes and six sets of parentheses. After you have made your corrections, rewrite the entire passage on a separate piece of paper and hand it in to your instructor.*

One of Summers Special Delights

Unquestionably, blackberries' are one of Americas favorite fruits. In July, practically everyones table is graced with them. Surprisingly, however, blackberries have'nt always enjoyed such popularity. For example, the colonists' 1607 1776 had love hate feelings about this fruit. They did appreciate the delicious jellies, soups, deserts, and wines blackberries' could be used for. Incidentally, many colonists favorite recipe was one for blackberry wine. However, the colonists' resentment toward blackberries' was also a well known fact; they detested the blackberrys tendency to transform open fields to jungles of straggly thorns.

Americans' of the 1800s feasted on blackberry pies and cobblers. They did'nt, however, sweeten these desserts' with expensive sugar; instead, they used either molasses's or maple syrup. Another way they enjoyed blackberries' was in puddings layered with slices' of buttered bread.

Through the years, the blackberrys popularity has steadily increased. Today, thousands of Americans' grow patches of their own because theres little work involved; blackberries' seldom need 1 replanting, 2 pruning, 3 fertilizing, or 4 weeding. A persons hardest job and don't I know it is to wait patiently until the blackberries ripen in mid July. The wait, though, is certainly worth it as the blackberrys unique flavor, whether experienced straight from the vine or straight from the oven, is unmatchable.

NAME _____   DATE _____

Writing: Respond in writing to one of the following questions:

- **Would a bubblegum manufacturer or a lumberjack be more concerned about the plight of penguins?**
- **What connections might a poet make between rain and a bump in a road?**

Suggestions: **REVIEW** the writing suggestions contained in the preceding chapters as many of them are appropriate for this assignment.

REMEMBER your major obligations are to be clear what you are writing about and to support what you assert with convincing evidence, whether it be factual or fanciful.

ARRANGE your schedule so you have sufficient time to devote to this assignment; your writing will need to be creative and full of specific reasons and illustrations to be well-received.

LIMIT your final draft to one complete page, typewritten and doublespaced.

PROVIDE an attention-grabbing title.

PROOFREAD; don't let your writing be undermined by surface mistakes; check **PROOFREADING TIPS,** page 295.

Have you completed one of the **LONG-RANGE ASSIGNMENTS,**
pages 291–292?
If so, your instructor may want you to select another one to do.
If that's the case, be sure to check
with the **WRITING SUGGESTIONS,** pages 293–294,
before, while, and after completing this assignment.

CHAPTER TEN

Capital Letters

A. ESTABLISHING THE BACKGROUND

The following list provides reliable guidance for the appropriate use of capital letters.

- **PROPER NOUNS (Particular people, places, things) are capitalized:**

    Carlos Rivera

    Grand Canyon

    Chevrolet

    Brooklyn, New York

but not common nouns:

    man

    canyon

    car

    city, state

- **PROPER ADJECTIVES (describe nouns) are capitalized:**

    My boyfriend and I are taking a *French* cooking course on Monday evenings.

Derek is a *Canadian* citizen.

Professor Yoshio, a *Shakespearean scholar,* is studying in England.

but not common adjectives:

My boyfriend and I are taking a *foreign* cooking course on Monday evenings.

Derek is a *respected* citizen.

Professor Yoshio, a *drama* scholar, is studying in England.

● **HOLIDAYS, MONTHS and DAYS OF THE WEEK are capitalized:**

Thanksgiving

November

Thursday

but not the seasons of the year:

fall

winter

spring

summer

● **SPECIFIC GEOGRAPHIC REGIONS are capitalized:**

Many of the oldest colleges in the nation are located in the East.

The West has awesome scenery.

The economy of the South is booming.

Most of his relatives live in the North.

Herbert Hoover grew up in the Midwest.

Arizona and New Mexico are in the Southwest.

but not compass directions:

Aurora is forty miles west of Chicago.

We planted a lilac bush six feet south of our back porch.

An industrial park is being developed <u>north</u> of the city.

The gymnasium is on the <u>east</u> side of campus.

The <u>west</u> part of the parking lot is reserved for employees.

● **SCHOOL COURSES are capitalized when they are names of <u>languages</u> or have <u>letters</u> or <u>numbers</u> following them:**

<u>E</u>nglish

<u>S</u>ociology 100

<u>B</u>iology 2B

<u>but not</u> when they are used in a general way:

geography

physics

psychology

Example: Ruth is majoring in mathematics.

● **FIRST, LAST, and MAJOR WORDS OF TITLES are capitalized:**

book:	<u>A Short History of a Small Place</u>
magazine:	<u>Saturday Evening Post</u>
newspaper:	<u>The Washington Post</u>

<u>but not</u> when words like a, an, the, and, for, in, and of come within the title:

<u>The Just and the Unjust</u>

<u>The Making of a Surgeon</u>

<u>Lost in the Funhouse</u>

● **A TITLE USED WITH A PERSON'S NAME or WHEN THE TITLE TAKES THE PLACE OF A PERSON'S NAME is capitalized:**

<u>P</u>rofessor Lucerne

Captain Butler

Uncle Ralph

I understand, Doctor, that you attended Tulane University.

but not when the title is used in a general way or when my (or similar pronoun) precedes a term of kinship, such as father, mother, uncle:

She is a college professor.

Mark was promoted to captain.

Davida is studying to be a doctor.

I received a letter from my uncle.

- **FIRST WORD OF A SENTENCE, POEM, QUOTATION, and the PRONOUN I are capitalized:**

sentence:	Invitations were sent to all members.
poem:	The woods are lovely dark and deep,
quotation:	Lisa asked, "When will Dana be home?"
pronoun I:	Brenda was beginning to worry that you wouldn't get here in time, and so was I.

but not the first word of an interrupted quotation or when only part of a direct quotation is written . . .

interrupted quotation:	"After completing the test," Professor Carver said, "you can leave."
part of a direct quotation:	The critic wrote that the movie is "wonderful entertainment."

- **SPECIFIC ORGANIZATIONS, PRODUCTS, COMPANIES, and RELIGIOUS GROUPS are capitalized:**

Democratic Party

Toastmasters Club

Papermate pen

Coca Cola

Stratton Tire Company

Presbyterians

but not when referred to in a general way . . .

political party

social club

pen

cola

company

church members

● **HISTORIC DOCUMENTS, EVENTS, and GOVERNMENT AGENCIES are capitalized:**

Declaration of Independence

Spanish Civil War

Federal Bureau of Investigation

● **LANGUAGES, NATIONALITIES, and RACES are capitalized . . .**

French

Swedish

Caucasian

Do the Exercises in Section B.

B. GAINING THE EXPERIENCE

Exercise 1:   *On the line below each sentence correctly rewrite any word or words that should or should not be capitalized; if the sentence is written correctly, then write Correct.*

1. has anyone heard from Sheila since she moved to atlanta, georgia?

    _____

    _____

2. my Wife drives a honda to work.

    _____

    _____

3. Our Vacation begins on the friday before easter.

    _____

    _____

4. my Husband and i watched the movie From Here to Eternity on television last saturday evening.

    _____

    _____

5. Mark, who is majoring in Religion, is taking Philosophy 350, Mathematics 100B, German and an american literature course.

    _____

    _____

6. When my grandparents retire, they plan to move to the South.

    _____

    _____

7. Mr. Powers asked, "can anyone work the tuesday evening shift?"

    _____

    _____

8. "Did you receive permission from captain Keller?" asked the clerk.

    _____

    _____

NAME _____   DATE _____

9. Is Randolph Street East or West of Longfellow Avenue?

_____

_____

10. Do you prefer Pepsi Cola, Sprite, or Dr. Pepper?

_____

_____

11. All National Parks are under the jurisdiction of the department of the interior.

_____

_____

12. Tell me, reverend, how long have you been a methodist minister?

_____

_____

13. Rita has a Cousin in the Air Force who is stationed in italy.

_____

_____

14. Our History class is studying the holocaust, which took place during World War II.

_____

_____

15. We plan to drive through the New England States to see the Fall foliage.

_____

_____

16. Coach Warner was obviously disappointed by the loss, but he said his team played hard and "Never gave up."

_____

_____

17. My mother and father, who were married in June, will celebrate their twentieth anniversary in Hawaii this spring.

_____

_____

18. My Roommate, who's majoring in Economics, reads the <u>wall street journal</u> everyday.

_____

_____

NAME _____   DATE _____

19. I need to run some errands, including going to the Post Office, Grocery Store, and Cleaners.

_____

_____

20. After graduating from High School, Helen worked as a Telephone Operator before attending Indiana University.

_____

_____

Exercise 2: *Correctly rewrite on the line any word or words that should or should not be capitalized; write Correct if all words are correct. (NOTE: The phrases do not need to begin with a capital letter, but the sentences do.)*

1. _____ when is her Birthday?

2. _____ henry moved to louisiana, I believe.

3. _____ traveled throughout the West.

4. _____ "Why don't you," Mike replied, "Come with us?"

5. _____ attends Iowa State university.

6. _____ graduated from Villisca high school

7. _____ taking courses in French and Sociology 101

8. _____ (poem title) "A web of feeling"

9. _____ You drive South for three blocks, then turn right.

10. _____ employed at southeast paint company

11. _____ leaves for College on labor day

12. _____ studying to be a lutheran Minister

13. _____ She is the Captain of the field hockey team

14. _____ Roger's account is with Illinois National bank.

15. _____ little rain during august

16. _____ (song title) "You Ain't Nothin' But a Hound dog"

17. _____ a musical legend

NAME _____   DATE _____

18. _____ special issue of <u>Sports Illustrated</u>

19. _____ Thornton bought Potato Chips, Bananas, and Rolaids.

20. _____ Yellowstone National Park is in California.

21. _____ "use the Microscope," professor Holden suggested.

22. _____ a son in Junior High

23. _____ Thanksgiving is a Week from thursday.

24. _____ (book title) <u>Stepping down from the Star</u>

25. _____ (directions) north, south, east, west

26. _____ works for the department of defense

27. _____ the Tournament begins this friday.

28. _____ When did you have a course in Surveying?

29. _____ in our Spanish class

30. _____ martha received a check from her Grandmother.

NAME _____   DATE _____

Chapter 10
Review Exercise: A. *Rewrite any word or words that should or should not be capitalized; if the sentence is written correctly, write* Correct.

1. We flew over lake Michigan and Chicago on our flight to montreal.

   _____

2. This year, easter is on sunday, april 9.

   _____

3. One of my uncles just bought a new Saturn from a car dealer on Hogan Road.

   _____

4. Ross is taking English, biology, Western Civilization 101, and sociology.

   _____

5. Dawn replied, "has anyone heard from Lauren since she moved out west?"

   _____

6. Last Winter, my boyfriend and I learned to ski at sugarloaf mountain.

   _____

7. The UCLA bruins and the Iowa hawkeyes are playing in the rose bowl on new year's day.

   _____

8. Midge and her family live on a farm five miles south of Clarinda.

   _____

9. After the Holidays, the Silver Spoon, a small but popular Boutique on Norman street, will be closed until Spring.

   _____

10. Before entering College, my roommate served in the Navy on the aircraft carrier *enterprize;* he spent one Summer and Fall in pearl harbor, Hawaii.

    _____

NAME _____   DATE _____

B. Write original sentences demonstrating the appropriate use of capital letters. An example has been done for you.

Example: proper noun: <u>We saw a double header at Fenway Park.</u>

1.   proper noun: _____

_____

2.   geographic region: _____

_____

3.   organization: _____

_____

4.   beginning a quotation: _____

_____

5.   book title: _____

_____

6.   proper adjective: _____

_____

7.   holiday, month, day: _____

_____

8.   title with a person's name: _____

_____

9.   specific school course: _____

_____

10.   religious group: _____

_____

NAME _____   **DATE** _____

C. APPLYING THE FINISHING TOUCH

(1) Proofreading: *Correct the thirty-three mistakes having to do with capital letters; there are twenty-seven words needing capital letters and six words that should not be capitalized. Check your corrections with those in the **Answer Key**.*

John Tyler: Tenth President, 1841–1845

John Tyler was born in greenway, virginia, on march 29, 1790. His Mother was of english descent; his Father was a successful Lawyer. After graduating from william and mary college, Tyler also became a Lawyer.

During the war of 1812, Tyler was a militia officer in the williamsburg-richmond area. In 1813, he married Letitia Christian, and they became the parents of eight children during their twenty-nine years of marriage.

After the war, Tyler embarked on a successful political career. He was elected to the United States house of representatives and then to the United States senate. In addition, Tyler served a term as governor of Virginia, as his Father had before him. In 1840, the whigs selected Tyler to be William Henry Harrison's running mate.

When president Harrison died a month after his inauguration, Tyler became the first vice-president to assume the presidency upon the death of his predecessor. Tyler's political foes, the democrats, soon referred to him as "His accidency."

Tyler's political philosophy, particularly his narrow interpretation of the *constitution of the United States* and his pro-slavery views, made him extremely unpopular not only with the democrats but also with the whigs.

NAME _____   DATE _____

The serious illness and eventual death of his wife in 1842 at the white house added to Tyler's problems. In 1844, President Tyler, fifty-four, shocked the nation when he married Julie Gardiner, twenty-four. This marriage produced seven children, so from both of his marriages Tyler was the Father of fifteen children.

Because of his extreme unpopularity, Tyler did not run for president in 1844. Years later, at the commencement of the civil war, Tyler was elected to the Confederate house of representatives; however, he died on january 18, 1862, at the age of seventy-one before he assumed his duties.

NAME _____   DATE _____

(2) Proofreading: *After correcting the capitalization errors, have your instructor check your work.*

Bad Weather Driving Tips

Because an accident can occur in a split-second, safety should be uppermost in your mind whenever you drive a car. When poor weather exists, however, concern for safety requires even more attention. Therefore, the following safety tips for driving during poor weather should be remembered.

If you must drive during foggy conditions, then follow certain procedures. For one, put your headlights on low-beam because high-beam only increases the glare. In addition, turn on your windshield wipers and defroster the moment you encounter fog to reduce the condensation on your windshield and windows. And even if it means that you will be hours late for thanksgiving dinner at your Grandparents, *slow down* to the point where you could stop within the stretch of highway illuminated by your headlights.

Also, you need to exercise special precautions when you drive in the rain. Your windshield washer, for example, should be used before turning on your wipers because the washer fluid will reduce the dirt and film that cause windshield smears and smudges. In addition, be sure to keep your distance from the car ahead of you; allow at least one car's length for every ten miles per hour you are driving. Remember also to drive slowly through large puddles to avoid shorting out your sparkplugs and saturating your brake linings. Also, keep in mind what a State Trooper in the midwest has

NAME _____   DATE _____

said, "slippery roads are caused as much by a mixture of rain and oil deposits as they are by a mixture of ice and snow."

Furthermore, Winter weather requires that you adopt additional safety practices. To promote maximum visibility, be sure to keep all of your car windows free from ice and snow, and be sure your headlights and taillights are kept clean. Be particularly mindful of possible icy patches in shaded areas and on bridges. Always keep a generous distance between you and the car ahead. If you should start to skid, turn in the direction that the rear of your car is sliding while keeping your foot off the brake and the accelerator. Be sure to allow yourself plenty of room for stopping, and gently pump your brakes when you do.

And whether you drive a buick century or a ford escort, prepare your car for stormy weather. In addition to attending to regular maintenance procedures, also make sure your car's tires are properly inflated to maximize traction. Wiper blades need to be in good condition, and the window washer periodically checked. Your car's heater, defroster, and brakes should be in top-notch order, and the exhaust system should be carefully examined for carbon monoxide leaks. Keep a flashlight in your glove compartment and jumper cables, flares, blanket, first-aid kit, and shovel in your trunk. And whether the bad weather comes during Winter or Summer, *always* drive defensively and *always* wear your seatbelt.

NAME _____ **DATE** _____

Writing: Select **one** of the following remarks and explain why it is more important to remember than the other two:

- **It ain't no use putting up your umbrella till it rains.**
- **The best way to quit smoking is to carry wet matches.**
- **There's never enough time to do all the nothing you want.**

Suggestions: **READ** aloud the first remark; is it a joke, good advice, or both? Jot down reasons why you believe the remark is on the money or off the wall; imagine occasions triggering such a remark.

DO the same for the other two remarks.

READ aloud all of your responses, then write some more; do this until you can select the <u>one</u> statement you believe has the most merit.

CONCENTRATE on developing <u>specific</u> reasons why that statement is the one to be remembered; discuss the merits and limitations of <u>all</u> of the remarks, but explain, nevertheless, there are sound reasons why it's more important to remember the remark you have selected than it is the other two.

DECIDE on the tone of your writing; your purpose is to persuade, but can you entertain as well?

REMEMBER, your writing will be well-received if it is comprised mainly of persuasive reasons reinforced with concrete illustrations, so invest whatever time it takes to do this.

LIMIT your final draft to one complete page, typewritten and doublespaced.

PROVIDE a title that reflects your paper's central message.

PROOFREAD, being mindful of capital letters and any other concerns that might need your attention.

Any **LONG-RANGE ASSIGNMENT** in the works?
If so, try to find time to work on it as well.

CHAPTER ELEVEN

Clarity — 1

A. ESTABLISHING THE BACKGROUND

Exploratory drafts can be as wordy and rambling as necessary so your thoughts have an opportunity to surface. However, once your main ideas and supporting details come into focus, clarity should be your major concern.

Clarity is aided by conciseness, so express your ideas as simply and as efficiently as you can. Always examine your sentences to see if there are vague, repetitious, or other unnecessary words that can be eliminated. What is eventually trimmed depends upon your own perceptions, but the words and phrases featured in this chapter are often unnecessary, so be mindful of them when you proofread.

REDUNDANCIES

Redundancies are words making needless repetition, such as "repeat again" or "sad mourners," so they should be eliminated from your sentences as they are in these examples:

My ~~personal~~ friend Scott is studying to be a teacher.

Marjorie's car is red ~~in color~~.

~~The reason~~ Josh left ~~was~~ because he had to go to work.

The fire ~~completely~~ destroyed the warehouse.

A bystander was ~~fatally~~ killed.

Witnesses were horrified ~~and shocked~~ by the accident.

Jackie's apartment is small ~~in size~~.

If we cooperate ~~together~~, the job will get done.

I thought ~~to myself~~, "Aren't we fortunate to be here?"

It's a ~~true~~ fact President Truman came from Missouri.

Do you think she'll ever write an autobiography ~~of her life~~?

The plane disappeared ~~from view~~ in a matter of minutes.

Felix is moving to ~~the state of~~ Illinois.

The college was founded in ~~the year of~~ 1868.

Will you return ~~back~~ to campus after the game?

When Lorraine was ~~at the age of~~ eighteen, she joined the air force.

OTHER UNNECESSARY WORDS

Frequently, *up, of, that, quite, both, really, very,* and *the* contribute nothing to the meaning of a sentence, so they can be omitted.

The ushers counted ~~up~~ the tickets sold.

We rested ~~up~~ before continuing our journey.

My sunglasses fell off ~~of~~ the dashboard.

We took the books off ~~of~~ the kitchen table.

I'm glad ~~that~~ Rico is on our team.

Heather said ~~that~~ she's tired of waiting.

Tyrone is ~~quite~~ confident he will get the job.

Were you ~~quite~~ pleased with your test scores?

~~Both~~ Jamie and Don attend Ohio State University.

~~Both~~ hamburgers and hot dogs were served at the picnic.

Phil and Marcia are ~~really~~ an attractive couple.

The noise from the planes taking off was ~~really~~ deafening.

Fortunately, the problem wasn't ~~very~~ difficult to solve.

The mall was ~~very~~ crowded with weary holiday shoppers.

~~The~~ players and ~~the~~ fans are in favor of a shorter season.

~~The~~ sponsors are urging all ~~the~~ boys and ~~the~~ girls to participate.

UNNECESSARY PHRASES

Readers realize you are expressing your opinion or what you believe or feel, so you should eliminate phrases like *in my opinion, I believe,* or *I feel* from your sentences.

~~In my opinion~~, Michael Jordan is the most exciting player in the NBA.

Most movies, ~~in my opinion~~, are a waste of time and money.

The Red Lion, ~~I believe~~, is the best restaurant in town.

Orange juice is good for most people, ~~I believe~~.

Martha is, ~~I feel~~, the most qualified person for the job.

Traveling, ~~I feel~~, is educational.

Also, certain phrases can often be eliminated, as demonstrated in the following sentences:

There is, There are, There were

~~There is~~ a dormitory is being built near the fieldhouse.

~~There are~~ many factors that influenced Susan to join the air force.

~~There were~~ parades were held every Memorial Day and Fourth of July.

who are, which is

Children ~~who are~~ in fourth grade can participate in the band.

Veronica owns a painting ~~which is~~ worth thousands of dollars.

in order, kind of, sort of, to be, or not

Gretchen must leave now ~~in order~~ to be in Salem by noon.

All of the antiques were ~~kind of~~ expensive.

I'm ~~sort of~~ thinking of majoring in psychology.

After working all day, Rex finds swimming ~~to be~~ relaxing.

Roberta needs more information before deciding whether ~~or not~~ to sign the petition.

Express your ideas simply and concisely.

Do all Exercises in Section B.

B. GAINING THE EXPERIENCE

Exercise 1:   *Cross out redundancies in the following sentences.*

1. The happy players circled around their coach.
2. After the supplies arrived, our troops were able to advance forward.
3. The stage was round in shape.
4. In my hometown where I live, there are two popular pizza parlors.
5. Margaret will continue on with her studies.
6. Can you return the book back to me by next week?
7. A huge giant rescued the children.
8. Last night, two armed gunmen robbed the convenience store on McKinley Street.
9. Matt Henderson is attending college in the state of Nebraska.
10. Do you think cars will change much in the coming future?
11. The doctor is attending to an acute crisis in the emergency room.
12. I was twelve in age when we moved to Wyoming.
13. The kitten sank down into the sofa.
14. My grandparents are seldom ever home.
15. All of the morning classes will be switched to the afternoon.

Exercise 2:   *Cross out unnecessary words in the following sentences.*

1. Darrell was very upset not to get the job.
2. We decided to store up wood for the winter.
3. Sondra earned excellent grades in both biology and calculus.
4. Tom almost fell off of the ladder when he heard the very exciting news.
5. The police officer said that my driving was quite satisfactory.
6. Is anyone interested in drinking up the orange juice?
7. Martha was really delighted to hear about your engagement.

NAME _____   DATE _____

8. Although his music fell off of the stand and children were fussing in the audience, the pianist said that he was pleased with his recital.

9. The patient was quite relieved to hear the good news.

10. Both fans and players were really disappointed when the rain continued.

11. Some rich people with a lot of money are quite generous in giving and donating to charities.

12. In order to reduce the traffic of cars and trucks near campus, I think Central Avenue should be restricted to those walking or to those riding bikes.

13. Blake sort of believes that those people who are angry and mad about the problem should kind of meet this evening to talk over and discuss practical and workable solutions.

14. When Chuck is tired and wornout, he really likes to go camping in some isolated and remote place.

15. The fraternities are planning a long marathon carwash over the weekend in order to raise and collect money for the local charities in town.

Exercise 3: *Cross out unnecessary phrases in the following sentences.*

1. In my opinion, my folks should remodel their kitchen.

2. When I refused to loan Mike my car, he got kind of mad.

3. There are people waiting to see you.

4. Vincent read the book, which is a mystery, in three hours.

5. Phil needs a course in statistics in order to do his research.

6. I believe my children watch too much television.

7. There is an old car parked in my neighbor's driveway.

8. Fortunately, Dorothy finds writing to be rewarding as well as frustrating.

9. Teen-agers were sort of wandering throughout the mall.

10. I feel hockey officials should make the penalties for fighting more costly.

11. Sheila's unsure whether or not justice was done.

12. There were a few guests staying at the old inn.

13. Students who are sitting in the back of the room will have difficulty seeing the slides.

14. Marcie runs five miles every other day in order to stay in shape for basketball.

15. Physical education, I believe, should be compulsory.

NAME _____ DATE _____

Chapter 11
Review Exercise: *Cross out redundancies and other unnecessary words and phrases in the following sentences.*

1. If these chemicals were to be combined together, an explosion would occur.

2. Shane lifted weights all summer in order to be stronger for football in the fall.

3. Edith was sort of tired after work, so she didn't go to the game with us.

4. The proposal was accepted by consensus of opinion.

5. Have you ever been convicted of any illegal crimes?

6. My sister and her husband have traveled all-throughout the Southwest.

7. Sid, be careful that the baby doesn't fall off of the porch.

8. I thought to myself, "Fred is acting really weird."

9. Workers who are on the night shift make fifteen dollars an hour.

10. These fingerprints are exactly identical.

11. Walter rents a room which is near the college.

12. The reason we went swimming was because it was very hot and quite humid.

13. Her eyes are green in color.

14. The children are cleaning up their room.

15. Our basketball coach, in my opinion, is not a very good recruiter.

16. My father suggested that I learn the basic fundamentals of carpentry.

17. I'm going to college in order to prepare for my future life.

18. Whether or not you ask Gail for a date is quite up to you.

19. The coach said that he was very surprised by both Jim's speed and strength.

20. Wouldn't you love to spend a summer season in Alaska?

21. Students who are interested in going to the state of Florida during spring break should call the airlines in order to see if any special and exceptional deals are available for the month of March.

22. We were really amazed and surprised to hear that Sue and Rick are back together again.

23. Toward the last of the year's end, business started to improve and get better.

24. After getting average and mediocre grades in high school, my brother wasn't confident and sure he would succeed in college.

25. According to a biography of her life, it's a true fact that she married when she was sixteen years of age.

NAME _____   DATE _____

26. There is a research study which indicates college students in their thirties and forties earn very high grades.

27. Joan's job requires her to drive very frequently and often, so she really sorta likes to stay home on the weekend.

28. Taxi driver, chef, waiter, motel desk clerk. and gas station attendant are among the jobs and occupations Harold, who's an accountant, had before he was twenty-five years old.

29. Aunt Bertha and Uncle Charlie are optimistic and hopeful they can come and attend my graduation in May.

30. Until we reached eighth grade in junior high, most of my friends and pals and I were too embarrassed and self-conscious to ask a girl for a date.

31. The famous celebrity, who is a personal friend of mine, gets tired and weary of answering and responding to the same old questions.

32. When I was eight years of age, I climbed up a tall, high tree, but then I was too scared and frightened to climb down, so a neighbor who lived close by had to come and rescue me.

33. After the car disappeared from view, John and Avery continued on walking toward town.

34. There are many factors, I feel, that influenced the jury's very surprising verdict.

35. My teammates and I rose up from our seats in shock and astonishment when the tall giants on the opposing team strolled into the gym.

C. APPLYING THE FINISHING TOUCH

(1) Proofreading: *Cross out the twenty-one redundancies and other unnecessary words contained in this passage. Check your work with that in the **Answer Key**.*

James K. Polk: Eleventh President, 1845–1849

James K. Polk, the eldest of ten children, was born in the state of North Carolina in 1795. He was raised up there and in Tennessee, where he moved with his family in 1806. Polk returned back to North Carolina in the year of 1815 in order to attend the state university. In the years that followed, Polk became a lawyer, entered politics, and married Sarah Childress.

Polk, who was known as "Young Hickory," served in Congress for fourteen years, and he was elected governor of the state of Tennessee in 1839. The reason Polk was called "Young Hickory" was because he was a personal friend and really an admirer of President Andrew Jackson, who was called "Old Hickory." Whether or not Polk appreciated his nickname is not known.

In the 1844 presidential election, Polk, who was the Democratic candidate, defeated Henry Clay, who was the Whig candidate. Polk expanded and enlarged the territory of the United States more than any other president except Jefferson. The reason the expansion occurred was because of three events: (1) annexation of Texas, (2) settlement of the Oregon Territory dispute with Great Britain, and (3) the Mexican War, resulting in the United States gaining the territory of what is now the states of Arizona, New Mexico, Utah, Colorado, Nevada, California, and part of Wyoming.

Although hardworking and capable throughout his life, Polk was often sick in health, and he decided not to run for reelection in 1848. Three months after leaving office, Polk died at fifty-three years in age.

NAME _____   DATE _____

(2) Proofreading: *After crossing out the redundancies and other unnecessary words and phrases, rewrite the entire passage on a separate piece of paper.*

A Special Time

Early evening, I believe, is the very best time to go for a relaxing stroll, so that's when I take Piper, who is my dog, for a walk. Unless the weather is really bad and awful, Gracie, who is my cat, tags along. We usually walk down the hill to a spacious large pasture lined with trees and bushes.

After we reach our destination, I take the leash off of Piper's collar in order to let him roam and wander. I watch and see as Piper dashes from tree to tree, really smelling and sniffing each one; frequently, he lifts up one of his back hind legs in order to leave a deposit of damp moisture.

Gracie, on the other hand, quietly and silently heads for the bushes, very alert to the slightest sound or movement. She is a deadly killer as I often see her with the remains of a bird or mouse in her mouth.

Whether or not Piper or Gracie are really ready or not to go, I usually decide to head back home after a half-hour or so. They always join up with me by the time I reach the top of the hill.

The reason I look forward to my evening walk with Piper and Gracie is because I find their companionship to be relaxing after a busy day. In my opinion, the cost and expense of owning my pets is really repaid a thousand-fold by such a special time.

NAME _____   DATE _____

Writing: Write a short story beginning with this sentence:

> **I sank deeper into my easy chair and let him get on with it, barely hearing his erudite remarks about the Bonum, Baldwin, Gravenstein, Yellow Newton, Winesap, McIntosh, and Northern Spy.**

Suggestions: **PUT** your imagination to work; your purpose can be either to entertain or to inform or to do both; if you think it would be helpful, look up the meanings of any unknown words.

BUDGET your time wisely over the next few days so you will have sufficient time to do justice to this assignment.

READ AND REREAD what you write, then make any revisions you think are necessary; repeat this process over several days; don't do a disservice to yourself or to your readers by handing in a "one-shot" draft; write a story you're confident others will appreciate.

TYPE AND DOUBLESPACE your final draft, which can be of any length.

PROVIDE a unique title (a humorous one, if appropriate).

PROOFREAD, eliminating all redundancies and other unnecessary words and phrases; in addition, be alert for the types of errors you may have made in previous papers; review **PROOFREADING TIPS,** page 295.

Is completing a **LONG-RANGE ASSIGNMENT** among your responsibilities?
If so, touch base with the **WRITING SUGGESTIONS,**
pages 293–294, once in a while.

CHAPTER TWELVE

Clarity — 2

A. ESTABLISHING THE BACKGROUND

WORDY PHRASES

Single words often convey more meaning and clarity than phrases do:

John <u>has a need for</u> a computer.
John <u>needs</u> a computer.

The flag <u>is representative</u> of our nation.
The flag <u>represents</u> our nation.

Our company <u>must make adjustments</u> in its budget.
Our company must <u>adjust</u> its budget.

A citizens' group <u>has the belief that</u> the zoning laws are outdated.
A citizens' group <u>believes</u> the zoning laws are outdated.

Jordan was there <u>at the time</u> when the accident happened.
Jordan was there <u>when</u> the accident happened.

<u>On a few occasions</u>, I've returned to my old neighborhood.
<u>Occasionally</u>, I've returned to my old neighborhood.
Henry often works overtime <u>despite the fact that</u> he doesn't need the money.

Henry often works overtime <u>though</u> he doesn't need the money.

● **Your writing will be clearer if you replace wordy phrases with a word or two:**

AVOID	USE
arrived at a decision	**decided**
as a result of	**because**
assuming that	**if**
at all times	**always**
at which time	**when**
be acquainted with	**know**
be aware of	**know**
bring to a conclusion	**finish**
by means of	**by**
came to a stop	**stopped**
despite the fact that	**although**
draws to a close	**ends**
due to the fact that	**because**
during the time that	**while**
enclosed herein	**enclosed**
exchanged wedding vows	**married**
filed a lawsuit	**sued**
full and complete	**(use either <u>full</u> or <u>complete</u>)**
gave the nod to	**approved**
gave consideration to	**considered**
has got to	**has to**
has the ability to	**can**
had an effect on	**affected**
if and when	**(use either <u>if</u> or <u>when</u>)**
in the event that	**if**
in view of the fact that	**because**
is going to	**will**
made a speech	**spoke**
made the acquaintance of	**met**
makes one's home	**lives**
on the grounds that	**because**
on the occasion of	**when**

prior to	**before**
promoted to the rank of	**promoted to**
put into effect	**started**
registered approval of	**approved**
revised downward	**lowered**
spelled out	**explained**
sprung a surprise	**surprised**
take into account	**consider**
tendered his resignation	**resigned**
united in holy matrimony	**married**
until such time as	**until**
voiced objections	**objected**
was in possession of	**had**

Do Exercise 1 in Section B.

POMPOUS WORDS

Some writers, in attempting to impress, use high-sounding words; however, pompous language can interfere with understanding. A good rule to follow, then, is never use a big word when a smaller one will do.

In the examples, notice the improvement in clarity when the underlined pompous words are replaced with the simple ones in parentheses:

Were you cognizant of Ellen's unhappiness?   **(aware)**

Cedar trees are indigenous to California.   **(native)**

We were unable to utilize the washing machine because it was malfunctionary.   **(use, broken)**

The district manager vowed to maximize sales during the next business quarter by effectuating new advertising strategies.   **(increase, introducing)**

The contractor plans to expedite the project so that the major edifice is consummated by fall.   **(speed up, building, finished)**

In lieu of flowers, people should contribute to their favorite charity. **(instead of)**

The Rams are playing well at this point in time.   **(now)**

Before I depart, I need to buy some dentifrice.   **(leave, toothpaste)**

● **If you spot pompous words in your writing, replace them with simpler words:**

AVOID	USE
affirmative	**yes**
ascertain	**find out**
commence	**begin**
crafted	**made**
downsizing	**reducing**
educator	**teacher**
endeavor	**try**
enhance	**improve**
ensuing	**following**
expired	**died**
feasible	**possible**
finalize	**complete**
imbibe	**drink**
impacted	**affected**
implement	**do**
incursion	**invasion**
indisposed	**ill**
innovative	**original**
instrumental	**helped**
interface	**connect, meet**
inundate	**flood**
misinformation	**lies**
modicum	**some**
networking	**joining, meeting**
oftentimes	**often**
ongoing	**continuing**
parameters	**limits, dimensions**
peruse	**examine**
populace	**people**
prioritize	**rank**
procure	**buy, get**
purloin	**steal**
remunerate	**pay**
retain	**keep**

subsequent	**later**
sustain	**suffer**
terminate	**stop**
transpired	**occurred**
viable	**possible**

Do Exercise 2 in Section B.

CLICHÉS

Clichés are expressions that have been used so frequently they have lost their freshness and power. Although writing clichés in exploratory drafts is acceptable, these stale phrases should be eliminated from your final paper, as was done in these sentences:

On Monday, it <u>rained cats and dogs</u> most of the day.
On Monday, the rain fell steadily until almost midnight.

Kirk enjoys the <u>finer things in life</u>.
Kirk enjoys reading, music, and art.

Juanita is as <u>sharp as a tack</u>.
Juanita is perceptive and intelligent.

Here are other examples of clichés that should be deleted from your final draft:

after all is said and done	breathless anticipation
all in a day's work	burning desire
all walks of life	burn the midnight oil
apple of one's eye	but one thing is certain
as far as the eye could see	by hook or by crook
at a loss for words	by leaps and bounds
at long last	
	calm before the storm
beginning of the end	calm, cool, and collected
best left unsaid	cold as ice
better late than never	cool as a cucumber
blanket of snow	crack of dawn
bolt from the blue	crazy as a loon
breakneck speed	crystal clear

dashed the hopes
depths of despair
diamond in the rough
dig in their heels
do your own thing
dog tired

easier said than done
every dog has its day

face the music
few and far between
follow in the footsteps of
fond memories
food for thought
fools rush in
frisky as a pup
from time immemorial

generous to a fault
given the green light
goes without saying
gone but not forgotten
green with envy

hale and hearty
happy as a lark
heart of gold
heaved a sigh of relief
hit the nail on the head
hook, line, and sinker
hungry as a bear
hustle and bustle

in full swing
in high gear
in the nick of time
in a nutshell
in the same boat
in this day and age
innocent as a newborn babe
it goes without saying

labor of love
ladder of success
last but not least

last-ditch effort
leaps and bounds
leave no stone unturned
legend in his or her own time
lend a helping hand
like a bolt from the blue
long arm of the law

matter of life and death

neat as a pin
never a dull moment
nick of time
nipped in the bud
no place like home
no sooner said than done
nose to the grindstone
nothing ventured, nothing
  gained

off his rocker
off the beaten path
on a roll
on the cutting edge
over and above
own worst enemy

paint the town red
pale as a ghost
pass the buck
picture of health
pleased as punch
pure as the driven snow

quick as a wink
quiet as a mouse

rat race
red-letter day
reins of government
remains to be seen
remedy the situation
ripe old age
road to recovery
rose to new heights
rude awakening

sadder but wiser
salt of the earth
sink or swim
slowly but surely
smart as a whip
smooth as silk
sneaking suspicion
stick to your guns
sticks out like a sore thumb
storms of protest
straight and narrow path
strike while the iron is hot
stubborn as a mule

take the bull by the horns
this day and age
throw caution to the wind
too numerous to mention

turned thumbs down
twinkling of an eye

untiring efforts
up in arms
upset the apple cart

vanish into thin air
view with alarm

walk of life
warm as toast
wee, small hours
wet blanket
white as snow
words fail to express
worse for wear
writing on the wall

Do Exercise 3 in Section B.

VAGUE LANGUAGE

Writing clarity requires thorough knowledge of the topic. However, attention to preciseness, as well as conciseness, contributes to clarity. Therefore, during your rereadings of your drafts, be alert to the possibility of replacing general, abstract words with specific, concrete ones. Notice the improvement in clarity when this is done:

The old man walks downtown every morning to buy a newspaper.

Every morning, eighty-year-old Mr. Pasquel shuffles downtown to Honeyman Drugstore to buy the <u>Des Moines Register</u>.

The minister displayed nervousness when she began speaking.

The young minister's voice cracked and her hands shook when she began speaking.

She was discouraged by a number of things.

Sheila was discouraged by Paul's indifference, a D grade on a physics test, and a failure to lose weight.

When you spot words in your writing like those on the left, try to replace them with words like those on the right:

car	**Pontiac**
fruit	**bananas**
book	**A Matter of Honor**
month	**June**
friend	**Butch Merritt**
uncle	**Uncle Orville**
walked	**strolled**
gave	**tossed**
asked	**demanded**
spoke	**whispered**
breathed	**panted**
gloom	**fog, rain**
fear	**gasps, tremors**
affection	**hug, kiss**
anger	**scream, curse**
cheerfulness	**laughter, smiles**
ridicule	**sneer, mockery**
disappointment	**cries, sighs**

Do Exercise 4 in Section B.

SEXIST LANGUAGE

People should be portrayed fairly; sexist language, however, often reflects stereotyping or insensitivity. The following guidelines can contribute to your ability to achieve gender fairness in your writing.

● **USE NEUTRAL OCCUPATIONAL TITLES:**

AVOID	**USE**
authoress, poetess	**author, poet**
policeman, policewoman	**police officer**
salesman, saleswoman	**sales representative**
workman	**worker**
fireman	**firefighter**
weatherman	**meteorologist, weather forecaster**
chairman, chairwoman	**chairperson, presiding officer**

mailman	**mail carrier**
steward, stewardess	**flight attendant**
foreman	**manager**
craftsman	**artisan**
cameraman	**camera operator**
newsboy	**news carrier**

● **USE GENDER-INCLUSIVE TERMS:**

AVOID	USE
mankind	**humanity, the human race**
man-hours	**hours, employee hours**
man's history	**human history**
man-made	**manufactured**
manpower	**personnel**
freshmen	**first-year students**
coeds	**students**
Englishmen, Frenchmen, Irishmen	**English, French, Irish**

● **USE RESPECTFUL TERMS:**

AVOID	USE
breadwinner	**worker, professional, wage earner**
better half	**wife, husband**
female attorney	**attorney**
lady doctor	**doctor**
male nurse	**nurse**
foxy lady	**attractive woman**
a hunk	**attractive man**

● **USE BALANCED PRONOUNS AND NOUNS:**

AVOID	USE
Everybody must hand in his paper by Friday.	Everybody must hand in his or her paper by Friday.
	or
	Students must hand in their papers by Friday.
	or
	Papers must be handed in by Friday.

Every person has <u>his</u> own mailbox.	Every person has <u>his</u> or <u>her</u> own mailbox.
	or
	Every person has a mailbox.
<u>Each</u> coach arranges <u>his</u> own practice schedule.	<u>Each</u> coach arranges <u>her</u> or <u>his</u> own practice schedule.
	or
	<u>Coaches</u> arrange <u>their</u> own practice schedules.
<u>Nobody</u> in <u>his</u> right mind would refuse such an offer.	<u>Nobody</u> in <u>her</u> or <u>his</u> right mind would refuse such an offer
	or
	<u>People</u> in <u>their</u> right minds would never refuse such an offer.
Many <u>men</u> and <u>ladies</u> from our community work at the auto plant.	Many <u>men</u> and <u>women</u> from our community work at the auto plant.
	or
	<u>Many citizens</u> from our community work at the auto plant.
A <u>man</u> and <u>his wife</u> sang a duet at the service.	A <u>husband</u> and <u>wife</u> sang a duet at the service.
	or
	A duet was sung at the service.
<u>George Allenson</u> and <u>his wife</u> Bette will represent our organization at the conference.	<u>Mr. and Mrs. Allenson</u> will represent our organization at the conference.
	or
	<u>George and Bette Allenson</u> will represent our organization at the conference.

Do Exercise 5 and the Review Exercises in Section B.

B. GAINING THE EXPERIENCE

Exercise 1: *Cross out the wordy phrases that have been underlined and replace them with single words. An example has been done for you.*

stopped

Example: The bus ~~came to a stop~~ in front of the school.

1. Most senators <u>registered their approval</u> of the President's nominee for the Supreme Court.

2. Charges against the suspect were dropped <u>on the grounds</u> of insufficient evidence.

3. The city manager <u>tendered her resignation</u> at yesterday's council meeting.

4. The new regulations go into effect next month.

5. <u>If and when</u> you go to England, be sure to visit Oxford University.

6. Coach Mannis <u>arrived at a decision</u> to start Del Greco at quarterback.

7. After her work day <u>drew to a close</u>, Felicia went shopping at the mall.

8. The happy couple <u>will exchange marriage vows</u> in June.

9. My brother plans to save money for college <u>during the time that</u> he's in the navy.

10. The job is yours, <u>assuming that</u> you're still interested.

11. Exams are on everybody's mind when the semester <u>draws to a close</u>.

12. <u>If and when</u> you hear from Gene, give him my congratulations.

13. Her driving license was suspended <u>as a result</u> of her previous offenses.

14. During Homecoming Weekend, I was happy to <u>make the acquaintance</u> of my boyfriend's parents.

15. <u>In the event that</u> Harry can't work tonight, can you?

Exercise 2: *Replace the underlined pompous expressions with simpler words. An example has been done for you.*

drink

Example: My grandparents don't ~~imbibe~~ alcoholic beverages.

1. In the <u>ensuing</u> weeks, the dictator <u>endeavored</u> to <u>terminate</u> the <u>populace's</u> unrest.

2. Unless you can suggest a <u>viable</u> alternative, we will have to <u>utilize</u> our reserve funds.

NAME _____   DATE _____

3. The engineers are <u>interfacing</u> with the construction crew to discuss the <u>parameters</u> of the project.

4. After <u>prioritizing</u> his goals, Kirk developed <u>innovative</u> strategies for <u>finalizing</u> them.

5. <u>At this point in time</u>, we should <u>ascertain</u> if it's <u>feasible</u> to <u>initiate</u> such changes.

6. After the meal <u>terminated</u>, Jane's <u>spouse exhibited</u> slides of British Columbia.

7. It is <u>feasible</u> seasoning would enhance the chowder.

8. After what had <u>transpired</u>, it was obvious we had to establish <u>parameters</u> to <u>retain</u> control.

9. The young man may be indicted for perjury because his <u>feedback</u> to the judge's <u>inquiries</u> contained <u>misinformation</u>.

10. Although his job requires him to move frequently, Mickey <u>endeavors</u> to make friends wherever his residence happens to be.

11. Judy was <u>instrumental</u> in explaining the <u>options</u> I had.

12. Be sure to <u>peruse</u> the contract because its terms would <u>impact</u> not only you but also the <u>populace</u> you represent.

13. Are you <u>cognizant of the fact</u> that <u>in lieu of</u> overtime pay workers would get additional vacation time?

14. We hope you will <u>utilize</u> your influence to have this clause changed before negotiations are <u>finalized</u>.

15. <u>At this point in time</u>, some workers would have difficulty <u>complying with</u> your orders.

Exercise 3:   *A. Underline the clichés in the following sentences.*

1. The hustle and bustle of New York City is a rude awakening to most first-time visitors.

2. In this day and age, it's easy to become green with envy because of the salaries professional athletes make.

3. Due to the members' untiring efforts, the goal was slowly but surely reached.

4. Sheila fell for his excuse hook, line, and sinker because she thought he looked as innocent as a newborn babe.

5. To make a long story short, she became as pale as a ghost when she found out he had been lying.

NAME _____   DATE _____

6. Our business is in full swing, and in a nutshell, we are confident we are on the cutting edge of success.

7. My old dog, who was the apple of my eye, is gone but not forgotten.

8. It goes without saying that if you keep doing your own thing, you are going to have to face the music one of these days.

9. Bucky, who hopes to follow in the footsteps of his two older brothers, is waiting with breathless anticipation to see if he's been accepted at the state university; if so, he'll be as happy as a lark.

10. Although she knows it's easier said than done, Marla has a burning desire to hike the entire length of the Appalachian Trail.

B. Rewrite each sentence, replacing the underlined cliché with specific words. An example has been done for you.

Example: For some reason, Grover was as <u>jumpy as a cat on a hot tin roof</u>.

For some reason, Grover was so nervous he couldn't eat, sleep, or concentrate.

1. <u>After all is said and done</u>, good health remains our most important possession.

_____

_____

2. Shelby discovered making straight A's was <u>easier said than done</u>.

_____

_____

3. Although there was a twinkle in her eyes, Amanda looked as <u>innocent as a newborn babe</u>.

_____

_____

4. Someone will have to <u>take the bull by the horns</u> if this project is to be completed.

_____

_____

5. Dexter jumped at the opportunity, believing that <u>nothing ventured, nothing gained</u>.

_____

_____

NAME _____   DATE _____

Exercise 4: *Rewrite each sentence replacing general and abstract words with specific and concrete ones. An example has been done for you.*

Example: After reading about the crime in the newspaper, my friend was sad.

After reading about the tragic kidnapping in the <u>Dallas Morning News</u>, *Scott's eyes filled with tears.*

1. One evening last week, the sunset was especially beautiful.

   _____

   _____

2. Mickey's car has a number of accessories.

   _____

   _____

3. My friend has a pleasing personality.

   _____

   _____

4. Some of the fans were out of control.

   _____

   _____

5. He was an effective president for a number of reasons.

   _____

   _____

6. Ginny cooked an unusual dinner one evening this week.

   _____

   _____

7. The patient complained of several aches and pains.

   _____

   _____

8. I experienced various emotions at my high school reunion.

   _____

   _____

9. My job gives me few opportunities to relax.

   _____

   _____

10. Don is a versatile athlete.

    _____

    _____

NAME _____   DATE _____

Exercise 5: *Rewrite the following sentences so that sexist language is avoided. An example has been done for you.*

Example: Each relative indicated his surprise when Sheldon announced he was resigning his mailman's job to become a male nurse.

Each relative indicated his or her surprise when Sheldon announced he was resigning his mail carrier's job to become a nurse.

or

Relatives indicated their surprise when Sheldon announced he was resigning his mail carrier's job to become a nurse.

1. Man's history has always reflected his belief in supernatural powers.

_____

_____

_____

2. Some colleges do not allow a freshman to have his car on campus.

_____

_____

_____

3. Roscoe's better half is a lady lawyer.

_____

_____

_____

4. Mr. Scrontas, a policeman, and his wife Courtney, a stewardess, are chairmen of the planning committee.

_____

_____

_____

5. Men and ladies over twenty-one are eligible to take the fireman's test.

_____

_____

_____

NAME _____   DATE _____

6. Any senior interested in interviewing for salesmen positions should make an appointment with one of the lady secretaries at the Career Center.

    _____

    _____

    _____

7. Everybody in our senior class had the time of his life during Skip Days.

    _____

    _____

    _____

8. Giselle, who works as a cameraman at the campus television station, is studying to be a weatherman.

    _____

    _____

    _____

9. A student in his first semester is ineligible to be chairman of the committee.

    _____

    _____

    _____

10. This section of the city was settled by Irishmen, and their descendants are among the leading citizens of the community, including a prominent lady judge.

    _____

    _____

    _____

NAME _____   DATE _____

Chapter 12
Review Exercise: *Improve the clarity of the following sentences by replacing the wordy phrases, pompous words, clichés, vague terms, and sexist language.*

1. No one should leave his car parked in the street overnight.

   _____

   _____

2. The movie was entertaining.

   _____

   _____

3. Despite the fact that she worked out only three times a week, Gloria lost weight by means of exercising.

   _____

   _____

4. When my friends initiated the ambitious project, they believed their networking of resources would make it feasible for them to consummate it by the end of the summer season.

   _____

   _____

5. The weather became bad, but my car performed beautifully.

   _____

   _____

6. Margaret remains calm, cool, and collected when she makes a speech.

   _____

   _____

7. Both men students and coeds provided the manpower for the charity drive.

   _____

   _____

8. Gino arrived just as the meeting drew to a close.

   _____

   _____

9. After prioritizing his options, Barry utilized his mechanical skills to procure a job.

   _____

   _____

10. After all is said and done, Ashley remains the apple of Jim's eye.

    _____

    _____

NAME _____   DATE _____

C. APPLYING THE FINISHING TOUCH

(1) Proofreading: *This passages contains five wordy phrases, three clichés, and two examples of sexist language. After making the necessary changes, check your work with that in the **Answer Key.***

Zachary Taylor: Twelfth President, 1849–1850

Zachary Taylor was the seventh president born in Virginia. However, a few months after his birth in 1784, Taylor and his family moved to Kentucky where he lived until entering the army.

Taylor became an excellent officer and climbed the ladder of success throughout his forty years in the army. Cool as a cucumber in battle, Taylor participated in the War of 1812, Indian disputes, and the Mexican War (1846–1848). He was called "Old Rough and Ready" due to the fact that he was tough, fearless, and down-to-earth.

A few years after entering the army, Taylor made the acquaintance of Margaret Smith, and they were united in holy matrimony in 1810. Although Taylor and Margaret were stationed at numerous army bases throughout their marriage, they always considered Louisiana their residence.

During the Mexican War, Taylor became a national hero after leading his 5,000 troops to a stunning victory over Santa Anna's 20,000 soldiers. Due to the fact that he was so popular, the Whigs nominated Taylor for president in 1848. Despite the fact that misinformation about his drinking was widely spread, Taylor won the close election. As president, Taylor faced a nation divided over whether slavery should be extended into the territories

NAME _____   DATE _____

acquired from Mexico. Taylor, although a slaveowner, strongly opposed the spread of slavery. After some senators indicated the South might secede from the Union over this issue, Taylor made it crystal clear that he would forcefully deal with any such attempt.

On July 4, 1850, at the laying of the cornerstone for the Washington Monument, Taylor became seriously indisposed from indigestion; he expired a few days later. Everybody in the nation was shocked when he heard the news. Taylor, president for only sixteen months, became the second Chief Executive to expire in office.

NAME _____   DATE _____

(2) Proofreading: *This passage contains clichés, wordy phrases, sexist language, and pompous as well as vague words. After making your corrections, rewrite the entire passage on a separate piece of paper.*

Laptops

The popularity of portable computers, commonly called laptops, is growing by leaps and bounds. The reason laptops are growing in popularity is due to the fact technological advances have been made. For example, when the first laptops were developed in the early 1980s, they weighed over twenty pounds, had fuzzy screens, and cost over $2000. At this point in time, however, many laptops weigh less than five pounds, have vivid screens, and cost less than $1000. In addition, today's laptop computers are so compact and portable they can be utilized while commuting to work or lounging around a pool. Technological improvements in laptops are also enabling a person to do his own thing, whether it's designing something or taking an inventory of things.

Laptops are used by people everywhere. According to stewardesses, there are always salesmen and other passengers pounding away on their computers during a flight. Laptops are also impacting on people in all walks of life. Alicia Garcia, a lady doctor, uses a laptop in her practice and her better half uses one in his florist shop. Selma Gretsky, an authoress, does most of her writing on a laptop.

If a person is considering buying a laptop, she should prioritize her computer needs before finalizing a purchase. In any instance, the laptop should have a crisp screen, responsive keyboard, a strong battery, ample storage, expansion slots, and light weight.

NAME _____   DATE _____

Writing: What emotions are contained in this passage?

> Someone in the crowd said to him, "Teacher, tell my brother to divide the inheritance with me."
>
> Jesus replied, "Man, who appointed me a judge or an arbiter between you?" Then he said to them, "Watch out! Be on your guard against all kinds of greed; a man's life does not consist in the abundance of his possessions."
>
> And he told them this parable: "The ground of a certain rich man produced a good crop. He thought to himself, 'What shall I do? I have no place to store my crops.'
>
> "Then he said, 'This is what I'll do. I will tear down my barns and build bigger ones, and there I will store all my grain and my goods. And I'll say to myself, 'You have plenty of good things laid up for many years. Take life easy; eat, drink and be merry.'
>
> "But God said to him, 'You fool! This very night your life will be demanded from you. Then who will get what you have prepared for yourself?'
>
> "This is how it will be with anyone who stores up things for himself but is not rich toward God."

Suggestions: **CONTINUE** to read the passage until you are confident you understand it.

JOT DOWN the emotions displayed by each speaker and any other emotions you feel come through in the passage.

LIST your reasons for citing each emotion.

DEVOTE a paragraph to each emotion; mention specific reasons why you believe each emotion is contained in the passage; if you feel some emotions are more important than others, make sure your reasons reflect this belief (and you might want to arrange your paragraphs from least important emotion to most important emotion).

CONSIDER linking your paragraphs with such words and phrases as *first, second, in addition, furthermore, most importantly, on the other hand, however;* also, be sure to put quotation marks around any direct quotes you cite from the passage.

IMPORTANT: MAKE SURE your paper is concerned with emotions; don't get sidetracked and end up writing a summary or an interpretation of the passage.

WRITE, READ, AND REWRITE until you are satisfied with what you have written; the length of your final draft, which should be typewritten and doublespaced, is up to you.

PROVIDE an appropriate title.

PROOFREAD; you now have an impressive background for proofreading, so make sure your paper isn't flawed by careless mistakes or unclear language; review **PROOFREADING TIPS,** page 295.

Does a LONG-RANGE ASSIGNMENT also deserve some of your attention?

After reviewing Chapters 9–12, take the MASTERY TEST provided by your instructor.

CHAPTER THIRTEEN

Spelling — Plurals

A. ESTABLISHING THE BACKGROUND

The external appearance of our writing is important. If our writing is neat and free from obvious errors, it likely will be read; however, if it is messy and marred by glaring errors, it likely will be ignored. Because correct spelling contributes positively to our writing's external appearance as well as to its clarity, this chapter and the one following are devoted to this subject.

-s

● **Most nouns (people, places, things) form the plural by adding -s:**

player	players
college	colleges
barrel	barrels

-es

● **Nouns ending in s, sh, ch, z, and x form the plural by adding -es:**

glass	glasses
dish	dishes
wrench	wrenches
buzz	buzzes
fox	foxes

-y Nouns

● **Plurals of nouns ending in y preceded by a vowel are formed by adding only s:**

key	keys
Tuesday	Tuesdays
attorney	attorneys

● **Plurals of nouns ending in y preceded by a consonant are formed by changing the y to ies:**

boundary	boundaries
party	parties
puppy	puppies

Note: **People's names ending in y, whether preceded by a vowel or consonant, are made plural by adding only s: Rileys, Kennedys**

Do Exercise 1 in Section B.
➡

-f, -fe Nouns

● **Plurals of nouns ending in f and fe are formed by changing the f to ves if the pronunciation of the root changes in the plural form:**

half	halves
self	selves
wife	wives
life	lives

● **However, if the root maintains its basic pronunciation, add only s:**

chief	chiefs
belief	beliefs
chef	chefs
cafe	cafes

-o Nouns

● **Plurals of nouns ending in <u>o</u> preceded by a vowel are formed by adding only <u>s</u>:**

boo	boos
rodeo	rodeos
studio	studios

● **Plurals of musical terms are also formed by adding only <u>s</u>:**

piano	pianos
solo	solos
soprano	sopranos

● **Plurals of nouns ending in <u>o</u> preceded by a consonant are formed by adding <u>es</u>:**

potato	potatoes
hero	heroes
mosquito	mosquitoes

Prominent Exceptions: **autos, photos, Eskimos, Filipinos**

Do Exercise 2 in Section B.

-is Nouns

● **Nouns ending in is form the plural by changing the <u>is</u> to <u>es</u>:**

parenthesis	parentheses
oasis	oases
analysis	analyses

Compound Words

● **Compound nouns form the plural by making plural the most important word:**

brother-in-law	brothers-in-law
maid of honor	maids of honor
attorney-at-law	attorneys-at-law

Irregular Plurals

● **Some nouns form the plural in irregular ways:**

man	men	datum	data
woman	women	ox	oxen
child	children	criterion	criteria
foot	feet	medium	media
tooth	teeth	goose	geese

Unchanging Nouns

● **Some nouns, usually the names of animals or fish, are spelled the same in the plural as in the singular:**

deer	deer
sheep	sheep
trout	trout

Do Exercise 3 and the Review Exercise in Section B.

B. GAINING THE EXPERIENCE

Exercise 1:   *Write the plural form for the following words.*

	Singular	**Plural**
1.	branch	_____
2.	picture	_____
3.	valley	_____
4.	lash	_____
5.	operation	_____
6.	buzz	_____
7.	army	_____
8.	porch	_____
9.	turkey	_____
10.	river	_____
11.	Wednesday	_____
12.	box	_____
13.	miss	_____
14.	university	_____
15.	wish	_____
16.	truck	_____
17.	apology	_____
18.	mix	_____
19.	alley	_____
20.	ally	_____
21.	ditch	_____
22.	chair	_____
23.	company	_____
24.	hush	_____
25.	building	_____

NAME _____   DATE _____

Exercise 2:   *Write the plural form for the following words.*

	Singular	**Plural**
1.	echo	_____
2.	leaf	_____
3.	shelf	_____
4.	radio	_____
5.	chief	_____
6.	solo	_____
7.	belief	_____
8.	embargo	_____
9.	hero	_____
10.	wolf	_____
11.	wife	_____
12.	veto	_____
13.	reef	_____
14.	soprano	_____
15.	volcano	_____
16.	buffalo	_____
17.	thief	_____
18.	banjo	_____
19.	calf	_____
20.	studio	_____
21.	life	_____
22.	half	_____
23.	potato	_____
24.	cello	_____
25.	piano	_____

NAME _____   DATE _____

Exercise 3: *Write the plural form for the following words.*

	Singular	**Plural**
1.	son-in-law	_____
2.	criterion	_____
3.	goose	_____
4.	diagnosis	_____
5.	deer	_____
6.	crisis	_____
7.	child	_____
8.	woman	_____
9.	sister-in-law	_____
10.	tooth	_____
11.	analysis	_____
12.	maid of honor	_____
13.	datum	_____
14.	neurosis	_____
15.	attorney-at-law	_____
16.	foot	_____
17.	parenthesis	_____
18.	moose	_____
19.	ox	_____
20.	salmon	_____
21.	psychosis	_____
22.	mouse	_____
23.	thesis	_____
24.	sheep	_____
25.	medium	_____

NAME _____   DATE _____

Chapter 13
Review Exercise: *If one of the words is misspelled, circle it, then spell it correctly in the space provided. If both words are spelled correctly, write* correct.

Examples:	ponies	(leafs)	*leaves*
	cups	dishes	*correct*
1.	buses	chieves	
2.	studioes	maps	
3.	ponies	diagnosises	
4.	citys	alleys	
5.	mountains	sopranos	
6.	lifes	attorneys-at-law	
7.	companys	teeth	
8.	dresses	buzzs	
9.	wishes	mother-in-laws	
10.	apologies	lakes	
11.	catches	babys	
12.	stitchs	varieties	
13.	deers	selves	
14.	sympathies	soloes	
15.	echoes	womans	
16.	banjos	crisises	
17.	armies	navies	
18.	porchs	neuroses	
19.	data	celloes	
20.	oxen	salmon	
21.	oases	valleys	
22.	slashs	journeys	
23.	wishes	maid of honors	
24.	media	fishes	
25.	thiefs	theses	

NAME _____   DATE _____

26.	radioes	tomatoes	_____
27.	knives	friends	_____
28.	thermometers	temples	_____
29.	analysises	trout	_____
30.	pianos	replys	_____
31.	daisies	tubas	_____
32.	portraits	opinions	_____
33.	heros	marriages	_____
34.	walnuts	sketchs	_____
35.	childrens	carriages	_____
36.	bicycles	dictionarys	_____
37.	privileges	computers	_____
38.	husbands	wifes	_____
39.	torches	fragments	_____
40.	partys	taxes	_____
41.	duties	pencils	_____
42.	Tuesdays	boxs	_____
43.	Kennedys	turkeys	_____
44.	potatoes	luxurys	_____
45.	synopses	maids of honor	_____
46.	activitys	chimneys	_____
47.	loaves	enemys	_____
48.	librarys	ladies	_____
49.	universities	colleges	_____
50.	foxes	wolfs	_____
51.	salarys	monkeys	_____

NAME _____   **DATE** _____

C. APPLYING THE FINISHING TOUCH

(1) Proofreading: *This passage contains nine misspellings. After making the necessary corrections, check your work with that in the **Answer Key**.*

Christa McAuliffe

After President Reagan announced in 1984 that a teacher would be chosen as the first private citizen to travel in space, over 11,000 teachers submitted their names for consideration. Through the following monthes, NASA officials sifted through piles of datum searching for the one teacher who met all of the criterion. Finally, on July 19, 1985, NASA officials announced that Christa McAuliffe, a social studys teacher at Concord High School, Concord, New Hampshire, was their choice.

Christa Corrigan McAuliffe was born in Boston, Massachusetts, in 1948 and raised in nearby Framingham. During her childhood, she joined the Girl Scoutes and took dance, voice, and piano lessons. In high school, Christa made the National Honor Society and participated in numerous activitys. including basketball, orchestra, and drama. In addition, she loved playing the guitar, piano, and singing soloes.

After graduating from high school, Christa attended the state college in Framingham where she majored in American history and secondary education. Despite taking a full load of courses, working nights as a clerk at a trucking firm, and babysitting, Christa found time to captain the debate

NAME _____   DATE _____

team, sing in the glee club, and perform in dramas. Christa always lived her philosophy, "To get the most out of life as possible."

In 1970, Christa married Steve McAuliffe, and they moved to Washington, D.C., where Steve attended law school and Christa began her teaching career. In 1978, they moved to Concord, New Hampshire.

As a teacher, Christa was enthusiastic, creative, and committed to her students. As a person, she was energetic, friendly, and devoted to her family, which included her husband and two childrens.

After undergoing monthes of training, Christa entered the *Challenger* spacecraft on the morning of January 28, 1986. Seventy-three seconds into the flight, the *Challenger* exploded, killing Christa and her six crew mates. A nation was plunged into mourning.

(2) Proofreading: *After correcting the ten misspellings in this passage, have your instructor check your work.*

Millard Fillmore: Thirteenth President, 1850–1853

Millard Fillmore, born in a log cabin in 1800, was raised in the Finger Lakes area of central New York, a region of deep vallies, thick woods, numerous lakes, and plentiful wildlife, including deer, mooses, and fish. Fillmore had eight brothers and sisters, and his family, like most familys living on a frontier farm, had a constant struggle to survive. Because of his parents' numerous financial crisises, Fillmore was apprenticed to a clothmaker.

Eventually, Fillmore became a successful lawyer and entered politics. Taking advantage of his opportunitys, Fillmore was elected to Congress. At the Whig convention in 1848, he was chosen as Zachary Taylor's running mate, and they won the national election. Two years later, after the steeple belles from the churchs in Washington, D.C., announced President Taylor's death, Millard Fillmore became the thirteenth president of the United States.

President Fillmore was admired for his calm and pleasant disposition, not for his intellectual facultys. As the nation became increasingly divided over slavery, Fillmore, who hated vetos, supported the Compromise of 1850. Although this compromise admitted California to the Union as a free state, it did contain a strict law requiring the return of runaway slaves.

Fillmore's endorsement of the Compromise of 1850 cost him the support of his own party, so he did not receive the presidential nomination in 1852. Four years later, however, Fillmore was nominated for president by the American Party, one of the new political partys that developed in the 1850s. However, this party, whose members were called "Know-Nothings," had little popular support, and Fillmore carried only Maryland in the election. In 1874, Fillmore died in Buffalo, New York.

NAME _____   DATE _____

Writing: Read these poems aloud several times:

Poem A

He who smacks the head of every nail,
Who misses not a trick,
Who always hits the bull's eye without fail,
Makes me sick.

Poem B

I never saw a purple cow,
I never hope to see one,
But I can tell you anyhow,
I'd rather see than be one.

Write a paper beginning with **one** of these assertions:

- **Poem A is superior to Poem B for several reasons.**
- **Poem B is superior to Poem A for several reasons.**
- **Poems A and B are unworthy of being called poems for several reasons.**
- **Poems A and B are good poems for several reasons.**

Suggestions: **REVIEW** the writing suggestions presented in the preceding chapters as some of them could prove helpful in doing this assignment.

WRITE AND REWRITE over several days, eliminating all general, vague, and obvious statements; your paper must be full of original as well as specific reasons to be persuasive.

INCLUDE at least <u>four</u> of these <u>eight</u> words or phrases in your paper and underline them: *furthermore, moreover, in addition, most importantly, another, however, on the other hand, consequently.*

LIMIT your final paper to <u>one complete page</u>, typewritten, doublespaced, and headed by an appropriate title.

PROOFREAD, being particularly mindful of your spelling.

If you are to do another one
of the **LONG-RANGE ASSIGNMENTS,** pages 291–292,
be sure to review the **WRITING SUGGESTIONS,** pages 293–294,
before, while, and after completing this assignment.

CHAPTER FOURTEEN

Spelling — Basic Guidelines

A. ESTABLISHING THE BACKGROUND

Although there are exceptions to the spelling guidelines presented in this chapter, they are sufficiently consistent to be helpful for the spelling of hundreds of words.

PREFIXES

- **Prefixes, such as <u>dis</u>-, <u>in</u>-, <u>mis</u>-, and <u>re</u>-, do NOT change the spelling of a word:**

dis + similar	dissimilar
in + capable	incapable
mis + spell	misspell
re + appoint	reappoint

COMPOUNDS

- **When two words are joined, omit NO letters:**

book + keeper	bookkeeper
extra + ordinary	extraordinary

fire + arms   firearms
room + mate   roommate

Do Exercise 1 in Section B.

EI AND IE WORDS

● Use <u>i</u> before <u>e</u> except after <u>c</u> or when sounded like <u>a</u> as in <u>neighbor</u> and <u>weigh</u>:

<u>I</u> BEFORE <u>E</u>

achieve
believe
chief
yield

EXCEPT AFTER <u>C</u>

ceiling
conceit
receive

**OR WHEN SOUNDED LIKE <u>A</u>
AS IN <u>NEIGHBOR</u> AND <u>WEIGH</u>**

freight
vein

Note: **Prominent exceptions to the preceding guidelines include ancient, neither, seize, leisure, and weird.**

Do Exercise 2 in Section B.

VOWEL SUFFIXES

- **When a word ends in silent e, DROP the e when adding a VOWEL suffix, such as -able, -ed, -ing, and -ous:**

desire	desirable
care	cared
become	becoming
fame	famous

Note: **For pronunciation purposes, words ending in -ce and -ge, such as peace and courage, retain the e: peaceable, courageous.**

CONSONANT SUFFIXES

- **When a word ends in silent e, KEEP the e when adding a CONSONANT suffix, such as -ful, -less, -ly, and -ment:**

E

care	careful
hope	hopeless
sincere	sincerely
excite	excitement

Note: **Prominent exceptions to the preceding guideline include argument, judgment, ninth, and truly.**

Do Exercise 3 in Section B.

DOUBLING CONSONANTS

- **When a one-syllable word ends in a single consonant preceded by a single vowel, double the final consonant when adding a vowel suffix:**

One-syllable Word	Vowel	Consonant	Double
bid	b	i	d	bidding, bidder
dig	d	i	g	digging, digger
drop	dr	o	p	dropping, dropped
slam	sl	a	m	slamming, slammed

- **Also, when a two-syllable word is accented on the SECOND syllable, and it ends in a single consonant preceded by a single vowel, DOUBLE the final consonant when adding a vowel suffix:**

Two-syllable Word Accent on Second Syllable	Vowel	Consonant	Double
admit	ad mit'	i	t	admitting, admitted
begin	be gin'	i	n	beginning, beginner
occur	oc cur'	u	r	occurring, occurred
refer	re fer'	e	r	referring, referred

When the preceding conditions do not exist, the final consonant remains single, as in these examples:

jump	jumped, jumping	The final consonant is NOT
perform	performed, performing, performer	doubled because the word ends in two consonants.
green	greener, greening	The final consonant is NOT
exceed	exceeded, exceeding	doubled because it is preceded by two vowels.
dif 'fer	differed, differing, difference	The final consonant is NOT doubled because the accent is on the first syllable.
equip	equipment	The final consonant is NOT
sad	sadness	doubled because the suffix begins with a consonant.

Do Exercise 4 in Section B.

COMMONLY MISSPELLED WORDS

These frequently used words are commonly misspelled:

1.	absence	26.	license
2.	accommodate	27.	marriage
3.	across	28.	necessary
4.	all right	29.	nickel
5.	a lot	30.	occasion
6.	always	31.	parallel
7.	amateur	32.	peculiar
8.	among	33.	pleasant
9.	calendar	34.	prejudice
10.	cemetery	35.	prevalent
11.	committee	36.	privilege
12.	cousin	37.	probably
13.	criticize	38.	professor
14.	definite	39.	prominent
15.	description	40.	pronunciation
16.	discipline	41.	psychology
17.	doctor	42.	quantity
18.	eligible	43.	questionnaire
19.	embarrass	44.	realize
20.	exercise	45.	recommend
21.	explanation	46.	ridiculous
22.	familiar	47.	restaurant
23.	finally	48.	separate
24.	forty	49.	similar
25.	guarantee	50.	succeed

Do Exercises 5 and 6 and the Review Exercises in Section B.

B. GAINING THE EXPERIENCE

Exercise 1:   *After adding the prefix or whole word, write each word in the space provided.*

1. dis + approve   _____

2. in + frequent   _____

3. wind + shield   _____

4. re + examine   _____

5. un + conscious   _____

6. extra + ordinary   _____

7. dis + agree   _____

8. with + hold   _____

9. mis + spell   _____

10. pre + view   _____

11. in + adequate   _____

12. book + keeper   _____

13. ear + ring   _____

14. dis + appear   _____

15. never + the + less   _____

16. finger + nail   _____

17. mis + use   _____

18. knick + knack   _____

19. in + convenient   _____

20. mail + box   _____

21. room + mate   _____

22. re + enter   _____

23. un + pleasant   _____

24. pre + eminent   _____

25. news + stand   _____

NAME _____   DATE _____

Exercise 2: *Write the correctly spelled word in the space provided; remember, it's "i before e except after c or when sounded like a as in neighbor and weigh."*

1. deceive, decieve   _____
2. mischief, mischeif   _____
3. grief, greif   _____
4. weight, wieght   _____
5. beleive, believe   _____
6. seige, siege   _____
7. friend, freind   _____
8. riegn, reign   _____
9. feild, field   _____
10. vein, vien   _____
11. shreik, shriek   _____
12. receipt, reciept   _____
13. sleigh, sliegh   _____
14. neighbor, nieghbor   _____
15. breif, brief   _____
16. receive, recieve   _____
17. neice, niece   _____
18. releif, relief   _____
19. acheive, achieve   _____
20. conceit, conciet   _____
21. preist, priest   _____
22. quiet, queit   _____
23. cashier, casheir   _____
24. viel, veil   _____
25. yield, yeild   _____

NAME _____   DATE _____

Exercise 3:   *Write the correctly spelled word in the space provided; remember, the <u>e</u> is kept with a consonant suffix but dropped with a vowel suffix.*

1.	hope + ful	hopeful, hopful	_____
2.	examine + ing	examineing, examining	_____
3.	care + less	careless, carless	_____
4.	immediate + ly	immediatly, immediately	_____
5.	advance + ment	advancement, advancment	_____
6.	complete + ing	completeing, completing	_____
7.	scrape + ed	scraped, scrapeed	_____
8.	love + ly	lovely, lovly	_____
9.	fame + ous	famous, fameous	_____
10.	promise + ed	promiseed, promised	_____
11.	notice + ed	noticed, noticeed	_____
12.	cute + er	cuteer, cuter	_____
13.	manage + ment	managment, management	_____
14.	stare + ing	stareing, staring	_____
15.	have + ing	having, haveing	_____
16.	tape + ing	tapeing, taping	_____
17.	perspire + ing	perspiring, perspireing	_____
18.	time + ly	timly, timely	_____
19.	excite + able	excitable, exciteable	_____
20.	noise + less	noisless, noiseless	_____
21.	achieve + ment	achievement, achievment	_____
22.	sincere + ity	sincereity, sincerity	_____
23.	peace + ful	peaceful, peacful	_____
24.	lone + ly	lonly, lonely	_____
25.	remove + able	removeable, removable	_____

NAME _____   DATE _____

Exercise 4: *After observing the base word on the left, write its correct form after a vowel suffix has been added. Remember, one-syllable words and words accented on the last syllable should have their final consonant doubled if the consonant is preceded by a single vowel.*

Example:	peg	peged (pegged)	*pegged*
1.	win	wining, winning	_____
2.	bump	bumped, bumpped	_____
3.	omit	omited, omitted	_____
4.	ship	shiped, shipped	_____
5.	contain	containing, containning	_____
6.	regret	regreted, regretted	_____
7.	travel	traveled, travelled	_____
8.	benefit	benefited, benefitted	_____
9.	wrap	wraped, wrapped	_____
10.	prefer	prefered, preferred	_____
11.	detour	detoured, detourred	_____
12.	commit	commited, committed	_____
13.	develop	developing, developping	_____
14.	pad	paded, padded	_____
15.	infer	infered, inferred	_____
16.	tear	tearing, tearring	_____
17.	step	steping, stepping	_____
18.	sand	sanding, sandding	_____
19.	occur	occured, occurred	_____
20.	mark	marked, markked	_____
21.	read	reading, readding	_____
22.	submit	submiting, submitting	_____
23.	flood	flooding, floodding	_____
24.	forget	forgeting, forgetting	_____
25.	regard	regarded, regardded	_____

NAME _____   DATE _____

Exercise 5: *In the space provided, spell the word suggested in parentheses. The dash (-) can indicate either a letter or letters need to be added.*

Example: *describe*   Can you (des - be) the car?

1. _____   Mr. Lopino promises to make a (def - n - te) decision by Friday.

2. _____   Were you satisfied with her (expl - n - tion)?

3. _____   My parents' plane (fin - ly) arrived at 7:00 o'clock.

4. _____   The (doct - r) is pleased with your progress.

5. _____   Lois is serving on the publicity (com - t - ee).

6. _____   Our van can (ac - modate) nine passengers.

7. _____   Do you have an excuse for your (ab - en - e)?

8. _____   My husband attends an (ex - ise) class that meets three times a week.

9. _____   Charlie has the (dis - pline) to stay on his diet.

10. _____   The cam recorder comes with a sixty-day (g - rantee).

11. _____   The small (cem - t - ry) is located two miles north of the village.

12. _____   You might (emb - rass) him if you ask that question.

13. _____   Tony works in the store (a - ross) the street from the bank.

14. _____   All members are (el - g - ble) to vote.

15. _____   Scott talks (alot, a lot) about changing jobs.

16. _____   He was (f - rty) years old when he started college.

17. _____   My (co - sin) is moving to New Mexico.

18. _____   She is an excellent (am - t - r) painter.

NAME _____   DATE _____

19. _____ My dog (a - ways) gets frightened when it thunders.

20. _____ Linda provided an interesting (des - ri - tion) of her new job.

21. _____ Do you have anything written down on the (cal - nd - r) for that date?

22. _____ There was not a good mechanic (am - ng) us.

23. _____ I'm not (fam - l - r) with that part of the city, are you?

24. _____ Do you think it would be (all right, alright) for me to borrow her car?

25. _____ He tried, so don't (crit - ze) him.

Exercise 6: *The directions for this exercise are the same as for the preceding one.*

1. _____ Sheila's aunt is a (prof - ss - r) at U.C.L.A.

2. _____ The announcer's (pron - nci - tion) of the players' names was flawless.

3. _____ Oak Street runs (par - l - l) to Stetson Boulevard.

4. _____ A large (quan - ty) of supplies will be needed for the expedition.

5. _____ It's (ne - es - ary) that all cast members attend the dress rehearsal.

6. _____ Can you (rec - mend) a dentist for me to see?

7. _____ Some people have a (pr - jud - e) against lawyers.

8. _____ The movie was (ridic - l - us), but I enjoyed it.

9. _____ We need to get a (prom - n - nt) person to deliver the commencement address.

10. _____ Molly and Clark's (marr - ge) took place on June 12th.

NAME _____   DATE _____

11. _____   I had a (pleas - nt) conversation with my elderly neighbor today.

12. _____   The governor believes the economy will (prob - ly) improve by fall.

13. _____   The (question - re) took five minutes to answer.

14. _____   Carlene has a pilot's (li - en - e).

15. _____   Why are colds more (prev - l - nt) during the winter months?

16. _____   Some married couples keep (sep - r - te) bank accounts.

17. _____   Bob and Alice took advantage of the (oc - s - on) to announce their engagement.

18. _____   Our (p - yc - logy) test has been postponed until next week.

19. _____   The witnesses gave (sim - l - r) accounts of the incident.

20. _____   Can you buy anything in this store for a (nick -)?

21. _____   I'm confident you will (suc - ed) in reaching your goal.

22. _____   My boss has been acting (pecul - r) lately.

23. _____   I didn't (re - l - ze) Dana was such a good athlete.

24. _____   Our banquet was held at an Italian (resta - r - nt).

25. _____   It was a (priv - l - ge) to be on the same team as Ted.

NAME _____   **DATE** _____

Chapter 14
Review Exercise: A. PREFIXES, COMPOUNDS: *Write the correctly spelled word in the space pro-vided.*

1.   roommate, roomate   _____

2.   unecessary, unnecessary   _____

3.   gloworm, glowworm   _____

4.   withold, withhold   _____

5.   extrodinary, extraordinary   _____

6.   mispell, misspell   _____

7.   interelated, interrelated   _____

8.   newsstand, newstand   _____

9.   disimilar, dissimilar   _____

10. bookkeeper, bookeeper   _____

B. EI, IE WORDS: *Write the correctly spelled word in the space provided.*

1.   beleive, believe   _____

2.   receive, recieve   _____

3.   neighbor, nieghbor   _____

4.   peice, piece   _____

5.   freind, friend   _____

6.   receipt, reciept   _____

7.   neice, niece   _____

8.   ceiling, cieling   _____

9.   weigh, wiegh   _____

10. sheild, shield   _____

C. SUFFIXES AND SILENT E: *Write the correctly spelled word in the space pro-vided.*

1.   write   writer, writeer   _____

2.   remove   removeing, removing   _____

3.   sincere   sincerity, sincereity   _____

4.   love   lovly, lovely   _____

5.   care   caring, careing   _____

6.   price   priceless, pricless   _____

NAME _____   DATE _____

7. advance   advancement, advancment   _____

8. excite   exciteing, exciting   _____

9. desire   desireable, desirable   _____

10. lone   lonely, lonly   _____

D. DOUBLING CONSONANTS: *Write the correctly spelled word in the space provided.*

1. beat   beating, beatting   _____

2. refer   refered, referred   _____

3. burn   burner, burnner   _____

4. occur   occured, occurred   _____

5. swim   swiming, swimming   _____

6. begin   beginer, beginner   _____

7. bleed   bleeding, bleedding   _____

8. skip   skiping, skipping   _____

9. pardon   pardoned, pardonned   _____

10. commit   commiting, committing   _____

E. COMMONLY MISSPELLED WORDS: *In the space provided, spell the word suggested in parentheses. The dash (-) can indicate either a letter or letters need to be added.*

1. _____ Karl, hang the (cal - nd - r) on the door.

2. _____ Do you (ex - ise) regularly?

3. _____ We divided the responsibilities (am - ng) the four of us.

4. _____ During Brittany's (ab - en - e), Meredith will be in charge.

5. _____ Did you ever (emb - rass) your parents when you were a child?

6. _____ Ann Martin has a real estate (li - en - e).

7. _____ Please put our orders on (sep - r - te) checks.

8. _____ This is a nice (resta - r - nt).

9. _____ Larry says it's (ne - es - ary) to bring our tools.

10. _____ Wayne considers it a (priv - l - ge) to have you as a guest.

NAME _____   **DATE** _____

C. APPLYING THE FINISHING TOUCH

(1) Proofreading: *This passage contains twenty misspellings. After making the necessary corrections, check your work with that in the **Answer Key**.*

Myths

Myths, regardless of how wierd they might be, have been captureing the imaginations of people for thousands of years. Not only are myths entertainning and exciteing, but also they are inspireing and instructive. Myths teach us that whatever is occuring in our lives, it is our personal qualities, not our acheivments, that are most important.

Classical myths originated in anceint Greece and were orally passed from generation to generation. Eventually, Homer (8th century B.C.) wrote down many of the myths, and Euripides (484–406 B.C.) and other dramatists wrote plays about them. In most cases, the gods and goddesses were presentted as the Greek people of that time percieved them.

Later, the Romans adoptted the Greek gods and goddesses but gave them new names; for example, Zeus became Jupiter and Eros became Cupid. For the Greeks and Romans, myths provided explainations about history, religion, pshycology, and nature. (Thunder, for example, occured when Apollo, the sun god, shook his sheild.)

Although most people no longer beleive in myths, those familiar with these anceint tales insist that these particular myths still provide valueable insights about ourselfs and the world in which we live.

NAME _____   DATE _____

(2) Proofreading: *This passage contains fourteen misspellings. After making the necessary corrections, have your instructor check your work.*

Franklin Pierce: Fourteenth President, 1853–1857

Franklin Pierce, son of a Revolutionary War officer, was born in 1804 in Hillsboro, New Hampshire. He graduated from Bowdoin College in Maine where Henry Wadsworth Longfellow and Nathaniel Hawthorne were amoung his classmates. Hawthorne and Pierce remainned liflong freinds.

After becomeing a successful lawyer, Pierce joined the Democratic Party and enterred politics. He was elected to the House of Representatives and then to the Senate. During the Mexican War of 1846–1848, Pierce, who was fourty-two, served as an army officer.

At the Democratic National Convention in 1852, Pierce, who was not nationally fameous, became the unexpected choice for president. In the fall election, he recieved the most votes and easily defeated Winfeild Scott, the Whig candidate.

Pierce's presidency was a failure. He selected ineffective people to serve in his cabinet, and he was unable to halt the increasing conflicts over slavery. After the Kansas-Nebraska Act, which Pierce supportted, pro- and anti-slavery people in Kansas killed one another in such numbers that the territory became known as "Bloody Kansas." By 1856, Pierce was being critized so severely throughout the country that the Democrats were too embarassed to renominate him for President.

Pierce's private life was mared by tragedy. One son was killed in a railroad accident shortly before Pierce was to assume the presidency. Mrs. Pierce never fully recovered from this sorrow. She died in 1863 and Pierce, who struggled with alcoholism much of his life, died six years later.

NAME _____ DATE _____

Writing: Choose **one** of the following with which to begin a short story:

- **The evidence was so overwhelming, the logic so compelling, and her words so impressive that Albert could say nothing but, "You're wrong!"**
- **"Why are you weeping? Did you imagine I was immortal?"**
- **Connor finally returned from the orphanage across the river where she had been making her weekly appearance.**

Suggestions: **TO PROVIDE PLEASURE**—make that the <u>purpose</u> of your story.

JOT DOWN story ideas and descriptions of characters coming to mind over the next few days; let your imagination roam.

COMMIT yourself to writing and rewriting until you are confident you've written a story bringing pleasure.

QUOTE the direct words of your characters at least four times; if necessary, review the section on quotation marks in Chapter Eight.

LIMIT your story to no more than five typewritten, doublespaced pages.

PROVIDE a clever title reflecting the story's contents.

PROOFREAD; again, you may find it helpful to review **PROOFREADING TIPS,** page 295.

If you are working on a **LONG-RANGE ASSIGNMENT,**
continue to do so once you have completed your short story.

CHAPTER FIFTEEN

Frequently Confused Words — 1

A. ESTABLISHING THE BACKGROUND

Clarity, the chief obligation of a writer, requires the accurate use of all words. Therefore, this chapter and the one following will enable you to distinguish between words often confused with one another.

1. **accept**—to receive

    Do you think Don will <u>accept</u> the job offer?

    except—all but

    My son likes all fruits <u>except</u> for grapefruit.

2. **advice**—a suggestion

    Sandy's <u>advice</u> was to sign the lease.

    advise—to provide a suggestion

    What did the lawyer <u>advise</u> you to do?

3. **affect**—to influence

    Economic predictions often <u>affect</u> the stock market.

    effect—a result

    The economic predictions had a positive <u>effect</u> on the stock market.

4. **among**—refers to three or more

    Responsibility for the event was divided <u>among</u> the five committee members.

between—refers to two

The argument <u>between</u> the manager and umpire delayed the game for almost five minutes.

5. **brake**—a device used to stop a vehicle; to slow down or stop

The bicycle's <u>brake</u> needs to be replaced.

I had to <u>brake</u> the car because of the sharp curve.

break—to smash; a timeout

Be sure the cat doesn't <u>break</u> the lamp.

We took a short <u>break</u> after we finished the yard work.

6. **breath**—the act of inhaling and exhaling

Tom took a deep <u>breath</u> before beginning his speech.

breathe—to draw air into and expel it from the lungs

The high humidity made it difficult to <u>breathe</u>.

7. **capital**—city serving as a seat of government; accumulated wealth; uppercase letter

Springfield is the <u>capital</u> city of Illinois.

The Bryans are attempting to raise enough <u>capital</u> to begin their own business.

The first word of a sentence should begin with a capital letter.

capitol—building in which a legislative body meets

My child's class took a tour of the <u>capitol</u> building in Albany.

8. **character**—what a person is actually like

Jennifer's <u>character</u> is one of compassion and integrity.

reputation—what others think a person is actually like

The judge has the <u>reputation</u> for giving harsh sentences.

9. **choose**—to select or decide

Maurice found it difficult to <u>choose</u> a college major.

chose—past tense of choose.

He finally <u>chose</u> biology.

10. **cite**—to quote or refer to

Can you <u>cite</u> any authorities to support your controversial statements?

sight—see; glimpse

The long-awaited train finally came into <u>sight</u>.

site—position or location

The Jenkins' property was selected as the <u>site</u> for the shopping mall.

11. **coarse**—rough; vulgar

    Burlap is a coarse material.

    I never heard my father use coarse language.

    course—path; school subject and all other meanings

    You can follow this course to reach the highway.

    Virginia's favorite course is chemistry.

    Of course you can ride with us.

12. **collaborate**—to work with another person or persons

    Local architects will collaborate in designing the new civic center.

    corroborate—to confirm or verify

    No one was able to corroborate the defendant's alibility.

13. **complement**—something that completes

    Does this scarf complement my outfit?

    compliment—flattering remark

    I would like to compliment you for your beautiful solo.

14. **confidant**—a person in whom on can confide personal information

    Archie Goodwin is Nero Wolfe's closest confidant.

    confident—self-assured

    The Bulls' coach is confident his team will win the title.

15. **conscience**—sense of right and wrong

    Ray's conscience began to bother him, so he apologized to his neighbor.

    conscious—awake; aware

    The patient is now conscious.

    Were you conscious of what your friends were doing?

16. **council**—a group of people that makes decisions

    The city council has approved the building of a new fire station.

    counsel—to provide advice; recommendation

    Our coach did counsel us to stay in good shape over the holidays.

    Thanks to Ms. Bailey's counsel, our trip went smoothly.

17. **covert**—secret, hidden

    Spies engage in covert activities.

overt—open, obvious

The suspect made an <u>overt</u> attempt to escape, so the police officer handcuffed him.

18. **decent**—proper; mannerly; kind

Ralph is the most <u>decent</u> person I have ever known.

descent—a downward direction; plung

Despite the stormy weather, the plane's <u>descent</u> went smoothly.

dissent—to disagree; a difference of opinion

Molly was the only person to <u>dissent</u> with the committee's recommendation.

There is considerable <u>dissent</u> in the community over whether a new elementary school should be built.

19. **desert**—dry barren land; forsaking one's duty

During the summer, the territory becomes a <u>desert</u> because of the scant rainfall.

Employers should never <u>desert</u> their obligations to employees when a merger occurs.

dessert—the last course in a meal

You can have either chocolate ice cream or strawberry yogurt for <u>dessert</u>.

20. **device**—an object

This <u>device</u> is designed to remove car oil filters.

devise—to plan, invent

City engineers are being pressured to <u>devise</u> a better traffic pattern for the metropolitan area.

21. **disinterested**—impartial; not influenced by personal interest

Joyce was obviously <u>disinterested</u> in the outcome, so she was asked to be the judge.

uninterested—indifferent; not interested

Michael appeared <u>uninterested</u> in going to the movies.

22. **elicit**—draw forth, bring to light

Police officers are attempting to <u>elicit</u> information about the accident.

illicit—unlawful

Many people suspect that my neighbor acquired his great wealth through <u>illicit</u> means.

23. **eminent**—famous, outstanding

    Senator Vignali is the most <u>eminent</u> person to come from our community.

    imminent—about to happen, threatening

    A storm seemed <u>imminent</u>, so we canceled the boat trip.

24. **explicit**—clearly expressed

    Wendy's <u>explicit</u> directions enabled me to find her home without any difficulty.

    implicit—not directly expressed; suggested

    Shelby didn't say "No," but his frown made it <u>implicit</u> that he didn't want to loan me his car.

25. **formally**—in a dignified, formal manner

    People attending the banquet are to dress <u>formally</u>.

    formerly—previously

    Craig <u>formerly</u> lived in New Jersey.

Do all of the Exercises in Section B.

B. GAINING THE EXPERIENCE

Exercise 1: *After reading the sentence, write the appropriate word in the space.*

1. _____ Abigail is (confidant, confident) her business will succeed.

2. _____ The host quickly apologized when he became (conscience, conscious) of the fact that his guests were offended by his remarks.

3. _____ The (cite, sight, site) from the bridge was spectacular.

4. _____ I enjoy every type of music (accept, except) modern jazz.

5. _____ Would you like a piece of lemon pie for (desert, dessert)?

6. _____ Three new members were chosen for the student (council, counsel).

7. _____ Because of the heavy traffic, I had to (brake, break) frequently.

8. _____ Did you thank George for his (advice, advise)?

9. _____ Anita was able to (device, devise) a clever way to stop the water leak.

10. _____ Jessica did (collaborate, corroborate) that Warren made every attempt to get here on time.

11. _____ Mrs. Steele attempted to (elicit, illicit) a smile from her baby grandson.

12. _____ Preparations were made for the submarine's (decent, descent).

13. _____ The construction work eventually made Brad's hands tough and (coarse, course).

14. _____ Jim Perrone, an (eminent, imminent) coach in our state, was the banquet speaker.

15. _____ Although I could be wrong, I believe Avon's silence was an (explicit, implicit) indication of his disapproval.

NAME _____ DATE _____

16. _____   The hot, humid weather didn't seem to (affect, effect) Charles like it did the rest of us.

17. _____   Dr. Knight was (formally, formerly) the president of a community college in Washington.

18. _____   Steve hopes that some season the World Series will be (among, between) the Chicago Cubs and the Boston Red Sox, his two favorite teams.

19. _____   Many of management's most important decisions are made in a (covert, overt) manner, which angers the employees.

20. _____   The members of the appeal board must be (disinterested, uninterested) in the cases to make fair decisions.

21. _____   Alan's (character, reputation) for practical jokes began during his high school days.

22. _____   Brown and yellow are colors that (complement, compliment) one another.

Exercise 2:   *After reading the sentence, write in the space the entire word suggested in parentheses.*

1. How did Ginger (br-) _____ her arm?

2. I (adv-e) _____ you to keep taking music lessons.

3. Spencer needs the measuring (dev-e) _____.

4. This book contains a picture of every (capit-l) _____ building in the United States.

5. Michael and Rachel will (co-borate) _____ in planning the activities for the special event.

6. My cousin claims to be the (confid-nt) _____ of a famous rock singer.

7. Luis is taking an advanced biology (co-rse) _____ this semester.

8. Although I didn't like the job, my supervisor was a (de-ent)

   _____ person.

9. After considerable thought, Hans (cho-e) _____ the sweater with the blue and red stripes.

10. Good soldiers never (des-rt) _____ their posts.

NAME _____   DATE _____

11. The crowded room was so hot and stuffy I could hardly (breat-)

   _____ .

12. Melissa had offered to help, so her (consci-) _____ was clear.

13. At the ceremony on January 16, Heather will be (form-ly)

   _____ installed as an officer of the club.

14. Did you (compl-ment) _____ Ryan for winning the race?

15. Before entering a plea, I urge you to seek a lawyer's (coun-l)

   _____ .

Exercise 3:   *Write original sentences for the following words.*

1. character: _____

   _____

2. breath: _____

   _____

3. effect: _____

   _____

4. cite: _____

   _____

5. dissent: _____

   _____

6. uninterested: _____

   _____

7. except: _____

   _____

8. overt: _____

   _____

9. eminent: _____

   _____

10. explicit: _____

   _____

NAME _____   DATE _____

Chapter 15
Review Exercise: *After reading the sentence, select the appropriate word and write it in the space provided.*

1. _____ Conrad was (among, between) the five people from the audience who participated in the magician's tricks.

2. _____ Jason expressed his joy over the exciting news in a number of (covert, overt) ways, including laughing, clapping, and hugging everyone.

3. _____ My paper was marked down because I forgot to (cite, sight, site) the sources for my information.

4. _____ We had gingerbread with whipped cream for (desert, dessert).

5. _____ Karen had to (brake, break) her car to avoid hitting the dog.

6. _____ Stacy, please (accept, except) my apology.

7. _____ What (coarse, course) of action do you think the President should take?

8. _____ How did your sudden fame (affect, effect) you?

9. _____ My (conscience, conscious) bothers me because I didn't take the time to visit my grandparents.

10. _____ Yesterday, we (choose, chose) new wallpaper for the dining room.

11. _____ Everyone was able to come (accept, except) Holly.

12. _____ Our Christmas (brake, break) begins next Thursday.

13. _____ It was obvious my neighbor didn't want any (advice, advise) from me.

14. _____ Benjamin was careful not to (brake, break) any of his wife's favorite dishes.

15. _____ The support David received from his friends had a positive (affect, effect) on his spirits.

16. _____ Members of the club will (choose, chose) new officers next month.

NAME _____ DATE _____

17. _____   I (advice, advise) you to take a vacation in the Wisconsin Dells.

18. _____   The Sahara (Desert, Dessert) is in the northern part of Africa.

19. _____   Vanessa got the old finish off the desk by using (coarse, course) sandpaper.

20. _____   Although intelligent and energetic, his (character, reputation) is flawed by arrogance and intolerance.

21. _____   After running up six flights of stairs, Mike was out of (breath, breathe).

22. _____   Recently, an expert did (collaborate, corroborate) that the painting was done by Winslow Homer.

23. _____   The college has raised sufficient (capital, capitol) to build a new dormitory.

24. _____   It became harder to (breath, breathe) the higher we climbed the mountain.

25. _____   The two professors plan to (collaborate, corroborate) in writing a history textbook.

26. _____   Des Moines is the (capital, capitol) city of Iowa.

27. _____   This campus was once the (cite, sight, site) of a large dairy farm.

28. _____   The appliance store on Hogan Boulevard has a good (character, reputation).

29. _____   Dustin suddenly became (conscience, conscious) of Jack's presence in the dark room.

30. _____   The responsibility will be shared (among, between) Raul and Greta.

31. _____   The (capital, capitol) building of New Hampshire is close to the downtown area of Concord.

32. _____   My (cite, sight, site) was blocked by the trees.

33. _____   Every sentence should begin with a (capital, capitol) letter.

34. _____   Let me (complement, compliment) you for your excellent work.

NAME _____   DATE _____

35. _____ Thanks to Marjorie's (council, counsel), we were able to solve our dilemma.

36. _____ A minister is often the (confident, confidant) of many people.

37. _____ Billy Graham, the (eminent, imminent) evangelist, was born in North Carolina.

38. _____ My brother, who is currently a student at Oklahoma State University, was (formally, formerly) in the army.

39. _____ Harper is enjoying her French (coarse, course).

40. _____ Most people in the community were shocked to learn that gambling and other (covert, overt) activities had been taking place in one of the local business establishments.

41. _____ Molly is (disinterested, uninterested) in this matter, so her decision will be based solely on the evidence.

42. _____ There is heated (decent, descent, dissent) in Congress over the President's proposed budget.

43. _____ Mr. Neilson hopes to (elicit, illicit) volunteers to help with the fund drive.

44. _____ Engineers hope to (device, devise) a more fuel-efficient car engine.

45. _____ At the wedding reception, the newlyweds were (formally, formerly) introduced as "Mr. and Mrs. Theodore Pelletier."

46. _____ Nola's technical knowledge should (complement, compliment) Forrest's business experience.

47. _____ The elevator's (decent, descent, dissent) was fast but smooth.

48. _____ The sergeant was (explicit, implicit): No one would be allowed off the base over the weekend unless the barracks was spotlessly clean.

49. _____ Because closing time was (eminent, imminent), we hurried to the cash register to pay for our merchandise.

NAME _____ DATE _____

50. _____ Mark was rooting for the Raiders to win, but I was (disinterested, uninterested) in the outcome.

51. _____ This is a handy (device, devise) for opening tightly sealed bottles.

52. _____ The sale and use of (elicit, illicit) drugs is one of the nation's most serious problems.

53. _____ Vicki is a capable, competent, and (confidant, confident) person.

54. _____ Mr. McGregor is a candidate for the city (council, counsel).

55. _____ Steve and Shawn are waiting for a (decent, descent, dissent) day to go golfing.

56. _____ Despite the criticism, I (council, counsel) you not to resign.

57. _____ The little boy's impish smile was an (explicit, implicit) indication of his mischievous nature.

58. _____ The teacher's sense of humor has a wonderful (affect, effect) on the children.

NAME _____ **DATE** _____

C. APPLYING THE FINISHING TOUCH

(1) Proofreading: *This passage contains fourteen words that are misused. After making your corrections, compare them with those in the Answer Key.*

Woods Hole

Woods Hole, a tiny seaport on Cape Cod in Massachusetts, is the sight of a major biological laboratory, a large fishery, and an imminent oceanographic institution. Though independent from one another, good communication exists between these three research centers, so their projects can sometimes be designed to compliment each other.

Since its founding in 1930, the Woods Hole Oceanographic Institution's character has grown throughout the world. Every year, hundreds of people and organizations seeking council about ocean matters contact the institution's scientists for their advise. Woods Hole oceanographers can provide valuable information about how the ocean's currents effect the climate. They can also site the sources for many of their important discoveries, including those concerning exotic marine life, vast underwater mountain ranges, and huge hot springs far below the ocean surface. People can even enroll in a marine science coarse or two at Woods Hole.

Woods Hole oceanographers are best known for their discovery of the *Titanic*. The *Titanic*, the most modern oceangoing vessel of its day, sank on its maiden voyage in 1912 after failing to break its forward progress toward an iceberg. Over 1500 passengers lost their lives. For seventy-three years, the precise location of the sunken *Titanic* was unknown. However, in 1985,

NAME _____   DATE _____

Woods Hole and French oceanographers were able to corroborate in their efforts and, by using various underwater devises, they were successful in locating the *Titanic* on the ocean floor about 370 miles off the coast of Newfoundland.

Because only one percent of the ocean floor has been explored, Woods Hole oceanographers are confidant many more exciting discoveries will be made in the years to come.

NAME _____   **DATE** _____

(2) Proofreading: *This passage contains twenty words that are misused. After making your corrections, have your instructor check your work.*

James Buchanan: Fifteenth President, 1857–1861

When James Buchanan became president in 1856, many people were confidant his political and government skills would so compliment one another that he would be able to break the nation's dissent into civil war. Buchanan appeared not only to possess an excellent background for the presidency, but also he had the character for conducting his official duties openly but formerly. It was hoped his election would bring a breathe of harmony to the nation.

Unfortunately, however, Buchanan's entire presidency was marked by frustration and failure for him and his country. In the beginning, Buchanan was not conscience of the seriousness of the split among the North and South; at the end, he was unable to chose a coarse of action, despite advise from many people, to deal with the South's secession from the Union.

James Buchanan was born in a rural area of Pennsylvania in 1791. He graduated from Dickinson College in 1809, and he served in the army during the War of 1812. He then became an imminent lawyer, and in 1819, he became engaged to Anne Coleman. However, Ms. Coleman decided to brake the engagement, and she died shortly thereafter. A rumor circulated that Ms. Coleman had committed suicide, but no one familiar with the circumstances of her death would ever collaborate that this was the case. Regardless, Buchanan later became the only president never to have been married.

In the years that followed, Buchanan became a successful politician,

NAME _____   DATE _____

and in 1856, he was elected president. Buchanan thought he could end the crisis among the North and South by appointing some Southerners to his cabinet and by getting Congress to except Kansas as a slave state. However, such steps did not even illicit the support of his own party, and the descent among the North and South grew worse. During the last days of Buchanan's administration, some of the Southern states began to secede from the Union.

When Abraham Lincoln succeeded him as president, Buchanan said to him, "If you are as happy in entering the White House as I shall feel on returning to Wheatland (his home in Lancaster, Pennsylvania), you are a happy man indeed." Buchanan lived for eight more years after leaving the presidency, dying in 1869 at the age of seventy-seven.

NAME _____ DATE _____

Writing: Which **ONE** of the statements below would you prefer to make to first-year high school students? Explain your choice to **THEM** in writing.

- **Never let a computer know you're in a hurry.**
- **A quiet, serious, and sensible person will just about ruin a party.**
- **Success isn't always green.**
- **Set your course by the stars, not by the lights of each passing ship.**
- **Cleverness is not wisdom.**
- **One reason people get into trouble is that trouble usually starts out being fun.**

Suggestions: **CHOOSE** the statement you **TRULY PREFER,** which may be different from the one you think you **SHOULD PREFER.**

EXPLORE your thoughts about the statement *and* first-year high school students by jotting down anything coming to mind; at this stage, accept what and how you write; consider whether you want to be funny, serious, or both.

WRITE AND REWRITE until specific reasons for your choice in relation to first-year high school students emerge.

WORK HARD to support your choice with unique but convincing reasons; avoid being too solemn or "preachy"; *keep* first-year high school students in mind.

WRITE your first complete draft, read it aloud, then make any changes you think would improve it; provide plenty of *particulars.*

FOCUS ON CLARITY because this is the type of paper that often becomes bogged down with generalizations, vague statements, and clichés; make sure your writing is *vivid, specific,* and *concrete.*

WRITE AGAIN, then read aloud what you have written and make improvements; keep doing this until you are satisfied with what you have written and the tone your writing reflects; once more, keep in mind first-year high school students, so try to give pleasure as well as information.

LIMIT your final draft to two or three typewritten, doublespaced pages.

GIVE your title some thought; it can make an important contribution to your paper.

PROOFREAD; you now possess a solid background for proofreading, so do a thorough job.

Does a LONG-RANGE ASSIGNMENT also need some of your attention?

CHAPTER SIXTEEN

Frequently Confused Words — 2

A. ESTABLISHING THE BACKGROUND

This chapter, as was true of the preceding one, will enable you to distinguish between words often confused with one another.

1. **forth**—forward; without notice

   Despite the difficulties, Dennis went <u>forth</u> with his plans.

   Suddenly, music broke <u>forth</u> from the upstairs window.

   fourth—after third

   Our bowling team is currently <u>fourth</u> in the league standings.

2. **hole**—an opening

   The plumber drilled a <u>hole</u> in the basement wall.

   whole—complete

   Sam ate the <u>whole</u> bag of cookies.

3. **illegible**—unreadable

   I have to write slowly or my writing becomes <u>illegible</u>.

   ineligible—unqualified; disqualified

   After serving two consecutive terms as mayor, Ms. Woolcott is now <u>ineligible</u> for this office.

4. **imply**—to suggest; say indirectly

   Avery's hesitation seemed to <u>imply</u> that he had second thoughts about our decision.

infer—to draw a conclusion

We could <u>infer</u> Sabrina felt better by her laughter and lively talk.

5. **instance**—an example

    Mr. Murphy's contribution is another <u>instance</u> of his generosity.

    instants—moments of time

    For a few <u>instants</u>, we were afraid our canoe was going to overturn.

6. **lessen**—to make less; decline

    The snow began to <u>lessen</u> by late morning.

    lesson—something to be learned, studied, or taught

    My son has a piano <u>lesson</u> after school.

7. **loose**—not tight; unfastened

    The little girl's front teeth were <u>loose</u>.

    The door was <u>loose</u> from its hinges.

    lose—misplace; opposite of win

    Carmelo seldom wears the pendant because she's afraid she might <u>lose</u> it.

    We will <u>lose</u> the game unless we play harder.

8. **marital**—refers to marriage

    My uncle and aunt's <u>marital</u> problems eventually led to a divorce.

    martial—refers to the military

    The soldiers patrolled the streets after <u>martial</u> law was declared.

9. **medal**—an award or decoration

    The state trooper received a <u>medal</u> for bravery.

    metal—a substance like gold, copper, or iron

    The old vacuum cleaner was made of heavy <u>metal</u>.

10. **moral**—concerned with right and wrong

    The judge said the defendant's selfishness was a <u>moral</u> problem, not a legal one.

    morale—refers to a person's emotional condition

    Cindy's <u>morale</u> soared after she received the promotion.

11. **passed**—past tense of pass

    Gene <u>passed</u> a number of other runners as he jogged around the track.

After learning we had <u>passed</u> our mid-term exams, my roommate and I pigged out on pizzas.

past—no longer current; time gone by

We have had sunny weather for the <u>past</u> two weeks.

12. **patience**—calmness; self-control

The police officer maintained his <u>patience</u> despite being taunted by some people in the crowd.

patient—sick or ill person; uncomplaining

The movie star is currently a <u>patient</u> in a Los Angeles hospital.

The <u>patient</u> teacher waited until all the students were finished with the assignment.

13. **personal**—concerned with private matters

I didn't ask Todd his age because I thought the question was too <u>personal</u>.

personnel—a group of people working for the same organization; concerned with employees

The plant's <u>personnel</u> office is located on the top floor.

14. **principal**—most important; head of a school; money

The <u>principal</u> reason Josh joined the navy was to see the world.

Ms. Higgins is the <u>principal</u> of Lincoln Elementary School.

I'm paying 11% interest on the <u>principal</u> I borrowed from the bank.

principle—rule or standard

Concern for others is a <u>principle</u> my parents always stressed.

15. **quiet**—silent; peaceful

Villisca is a <u>quiet</u> little village in Iowa.

quit—to stop; to give up

We <u>quit</u> work at 4:30 p.m.

quite—really; entirely

Felicia and Andy's wedding was <u>quite</u> impressive.

16. **role**—a part played by an actor

Who's playing the <u>role</u> of Lysander in Shakespeare's *A Mid-summer Night's Dream?*

roll—to move; a list of names; a type of bread

I can't <u>roll</u> my wheel-barrow because it has a flat tire.

According to the class <u>roll</u>, Otis hasn't any absences.

I need some butter for my <u>roll</u>.

17. **shone**—past tense of shine

Friday was the first day the sun <u>shone</u> all week.

shown—past tense of show

One of Kelly's favorite movies was <u>shown</u> on television last night.

18. **stationary**—unmoving; still

The troops remained <u>stationary</u> throughout the lengthy ceremony.

stationery—writing paper

Melanie bought some colorful <u>stationery</u> at the gift shop.

19. **statue**—work of sculpture; a carving

The <u>statue</u> of Robert E. Lee was completed in 1897.

stature—refers to one's reputation, standing, or qualities

After winning the award, Hector's <u>stature</u> increased among his friends.

statute—regulation; rule; law

A community <u>statute</u> prohibits the drinking of alcoholic beverages in the city parks.

20. **than**—used in comparisons

I liked the book better <u>than</u> the movie.

then—at that time; when

After washing her car, Terry <u>then</u> waxed it.

21. **threw**—the past tense of throw

Roger <u>threw</u> the old newspaper clipping into his desk drawer.

through—from one side to the other; completed

We had to walk <u>through</u> the lobby to get to the elevator.

22. **to**—introduces a phrase containing a noun or verb

Nicholas is going <u>to</u> the movies.

Mr. Perkins is going <u>to</u> mow his lawn.

too—also; more than enough

Cynthia is going to the movies, <u>too</u>.

The crops are not doing well because of <u>too</u> much rain.

two—the number following one

We saw <u>two</u> cardinals in our apple tree today.

23. **waist**—the middle of the body

Brandon has lost two inches around his <u>waist</u> since he's been on his diet.

waste—discarded material; to squander

Factories are not permitted to dump waste into the river.

Jackie doesn't like to waste her time between classes, so she studies at the library.

24. **weather**—condition of climate

New England's cold weather continued into April.

whether—if

Cynthia is still unsure whether she can go with us.

25. **wear**—concerned with the act of wearing clothes

My son loves to wear corduroy pants.

were—a plural verb; also used with you

We were surprised by news of their engagement.

Were you surprised too?

where—relates to a place

Conway, Arkansas, is where my father was born.

Do all of the Exercises in Section B.

B. GAINING THE EXPERIENCE

Exercise 1: After reading the sentence, write the appropriate word in the space provided.

1. _____ The good news improved everyone's (moral, morale).

2. _____ The Millers' address is printed on their (stationary, stationery).

3. _____ Because of his ancestry, Ireland is the (principal, principle) country Patrick wants to visit.

4. _____ Basketball referees must never (loose, lose) their composure.

5. _____ If you take the morning train, (than, then) you'll arrive in Washington, D.C., by noon.

6. _____ My sisters (wear, were, where) members of the field hockey team.

7. _____ The (patience, patient) in Room 311 is going home today.

8. _____ The lampshade has a (hole, whole) in it.

9. _____ Marsha plans (to, too, two) remodel her apartment this summer.

10. _____ My grandparents, who recently celebrated their fiftieth wedding anniversary, are often asked the secret of (marital, martial) bliss.

11. _____ The President's news conference will be (shone, shown) on television.

12. _____ Buddy said he's going to (quiet, quit, quite) shaving for the next two months.

13. _____ Eventually, Ginny's disappointment began to (lessen, lesson).

14. _____ Don't (waist, waste) your time and money seeing that movie.

15. _____ The angry boy (threw, through) his toys around the room.

16. _____ October (weather, whether) is invigorating.

17. _____ We could (imply, infer) by Tyrone's big smile that he had a date.

NAME _____   DATE _____

18. _____ The expensive-looking ring is actually made of cheap (medal, metal).

19. _____ Pamela has a small but challenging (role, roll) in the drama.

20. _____ People who have resided less than six months in the district are (illegible, ineligible) to vote.

Exercise 2: *After reading the sentence, write in the space the entire word suggested in parentheses.*

1. Rhonda has a (person-l) _____ interest in the outcome as she's related to one of the candidates.

2. Humphrey Bogart's (stat-e) _____ as an actor reached its zenith in the 1940s.

3. Fans rushed (fo-th) _____ to get nearer their idol.

4. The sun was out for only a few (instan-) _____ this afternoon.

5. Mickey easily (pas-) _____ his driver's test.

6. During the winter months, Shannon rides a (station-ry) _____ bicycle for exercise.

7. You need to take immediate steps if you should (l-se) _____ your credit cards.

8. The spilled coffee has made Wayne's letter (i-gible) _____.

9. Please add your name to the (rol-) _____ if you're planning to go on the field trip next week.

10. Sculpturing requires talent, training, and a lot of (patien-) _____.

11. Glenda's carpentry skill is just one (instan-) _____ of her numerous abilities.

12. "The customer is always right" is a (princip-) _____ my boss believes in.

13. The art instructor is giving a (less-n) _____ on the use of water colors.

14. Kristen received a (me-al) _____ for being on the winning relay team.

15. The army band played some stirring (mar-al) _____ music.

NAME _____   DATE _____

Exercise 3:   *Write original sentences for the following words.*

1. past: _____

    _____

2. fourth: _____

    _____

3. waist: _____

    _____

4. imply: _____

    _____

5. whether: _____

    _____

6. personnel: _____

    _____

7. through: _____

    _____

8. moral: _____

    _____

9. whole: _____

    _____

10. shone: _____

    _____

NAME _____   DATE _____

Chapter 16
Review Exercise: After reading the sentence, select the appropriate word and write it in the space provided.

1. _____ When did your pain (lessen, lesson)?

2. _____ If you'll buy the sofa today, (than, then) I'll give you a 20% discount.

3. _____ By the way my date stared at me, I could (imply, infer) she didn't approve of the way I was dressed.

4. _____ Phil decided to (quiet, quit, quite) his part-time job because he was falling behind in his studies.

5. _____ It's the (forth, fourth) time Joan has sprained her right ankle.

6. _____ A (statue, stature, statute) of a Confederate soldier stands in the middle of the park.

7. _____ The spotlight's beam (shone, shown) brightly in the dark sky.

8. _____ Lance (threw, through) his books on the table.

9. _____ The song was about the (marital, martial) woes of a cowboy and his wife.

10. _____ The sergeant calls the (role, roll) every morning at five o'clock.

11. _____ Do you happen to know (wear, were, where) my car keys are?

12. _____ The upset victory boosted our team's (moral, morale).

13. _____ The trainer said I would have to be more (patience, patient) in working with my dog.

14. _____ Mr. Palmer told some (personal, personnel) stories about his famous brother.

15. _____ Cans, bottles, and other (waist, waste) were scattered across the deserted parking lot.

16. _____ In a matter of (instance, instants), the sky became overcast.

17. _____ Mildred received a (medal, metal) for perfect attendance.

NAME _____   DATE _____

18. _____ The exhausted doctor was looking forward to a (quiet, quit, quite) evening at home.

19. _____ The stage is lit by movable as well as (stationary, stationery) lights.

20. _____ Chuck's relatives provided the (principal, principle) he needed to begin his business venture.

21. _____ What is the (weather, whether) forecast for tomorrow?

22. _____ My writing looks (illegible, ineligible) compared to Lloyd's neat penmanship.

23. _____ In the (passed, past), this building was heated by a huge coal furnace.

24. _____ Somehow, my dog got (loose, lose) from his leash.

25. _____ Gloria says she is (to, too, two) busy to go with us.

26. _____ Paul said he was (quiet, quit, quite) surprised by my telephone call.

27. _____ The development of the tank is among the (marital, martial) subjects included in this history book.

28. _____ Are you trying to (imply, infer) I was unfair to you?

29. _____ The (patience, patient) was delighted to learn that he had no cavities.

30. _____ My wife and I (wear, were, where) pleased to meet your relatives.

31. _____ When Joyce got (threw, through) studying, she went jogging.

32. _____ Suddenly, (to, too, two) dogs pranced onto the field.

33. _____ Would you like a pecan (role, roll)?

34. _____ Thanks to the magic of radio and television, the important message went (forth, fourth) immediately to all areas of the state.

35. _____ I didn't think the champion would (loose, lose) to the challenger, did you?

NAME _____   **DATE** _____

36. _____ Mr. Neitzel, the (principal, principle) of Stokes School, will retire this spring.

37. _____ Brian had his first guitar (lessen, lesson) today.

38. _____ One of the sofa cushions has a (hole, whole) in it.

39. _____ The expansion of the industrial park is another (instance, instants) of our community's growing economy.

40. _____ Do you know (weather, whether) Don brought his camera?

41. _____ Bradley forgot (to, too, two) set his alarm clock.

42. _____ I gave him my word, so I have a (moral, morale) responsibility to keep it.

43. _____ There's a long line waiting to buy tickets, so you must be (patience, patient).

44. _____ The children (passed, past) their time by playing ping-pong and video games.

45. _____ Students with unsatisfactory grades are (illegible, ineligible) to participate in extracurricular activities.

46. _____ The (hole, whole) house, including the attic and basement, has been remodeled.

47. _____ A (statue, stature, statute) prohibits overnight parking in the streets during the winter months.

48. _____ Hal bought the pants because the length and (waist, waste) sizes were appropriate for him.

49. _____ A videotape of France was (shone, shown) after dinner.

50. _____ Hank decided to (role, roll) the grocery cart back to the store.

51. _____ The scandal destroyed his once lofty (statue, stature, statute) in the community.

52. _____ A (principal, principle) Betty recommends is never to complain about trivial matters.

NAME _____ DATE _____

53. _____   James Dean became well-known after his starring (role, roll) in *Rebel Without a Cause.*

54. _____   Arthritis is the (principal, principle) cause of my grandmother's discomfort.

55. _____   The fire chief was given permission to hire additional (personal, personnel).

56. _____   Plastic toys aren't as durable as (medal, metal) ones.

57. _____   Be sure to (wear, were, where) old clothes when you come over Saturday to help me.

58. _____   Jim likes basketball more (than, then) any other sport.

NAME _____   **DATE** _____

C. APPLYING THE FINISHING TOUCH

(1) Proofreading: *This passage contains twelve words that are misused. After making the necessary corrections, check your work with that in the **Answer Key**.*

Keeping Their Cool

Sports referees, tax assessors, telephone solicitors, and police officers usually do not enjoy a high statue in their communities; in fact, they are among those people for whom going fourth to work means the likelihood of enduring verbal and, possibly, physical abuse from their fellow citizens. Clearly, than, these jobs are not for everyone, especially those with sensitive or explosive temperaments.

Basketball referees, for example, must exercise self-control at all times despite being screamed at by hysterical fans and sometimes by furious coaches if their team should loose a close contest because of a foul called near the end of the game. Tax assessors, to, must remain patience, even when outraged citizens curse them because of their high tax bills.

Telephone solicitors must also maintain their poise and cheerfulness while being subjected to personnel insults of all kinds, many coming before they are even threw explaining the reason for their call. Police officers are frequently confronted not only with verbal but also physical abuse, particularly while making arrests, serving summons, or dealing with domestic disputes.

How, than, do people in these stressful occupations maintain their moral? Many indicate they have learned to "role with the punches" while keeping their sense of humor. They also say following the principal of "remaining calm while treating everyone with respect" helps to diffuse hostile confrontations.

NAME _____   DATE _____

(2) Proofreading: *This passage contains fifteen words that are misused. After making the necessary corrections, have your instructor check your work.*

Abraham Lincoln: Sixteenth President, 1861–1865

Abraham Lincoln, whose statute as president is unmatched, was born in a log cabin in Hardin County, Kentucky, on February 12, 1809. When Lincoln was eight, he and his family moved to a wilderness area in Indiana wear his mother died two years later. In 1819, his father married Sarah Bush Johnston, a widow with four children.

In 1830, the Lincoln family moved again, this time to a farm in Illinois. Shortly afterwards, Lincoln, who was twenty-one, went fourth on his own, settling in New Salem, a small frontier village in Illinois. For the next few years, he worked as a store clerk, postmaster, and surveyor. Lincoln also briefly experienced the marital life, serving as a volunteer during the Black Hawk War.

Although Lincoln had few opportunities to attend school, he always had a remarkable interest in learning. In 1836, after studying mostly on his own, he past an examination entitling him to practice law. Lincoln than moved to Springfield, Illinois, and in 1842, he married Mary Todd. Threw the years, they experienced much personnel sorrow as only one of their four sons lived to reach maturity.

Lincoln became a successful politician; however, after serving eight years in the state legislature and one term in the United States Congress, he abandoned politics for a number of years to concentrate on his law practice.

Lincoln's interest in politics was reawakened by the passage of the Kansas-Nebraska Act, which Lincoln believed would result in the spread of

NAME _____   DATE _____

slavery. He ran for the United States Senate against the sponsor of the Kansas-Nebraska Act, Stephen Douglas. Although Lincoln lost the election, he became nationally known as a result of his effective debating with Douglas.

Lincoln received the Republican nomination for president in 1860, and he won the election that fall. By the time Lincoln assumed the presidency, seven Southern states had left the Union and others, to, where preparing to secede.

The Civil War erupted in the spring of 1861 and lasted for four tragic years. On numerous occasions, it seemed likely the North would loose the war, yet Lincoln remained firm, patience, and committed to preserving the Union at all costs. Although his handwriting was considered ineligible by some people, Lincoln's eloquent speeches did much to maintain Northern moral throughout the years of conflict.

Lincoln won re-election in 1864, and the war finally ended with Lee's surrender to Grant on April 9, 1865. Five days later, while attending a play at Ford's Theatre in Washington, Lincoln was shot by the actor John Wilkes Booth, and Lincoln past away at 7:22 the next morning.

NAME _____   DATE _____

Writing: Copy a short passage (no longer than four or five paragraphs) from a book, magazine, newspaper, or other source that you believe is *clear, convincing,* and *interesting;* the passage can be fiction or non-fiction. Explain in writing the reasons for your opinion.

Suggestions: **BEGIN** your paper with the entire passage; mention its source, author, publication date, and other information about it you believe your readers need to know.

PRESENT as many reasons as you can why you believe the passage is clear, convincing, and interesting; examples from the passage should be cited (use quotation marks when you do) in explaining your reasons.

DON'T GET SIDETRACKED by writing about issues unrelated to your purpose, which is to explain why you believe the passage is *clear, convincing,* and *interesting.*

MAKE strong, confident statements; if your opinions are supported, you are entitled to them, so don't write wishy-washy statements like "I may be wrong, but I sort of think" or "This may be silly, but I believe."

DO YOUR BEST to make *your own writing* clear, convincing, and interesting.

YOUR FINAL DRAFT should be typewritten and doublespaced; its length should be sufficient to accomplish your purpose.

PROVIDE a title that relates to your purpose but doesn't make your readers yawn.

PROOFREAD with your eye and ear; check **PROOFREADING TIPS,** page 295.

Good luck to you if you're also completing
a **LONG-RANGE ASSIGNMENT.**

After reviewing Chapters 13–16,
take the **MASTERY TEST** provided by your instructor.

Long-Range Assignments

Periodically, your instructor may have you do one of these research assignments. Often framed as offbeat, humorous questions, these assignments actually require a thoughtful blending of facts and imagination to be done well, so always begin your work on one as soon as possible. **SUGGESTIONS FOR DOING THESE ASSIGNMENTS ARE PRESENTED ON PAGES 293–294.**

- Did any soldiers actually survive Custer's Last Stand?
- Who would have made the better football coach, Robert E. Lee or Ulysses S. Grant?
- Would Babe Didrikson Zaharias be a success today?
- Why did many women find John Wilkes Booth attractive?
- What was Lee Harvey Oswald's basic problem?
- Was Jean Harris treated fairly by our judicial system?
- Which story is more fascinating, the building of the Brooklyn Bridge or the building of the Hoover Dam?
- Was Beethoven ever in love?
- What would Sigmund Freud say about hula hoops?
- Would George Washington or Abraham Lincoln have been more likely to believe in UFOs?
- How come geese can fly farther than eagles?
- Would Beatrix Potter have written Peter Rabbit if she hadn't been discriminated against?
- Does Benjamin Banneker deserve to have a school named after him?
- Was the author of *A Winter in Majorca* a saint or a sinner?
- Is there anything fascinating about botany?

- Why can it be said that the apples and cider we enjoy every fall are the result of year-round work, skill, and good luck?
- What's the story behind Coca Cola?
- Was the Packard a good automobile?
- What in the world would Eleanor Roosevelt and Madonna have talked about over lunch?
- Who do you think Jack the Ripper was?
- What was unusual about Yasuo Kuniyoshi's style?
- Can anything bad be said about George Eastman?
- Who would have been a good choice to integrate baseball if Jackie Robinson had not been around?
- Who cared more about a song's lyrics, Elvis Presley or Janis Joplin?
- Is the ending of the movie *Casablanca* a good one?
- Is it true there are poisons that can't be traced in the human body?
- Would you rather attend college in San Juan, Rìo Piedras, or Mayaguez?
- What would happen if the moon suddenly disappeared?
- Will Michael Jackson, Michael Jordan, or Michael Landon be best remembered one-hundred years from now?
- What outdoor activities did Christa McAuliffe enjoy?
- Who do you think was the model for the Mona Lisa?
- Is Chuck Berry overrated?
- How many American Indian languages are still being spoken?
- What's the story behind the Miranda rule?
- Who has had the most effect on the musical life of Puerto Rico: Pablo Casals, Rafael Hernandez, the Figueroa family, or someone not included on this list?
- Should United States history books include a chapter about the Buffalo Soldiers?
- Did Fray Junipero Serra make any enduring contributions to American history?
- What's the story behind the Mayo Clinic?
- If Sacagawea were alive today, where would she travel?
- Why did the Edsel fail?
- Would Dolley Madison have enjoyed today's country music?
- Who's affected our society more, Malcolm X or Kenneth Clark?
- How do pilots figure out how to get from Houston to Minneapolis?
- What high school activities did James Dean participate in?
- What do you think happened to Judge Crater?

Writing Suggestions for the Long-Range Assignments

- **WRITE** from a fund of knowledge; fill your head with information about your topic by researching it in books, encyclopedias, journals, magazines, and newspapers; interview people who are informed about your topic; use at least three sources of information (don't be hesitant to ask library personnel for help); try to discover surprising or unusual facts about your subject; thorough knowledge will enable you to write confidently as well as to go beyond the trite and superficial.

- **CONCENTRATE** on answering the question you have selected, but be sure to provide sufficient background information about your subject so your readers can understand what you are writing about.

- **ORGANIZE** your notes and frequently read them.

- **JOT DOWN** the points you want to cover in your paper; state your central idea (thesis) and main ideas simply and clearly.

- **WRITE** your first draft rapidly; focus exclusively on content and ignore how you write (spelling, punctuation, and other such matters can be checked later).

- **READ** what you have written several times, then start revising; introduce your central idea (thesis) in the first paragraph; build each paragraph by placing the main sentence (topic sentence) in the beginning, then have the other sentences relate directly to it.

- **CHALLENGE** yourself to support your central point and main ideas with examples, illustrations, reasons, facts, and details; replace vague statements with specific ones; use *concrete* words—words referring to sight, sound, smell, taste, and feel; use *specific* words—words referring to particulars like name, age, make, weight, and type; work hard to provide clear explanations and sufficient, convincing support; your writing will be respected if you do.

- **BUDGET** your time so you will have ample opportunities to research, reflect, write, discuss, imagine, revise, and proofread; sufficient time will also enable you to produce original, engaging writing.
- **SHARE** your writing with someone to get her or his suggestions.
- **REVISE** until you can say, "This paper provides pleasure as well as information."
- **LIMIT** your final draft to four or five pages, typewritten and double-spaced.
- **LIST** your sources of information on a separate sheet and attach it to the end of your paper.
- **PROVIDE** a title arousing curiosity.
- **PROOFREAD**—check **PROOFREADING TIPS** which follow on the next page.

Proofreading Tips

- **Type your final draft.** This makes sentence errors easier to spot.
- **Place a ruler or pen under each line as you proofread.** This slows you down, enabling you to concentrate on each word.
- **Read your paper several times, including once when you read the last sentence first, then the next-to-last sentence, and so forth.** It is difficult to detect every error in one or two readings; reading backwards promotes attention to words, not context.
- **Look for mistakes you have made most frequently in the past.** This will likely eliminate most of your errors.
- **Check the spelling and capitalization of words you were unsure of.** These are among the easiest errors to make.
- **Make sure modifying words, phrases, and clauses are placed correctly.** This contributes to clarity and fluency.
- **Concentrate solely on clarity during one or two readings, eliminating wordiness, clichés, redundancies, pompous, vague, and omitted words.** Clarity is your major responsibility as a writer.
- **Set your paper aside for a while.** Fresh eyes are necessary to spot the least obvious errors.
- **Be patient and diligent.** Effective proofreading requires time and thoroughness; remember, you, not anyone else, are responsible for proofreading what you write.

Answer Key

CHAPTER ONE: Subjects and Verbs, pages 1–16

Exercise 1, page 7
(Answers will vary;
following are
typical responses.)

1. Jim
2. Hannah
3. we
4. alarm clock
5. contribution
6. Meredith
7. Tyrone, Rona
8. motorcycles
9. Mark, Sandy
10. cat

Exercise 2, page 7

1. Cagney
2. Lee
3. house
4. Windsor, Frank
5. You
6. magazines
7. Rhode Island
8. radio
9. We
10. temperature

Exercise 3, page 8

	subject	*prep. phrase*
1.	Buckets	of water
		to the horses
2.	dent	For two hundred dollars
		in your car door
3.	Karl	During the spring break
		to Florida
4.	number	of articles
		in the magazine
		with diet and exercise
5.	clock	on the wall
6.	cat	In the corner
		of the couch
7.	choir	from our college
8.	flowers	in the rock garden
9.	All	of the members
10.	road	before us

Exercise 4, page 8

(Answers will vary; following are typical responses.)

1.	read	6.	stacked
2.	was	7.	whined, cried, begged, did
3.	picked, packed	8.	petted
4.	spoke	9.	went, drove
5.	chased	10.	meets

Exercise 5, page 9

	subject	*verb*	*prep. phrase*
1.	dish	crashed	to the floor
2.	child	tossed, turned	In the darkened bedroom
3.	mail	is	*none*
4.	phone	disturbed	in the kitchen
5.	cat, dog	are	*none*
6.	spring, summer	were	For Jeff
7.	Felix	sang, danced	in the talent show
8.	flash	startled	of the camera
9.	Sam, Joyce	planned, built	Against all odds
10.	coffee	was	*none*

Exercise 6, page 9

1. Roy should have found (H H M)
2. everyone was wearing (H M)
3. Haley has bought (H M)
4. Mildred and Art are searching (H M)
5. Mike has forgotten (H M)

Exercise 7, page 10
(Answers will vary; following are
typical answers.)
1. are
2. has been
3. had, would have
4. Did
5. should

Exercise 8, page 10

	subject	verb
1.	envelopes	are
2.	wallet	is
3.	Joe	did get
4.	you	Did ask
5.	evidence	is
6.	you	do think
7.	coupons	are
8.	you	are leaving
9.	Elliot	was
10.	motorcycle	was

Review Exercise, page 11

Your instructor will check your answers.

C. APPLYING THE FINISHING TOUCH, CHAPTER ONE

Proofreading:
(1) Birth of the Presidency, page 13

	subject	verb
1.	delegates	met
2.	delegates	agreed, was needed
3.	efforts	led
4.	establishment	was
5.	citizens	became alarmed
6.	president	would differ
7.	They	objected
8.	president	controlled
9.	fears, objections	were overcome
10.	answer	lies
11.	George Washington	adhered, respected
12.	fears, objections	disappeared

(2) The White House, page 14

Your instructor will check your work.

CHAPTER TWO: Fragments, pages 17–32

Exercise 1, page 23

(Answers will vary; following are typical responses.)

1. (Fragment—lacks a subject)   *David* joined the army after high school.

2. (a *being* fragment)   Trina *is* courteous to all customers.

3. (Fragment—lacks a verb)   Joyce *was standing* near the stadium entrance.

4. Sentence

5. (Fragment—lacks a verb)   The television set's picture *kept* rolling all evening.

6. (a *being* fragment)   He *is* shy around strangers.

7. (Fragment—lacks a subject)   *Nick* annoyed everyone at dinner by cracking his knuckles.

8. Sentence

9. (Fragment—lacks a subject and a verb)   Bravely jumping into the cold lake, the *children were* soon squealing in delight.

10. Sentence

Exercise 2, page 24

(Answers will vary; following are typical responses.)

1. Sentence
2. After the rain came for two straight days, *the river's banks were in danger of overflowing.*
3. The restaurant that is on the corner of Spring and Elm Streets *specializes in Italian food.*
4. Sentence
5. Blaine, before he repaired his car yesterday, *was riding his bicycle to work.*
6. *Mr. McGraw is* the man who is well-known for building fireplaces.
7. Sentence
8. Because the meeting had already begun, *Catherine apologized for being late.*
9. Sentence
10. Pecan pie, which is my favorite dessert, *is not difficult to make.*

Exercise 3, page 25

(Answers will vary; following are typical responses.)

1. Household expenses in our city have risen dramatically this past year. For example, the cost of electricity and water *has risen over twelve percent.*

2. Sentence

3. Taking time to be kind *is* appreciated by most people.

4. Sentence

5. Clint leaned the broken shovel against the barn door, which was also broken.

6. Melissa and Vickie planned to visit many western states during the summer months, including Wyoming, Montana, Idaho, and Washington.

7. Dr. Williams, a general practitioner for many years, is a member of the school board *and* the city council.

8. Sentence

9. In the evening, but particularly by the lakeshore, *a* gentle breeze often brought a blessed relief from the day's oppressive heat.

10. Farming appeals to me, *e*specially after being a trucker for many years.

Review Exercise, page 27

Your instructor will check your answers.

C. APPLYING THE FINISHING TOUCH, CHAPTER TWO

(1) Proofreading:
George Washington: First President, 1789–1797, page 29

(An * indicates a line containing a correction; some commas are optional, so check with your instructor if you have any questions.)

George Washington was born in 1732 at a Virginia plantation. He apparently received little formal education, but he did learn surveying. At

* the age of sixteen, *Washington* joined a surveying group sent to the Shenandoah Valley by Lord Fairfax. For the next few years, Washington con-

* ducted surveys in the frontier areas, *p*articularly Virginia and what is now West Virginia.

Washington was commissioned a lieutenant colonel in 1754, and he saw action in the French and Indian War. In one battle, he escaped injury,
* although four bullets tore through his coat and two horses were shot from under him.
* In 1759, Washington married Martha Dandridge Curtis, *a* wealthy widow with two children. Until the outbreak of the American Revolution, he managed his lands around Mount Vernon and was involved in Virginia politics.

When the Second Continental Congress met in Philadelphia in May, 1775, Washington was selected as Commander-in-Chief of the Continental Army. After taking command of his poorly trained troops, Washington was
* confronted with a number of severe problems, *e*specially supplies. Eventually, however, Washington fashioned a well-trained army and overcame the other problems as well.
* After the Revolutionary War, which lasted six grueling years, Washington returned to his Mount Vernon estate. However, he soon realized the nation was not functioning well under its Articles of Confederation. Therefore, he joined other national leaders in taking steps leading to the Constitutional Convention in Philadelphia in 1787. After the Constitution was ratified by the states, Washington was elected president.
* Weary of politics and feeling old, Washington retire*d* *at* the end of his second term. He enjoyed less than three years of retirement at Mount
* Vernon, for he died on December 14, 1799.

(2) The Road, page 31
Your instructor will check your work.

CHAPTER THREE: Run-Ons, pages 33—53

Exercise 1, page 37

1. rude/she
2. funny/surprisingly
3. Canyon/it's
4. Oldsmobile/he
5. worms/they
6. like/we
7. college/her
8. you/don't
9. attention/he
10. tailgate/other
11. asked/my
12. shape/running
13. won/the
14. snowfall/it
15. assigned/the
16. back/reluctantly
17. called/the
18. impressive/her
19. hours/the
20. believed/the

Exercise 2, page 38

1. CS
2. C
3. C
4. CS
5. C
6. FS
7. CS
8. C
9. CS
10. C
11. FS
12. C
13. C
14. FS
15. C
16. FS
17. CS
18. C
19. C
20. CS
21. C
22. FS
23. C
24. C
25. CS

Exercise 3, page 39

1. The rain turned to sleet, <u>so</u> Cameron decided to postpone his trip until tomorrow.
2. Vickie is a violinist in the college orchestra, <u>and</u> she is also a member of the swimming team.
3. My parents, who need a new washing machine, rushed to Dotson's Home Store, <u>for</u> the owner was offering a 50% discount on all appliances.
4. Correct
5. Dr. Gray's office was finally empty, <u>but</u> she still had to see patients at the hospital.
6. Jim said that he mowed the lawn last week, <u>so</u> it's Steve's turn to do the mowing this time.
7. Lauren seemed like an old friend after just a couple of hours, <u>but</u> I had met her for the first time this morning.
8. Correct
9. Obviously, the garbage had been in the kitchen for many days, <u>and</u> there was also a sink full of dirty dishes.
10. You can leave with me today, <u>or</u> you can go with Karl on Tuesday.

Exercise 4, page 40

1. Amy is a serious student; she hopes to go to medical school next year.
2. In addition, there were many old cars in the parade; my favorite was a 1948 Plymouth convertible.
3. Bookshelves crammed with books stood against each wall; numerous magazines were scattered on top of the large coffee table.
4. You have to turn right on Route 16 to reach Linwood; didn't you know that?
5. Ross seldom uses his snowmobile anymore; apparently, he prefers to use his all-terrain vehicle even in the winter time.

Exercise 5, page 41

1. Mike saved his money for over two years; consequently, he was able to buy a dependable used car.
2. I discovered that the necklace was made of imitation pearls; moreover, the setting in the ring was actually glass.
3. My husband doesn't particular care for classical music; nevertheless, he generally attends each concert with me.
4. Lisa went to the shopping mall to buy a pair of jeans; however, she ended up buying a sweater.
5. Rain fell steadily for two days; as a result, the river was near the flood stage.

Exercise 6, page 42

1. My brother and I decided to apply for a job at Murphy's Stable after we had talked to two of our friends who work there.
2. Before Kim and I attended the wedding reception at the country club, we went to the House of Lights to pick up the lamp we had bought the happy couple.
3. While Eric attended his 8:30 class, Sabrina studied in the library.
4. Mr. Chasson said I should continue to sand the table top with very fine sandpaper even though it felt as smooth as glass to me.
5. Eric attended his 8:30 class while Sabrina studied in the library.
6. Even though Mr. Chasson said I should continue to sand the table top with very fine sandpaper, it felt as smooth as glass to me.
7. When the fire whistle blew in the small community, volunteer fire fighters got to the fire station as quickly as they could.
8. Barry has acquired two rare Canadian stamps since he attended last month's stamp meeting at the community center.
9. Because Don is easy to get along with, I like him as a roommate.
10. Until Stephanie sprained her ankle last week, she was jogging two miles a day.

11. Stephanie was jogging two miles a day <u>until</u> she sprained her ankle last week.
12. I took the bus to work <u>because</u> my car wouldn't start.

Exercise 7, page 43

1. In the morning, Erica leaves for New Mexico. She has always wanted to visit Santa Fe and Taos.
2. Didn't you know that Jefferson's Landscaping was hiring summer help? I thought everyone home from college was aware of that fact.
3. Mrs. Elliott opened the shutters. The brilliant morning sun streamed into the room.
4. Mr. Burnell, one of my neighbors, is ninety-years-old. He's in remarkably good health.
5. Water from the melting snow gushed down the mountainside. There was no immediate danger of flooding in the area, however.
6. Megan, what college does your fiancé attend? The newspaper would like to include that information in your engagement announcement.
7. The bus schedule has been changed. For the most part, I still find it convenient to ride the bus to work.
8. How many states have you been in? I counted up the other day, and I've been in thirty-eight states.
9. Doug is extremely considerate to his grandparents. He takes them to their doctor and dentist appointments, does chores around their house, and does most of their grocery shopping.
10. Hot dogs, baked beans, and brown bread are a traditional Saturday night meal in New England. Did you know that?

Exercise 8, page 45

1. I split the cord of wood, <u>and</u> Josh stacked it against one of the basement's walls.   (<u>but</u> could also be used)
2. It was a hot, humid day; Scott couldn't wait to go swimming.
3. Dad stopped by Miller's drugstore to buy a copy of the <u>New York Times</u>. He does this every Sunday morning after church.
4. <u>After</u> we played hockey for a couple of hours, we went to Karl's Pub for pizzas.
5. Rita's ankle was badly swollen; <u>however,</u> x-rays indicated that it was not broken.
6. When was the last time you had a dental check-up? You have a number of cavities.
7. <u>Because</u> Stella had her receipt for the merchandise, the courteous young clerk promptly refunded her money.
8. David has a bad case of the flu; the doctor prescribed antibiotics, fluids, and bedrest.

9. Margaret grew up on a large vegetable farm in New Jersey; <u>consequent-ly,</u> she's knowledgeable about gardening.   (<u>therefore</u> or <u>thus</u> could also be used)

10. The Hawks were the favorites to win the regional tournament, <u>but</u> the Bears upset them in the very first game.

Review Exercise, page 47

Your instructor will check your answers.

C. APPLYING THE FINISHING TOUCH, CHAPTER THREE

(1) Proofreading:
John Adams: Second President, 1797–1801, page 51

(An * indicates a line where a correction of a run-on is made. Typical corrections are presented, but others are possible; check with your instructor if you have any questions.)

John Adams was born in the Massachusetts Bay Colony in 1735. Adams was among the earliest members of the Continental Congress in favor

* of the colonies declaring their independence from Great Britain. <u>D</u>uring the Revolutionary War and for a number of years afterwards, Adams served his young nation as a diplomat in Europe.

After serving as Washington's vice-president, Adams was elected the

* second president of the United States. <u>H</u>e and his wife Abigail were the first couple to live in the White House. During his presidency, France and

* England were at war, <u>and</u> these countries interfered with American shipping.

* Many Americans urged President Adams to declare war, <u>but</u> he was

* determined to keep his young nation out of such a conflict; <u>however,</u> hostili-ties did break out between the United States and France at sea.

Although Adams kept the nation out of war, he was unable to keep his party united behind him, and Thomas Jefferson defeated him in the 1800 presidential election. Adams retired to his home in Quincy, Massachusetts, where he lived to be ninety-years-old. On July 4, 1826, the fiftieth

* ing the legislative, executive, and judicial branches, <u>was</u> established under
the Constitution of 1787, Jefferson became President Washington's
Secretary of State. Then after serving as John Adams's vice-president,
Jefferson was elected president in 1801.

As president, Jefferson kept the nation out of war, ended the raiding of
American ships in the Mediterranean Sea, and negotiated the purchase of
the Louisiana Territory from France, an acquisition that more than doubled
* the size of the United States. Each of these impressive achievements <u>was</u>
accomplished despite many difficulties and much criticism.

After his two terms as president, Jefferson retired to his beloved
Monticello, his handsome home overlooking Charlottesville, Virginia. There
* he <u>was</u> able to pursue his numerous interests for many years. Everybody
* who <u>learns</u> of the following fact seldom <u>forgets</u> it: Presidents Thomas
Jefferson and John Adams both died on July 4, 1826, the fiftieth
anniversary of the Declaration of Independence.

(2) The Model T Ford, page 69

Your instructor will check your work.

CHAPTER FIVE: Misplaced and Dangling Modifiers, pages 71—87

Exercise 1, page 75

1. C	5. M	9. M	13. M	17. C
2. M	6. C	10. C	14. C	18. M
3. M	7. C	11. C	15. M	19. C
4. C	8. M	12. C	16. M	20. M

Exercise 2, page 75

1. The young (man) in the maroon sweater plays the saxophone in the college band.
2. A funny looking (man) with two large packages struggled into the taxi.

   or

   With two large packages, a funny looking (man) struggled into the taxi

3. Working in the flower garden, (Mom) was stung by a bee.

   or

   (Mom,) working in the flower garden, was stung by a bee.

4. In jogging clothes, the (girl) watched the squirrel escape from the scolding birds.

   or

   The (girl) in jogging clothes watched the squirrel escape from the scolding birds.

5. Amy reheated the (casserole) that had become cold in the warm oven.

6. A (woman) driving a yellow convertible turned around in our way.

   or

   Driving a yellow convertible, a (woman) turned around in our way.

7. On the way to work, (Whitney) saw a bad accident.

   or

   (Whitney,) on the way to work, saw a bad accident.

8. Susan rented an (apartment) with a tiny kitchen during the school year.

   or

   An (apartment) with a tiny kitchen was rented by Susan during the school year.

9. Rick remembered with regret that he had forgotten to send his grandparents an anniversary card.

10. Because he knew most of the answers, Bob won nearly (five hundred dollars.)

Exercise 3, page 77

1. D	5. C	9. C	13. D	17. D
2. C	6. C	10. D	14. D	18. C
3. C	7. D	11. C	15. C	19. D
4. D	8. D	12. C	16. C	20. D

Exercise 4, page 78

(Answers will vary; typical answers are presented.)

1. After receiving the gift, (Bruno) jumped in the air.
2. (Chelsea,) while shopping at the mall, ran into her old boyfriend.
3. Since living in San Diego, (Kwan) has become a top-notch tennis player.
4. (Cory,) on hearing the news, offered to help.
5. Waiting for the mail to arrive, (Hilda) grew more and more impatient.
6. Stepping carefully, (I) climbed to the top of the ladder.
7. Answering the phone, (Dale) accidentally knocked over the vase of flowers.
8. The (scouts,) by beginning immediately, will be able to portage the rapids by sunset.

Exercise 5, page 79

1. Andy bought a (desk) with three drawers for his room.
2. Dozing on the couch, (Meredith) skimmed through a pile of magazines.
3. Frowning at Heidi, the (clerk) with the long beard in the jewelry department asked for her receipt.
4. The small boy wanted almost every (toy) in the store.
5. Baxter drove his 1957 (Chevrolet,) which was spotless, down the busy highway towards San Diego.

Exercise 6, page 80

(Answers will vary; typical answers are presented.)
1. Before going to bed, (you) should put the cat outdoors.
2. As (I) listened to the constant roar of the highway traffic, the motel room provided little rest.
3. Even though (we) wondered what would happen next in the comedy, the eventual outcome was always predictable.
4. Just before (Judy) finished the last wall, the paint ran out.
5. Because (Paul) had never run that great a distance before, his legs became stiff and sore.

Review Exercise, page 81

Your instructor will check your answers.

C. APPLYING THE FINISHING TOUCH, CHAPTER FIVE

(1) Proofreading:
Johns Hopkins Medical School, page 83

(An * indicates a line where a misplaced or dangling modifier has been corrected. Typical corrections are presented, but others are possible; check with your instructor if you have any questions.)

*   The citizens of Baltimore are understandably proud of Johns Hopkins University, one of the most esteemed universities in the world. Its various schools and departments are generally ranked among the best in the nation, but it is its medical school that often receives the highest acclaim.

The medical school, founded in 1893, became the first one associated with a university to admit men and women based solely upon objective qualifications. The Baltimore Women's Committee of that day was responsible for this distinction. After raising the funds to establish the medical school, the

* committee proposed two conditions. First, the committee insisted that men and women be admitted to the medical school "on the same terms."

* Dismayed, the president of Johns Hopkins objected to this condition. He believed women simply were not endowed with the same capacities for medical study as men; therefore, he maintained, lower standards would have to be applied if women were to be admitted. However, the women on the committee would not accept the president's contentions on this matter.

* Finally, the president reluctantly agreed to the "on the same terms" policy.

In addition, the Baltimore Women's committee insisted that only applicants with appropriate preparation in sciences and foreign languages be admitted to the medical school. Convinced few applicants would be capable

* of meeting these entrance requirements, the Johns Hopkins faculty voiced its

* opposition to this second condition. Standing firm once again, however, the

* determined Baltimore Women's Committee pushed through the requirements, the most stringent of any medical school at that time.

As a result of the enlightened policies insisted upon by the Baltimore Women's Committee, Johns Hopkins Medical School soon attracted some of the nation's most capable students, leading to the school's early credibility. As time passed, the school's credibility continued to increase for a variety of reasons. Now, as has been the case for many years, Johns Hopkins Medical School is considered one of the finest institutions of its kind in the world.

(2) James Madison: Fourth President, 1809–1817, page 85
Your instructor will check your work.

CHAPTER SIX: Parallel Structure, pages 89—102

Exercise 1, page 91

1. B	4. B	7. B	10. B
2. A	5. A	8. B	
3. A	6. B	9. A	

Exercise 2, page 92

1. A, <u>taking</u> . . . <u>working</u>
2. B, <u>to mow</u> . . . <u>to weed</u>
3. B, <u>who has</u> . . . <u>who wants</u>
4. A and B, <u>library</u> . . . <u>student union</u> . . . <u>fieldhouse</u>
5. B, <u>whether he was</u> . . . <u>whether he had</u>
6. A, <u>burned</u> . . . <u>needed</u>
7. B, <u>to wait</u> . . . <u>to help</u>
8. A, <u>to enjoy</u> . . . <u>to visit</u>
9. B, <u>reading</u> . . . <u>watching</u>
10. A, <u>to become</u> . . . <u>to live</u>
11. A, <u>mowing</u> . . . <u>weeding</u>
12. A and B, <u>shooting</u> . . . <u>playing to shoot</u> . . . <u>to play</u>

Exercise 3, page 93

1. yes	4. yes	7. no	10. yes
2. no	5. no	8. yes	11. yes
3. no	6. yes	9. no	12. no

Exercise 4, page 94

1. dependable	6. law enforcement
2. beautiful	7. intelligent
3. floating	8. gas mileage
4. illogical	9. began to darken
5. locks the doors	10. contests are conducted

Exercise 5, page 95

(Answers will vary; following are typical responses.)

1. peeling
2. we would receive a failing grade
3. an excellent athlete
4. wallpapering the hall
5. to play cards

6. slowly
7. practicing his music lesson
8. interesting
9. to sleep more soundly
10. incompetent

Review Exercise, page 96

Your instructor will check your answers.

C. APPLYING THE FINISHING TOUCH, CHAPTER SIX

(1) Proofreading:
Mary Baker Eddy, page 99

*(An * indicates a line where non-parallelism has been corrected. Typical corrections are presented, but others are possible; check with your instructor if you have any questions.)*

Mary Baker Eddy, founder of the Christian Science Church, was born in Concord, New Hampshire, in 1821. For the first forty years of her life,

* Eddy was often frail, sickly, and <u>emotional.</u> In 1862, she regained her health after a doctor convinced her that illness was often caused by the mind. After linking this and other beliefs, Eddy began publishing *Science and Health,* a

* handbook that was widely criticized as well as <u>widely praised.</u>

* Eddy was an inspiring teacher and an <u>effective organizer.</u> She

* maintained not only illness <u>but also death was unreal.</u> To further spread her

* teachings, Eddy established the Christian Science Association and <u>chartered</u>

* <u>the Church of Christ Scientist.</u> Her disciples were loyal, committed, and

* <u>devoted.</u>

* Though often criticized and <u>ridiculed,</u> Eddy was admired more <u>than she</u>

* <u>was attacked.</u> By the time of her death in 1910, Mary Baker Eddy and the church she had founded were well-known throughout America. She left most of her $2.5 million estate to her church, which numbered nearly 100,000 members.

(2) James Monroe: Fifth President, 1817–1825, page 100

Your instructor will check your work.

CHAPTER SEVEN: Verb Tense, Voice, and Person, pages 103–125

Exercise 1, page 111

Present Tense:

Millard Fillmore, who <u>becomes</u> president after the death of Zachary Taylor, <u>is</u> the second vice president to assume the highest office in the nation after the death of his predecessor; John Tyler <u>is</u> the first vice president to do so. Fillmore <u>assumes</u> the office on July 10, 1850. Fillmore <u>is</u> from the state of New York, and he <u>is</u> fifty-years-old at the time of his inauguration; his father <u>is</u> alive at this time. Fillmore <u>has</u> once <u>been</u> a lawyer, and he <u>has served</u> in the House of Representatives. He <u>is married</u> and the father of two daughters.

Past Tense:

Millard Fillmore, who <u>became</u> president after the death of Zachary Taylor, <u>was</u> the second vice president to assume the highest office in the nation after the death of his predecessor; John Tyler <u>was</u> the first vice president to do so. Fillmore <u>assumed</u> the office on July 10, 1850. Fillmore <u>was</u> from the state of New York, and he <u>was</u> fifty-years-old at the time of his inauguration; his father <u>was</u> alive at this time. Fillmore <u>had</u> once <u>been</u> a lawyer, and he <u>had served</u> in the House of Representatives. He <u>was married</u> and the father of two daughters.

Exercise 2, page 112

1. driven
2. began
3. drunk, eaten
4. blown, win
5. forgave, forgiven
6. taken
7. written, came
8. said, freeze
9. tore
10. shaken
11. stole, stolen
12. sprang
13. lain
14. told, taught
15. swear
16. saw
17. did
18. knew, left
19. swung
20. brought, sang

Exercise 3, page 113

Have your instructor check your sentences.

Exercise 4, page 114

1. Steve and Shawn cleaned the garage and basement.
2. The judge expressed appreciation to the jury.
3. The nervous waitress spilled coffee all over the counter.
4. A roaring lawnmower suddenly interrupted the peace and quiet.
5. A young man in a blue uniform filled the vending machines in the lobby.
6. Mr. Richards did all of the electrical work.
7. Miss Marple, Agatha Christie's most beloved detective, finally solved the puzzling murder case.
8. Frank took and developed the impressive photographs hanging in the hallway.
9. My parents made the final remodeling decisions.
10. When Ann and Gene announced their engagement, everyone expressed approval.

Exercise 5, page 116

Thank you, Lesley

Although I grew up in a state where skiing is popular, I never learned to ski as a youngster because I was convinced this sport required more skill and daring than I possessed. However, during my first year in college, my friend Lesley kept urging me to go skiing with her. I made one lame excuse after another about why I couldn't go before I finally admitted to her that I didn't know how to ski. Lesley said "no problem" as she would be glad to teach me, and I knew by the way she said it I couldn't make any more excuses.

But when the day arrived when I had agreed to go skiing with her, I actually drove over to Lesley's dormitory to tell her I had changed my mind. However, she was already waiting for me, standing in the dorm's parking lot with a big smile and ski equipment sprawled all around her. I couldn't chicken out now, so with fear and trembling, I was soon on my way to the slopes.

I never felt so awkward or as embarrassed in my life as the first few times I tried to stand wearing skis; I quickly concluded there was no way I would ever be able to maintain my balance, health, or dignity on skis.

However, within an hour, Lesley not only had me standing but also had me snowplowing down a short beginners' slope. As the day progressed, my skill and confidence slowly grew, and I could tell I was becoming hooked on skiing.

Lesley deserves the credit for my early progress on skis as she was a patient, understanding, and encouraging teacher. She didn't laugh at my fears or falls, and her comments were always helpful and reassuring. By the end of day, I was confidently skiing down the longest beginners' slope, and I was already looking forward to going skiing again.

Since that fateful day three winters ago, I have gone skiing many times. Although I have never become as accomplished a skier as Lesley or some of my other friends, I am able to ski most trails, a feat I would never have dreamed possible when I think back to my first day on skis. I will always be grateful to Lesley, for skiing has increased my self-confidence and brought me more pleasure than I could ever have imagined.

Review Exercise, page 118

Your instructor will check your answers.

C. APPLYING THE FINISHING TOUCH, CHAPTER SEVEN

(1) Proofreading:
Handling Criticism, page 121

(An * indicates a line containing a correction; check with your instructor if you have any questions.)

* Some people brush off criticism. However, I take criticism personally. I used to respond to faultfinding with either anger or sulkiness. Recently,
* however, I concluded that criticism is something I will encounter throughout
* life, so I should learn to deal with it as constructively as possible.

One way I have learned to cope with criticism is really to listen to what
* my critic is saying. Rather than interrupting with "You don't know what you're talking about" as I previously did, I now acknowledge the person's
* criticism with "I understand what you're saying." This response, I learned, leads to a positive exchange of viewpoints rather than to an escalation of bit-

*   ter remarks. In addition, I often discover the person's criticism is justified or
at least understandable, so the necessary steps leading to personal improvement or better communications can be taken.

*   Furthermore, I now recognize the fine line between criticism and praise.
For example, when someone recently criticized me for making hasty
decisions, I remembered the day before another person had complimented
me for my decisiveness. Thus, my ability to accept criticism more objectively
has improved since recognizing people sometimes reach vastly different con-

*   clusions about my behavior.

*   Finally, I handle criticism more effectively today because of a more sen-

*   sible reaction to it. By focusing on the possible merits of the criticism rather

*   than on the potential damage to my self-esteem, I put myself in a "no-lose"
position: either the criticism prompts me to improve in some way, or it
provides me with reassurance my conduct in this particular matter is appropriate despite the criticism.

*   Dealing with criticism is not easy for me, but the preceding approaches
have certainly helped.

(2) John Quincy Adams: Sixth President, 1825–1829, page 123
Your instructor will check your work.

CHAPTER EIGHT: Punctuation—1, pages 127–147

Exercise 1, page 137

1. Are you sure the store is open?
2. My goodness! Have you ever seen such a messy room? C
3. My folks just love to watch old movies on their videocassette recorder.
4. When did Lt. Means get transferred to Ford Ord? C
5. Look out! There's a child in the road! *or* Look out! There's a child in the
   road.
6. Kurt asked how much the job paid.
7. I understand that Larry Dennius, M. D., will be the luncheon speaker.
8. Gracious, you look terrible. *or* Gracious! You look terrible!
9. We asked the instructor when the test would be.
10. Charles, turn off your radio and get that paper written immediately! *or*
    Charles, turn off your radio and get that paper written immediately.

Exercise 2, page 137

1. The first four presidents of the United States were George Washington, John Adams, Thomas Jefferson, and James Madison.
2. No commas needed.
3. The doctor quickly reassured the parents, for he could see how worried they were.
4. David fell asleep watching television, but Roger and Keith played ping-pong until after midnight.
5. No commas needed.
6. Shelly will pick us up at the airport, or she will have a taxi waiting for us.
7. The Ortons raise corn, soybeans, and pigs on their Iowa farm.
8. No commas needed.
9. I didn't give the begging man any money, yet I felt sorry for him.
10. Marilyn was impressed by his sensitive, insightful reply.
11. The snow continued most of the night; nevertheless, the main streets had been plowed before I left for work.
12. I went to the drugstore intending to buy only a newspaper, but I ended up buying toothpaste, shampoo, vitamins, batteries, a magazine, and a newspaper.
13. They labored all day in the suffocating, sticky heat.
14. Jordan was a math major his first two years in college, but he switched his major to economics when he was a junior.
15. Lyman and his pals drove all night; thus, they got to Florida before we did.

Exercise 3, page 138

1. Bates College, which is located in Maine, is where my mother went to school.
2. Yes, I would like to have dessert.
3. Although he had promised to come, Ryan missed the meeting.
4. No commas needed.
5. No commas needed.
6. The Cranston bus, which is parked behind the Student Union, is the one that goes to the shopping mall.
7. However, I would be glad to drive you there.
8. Until Vanessa called me, I was uncertain about the outcome of the election.
9. Sidney, believe it or not, was elected our representative.
10. No commas needed.
11. *Charlotte's Web,* written by E. B. White, is a popular children's book.
12. Karen, a chemistry major, works part-time at a medical laboratory.
13. Slipping and sliding, the giggling couple clung to each other as they gingerly made their way across the icy parking lot.
14. My neighbor, the one who lives to the left of me, is a retired police officer.
15. Slowly and quietly, Tex made his way toward the refrigerator.

Exercise 4, page 139

1. No commas needed.
2. The company's headquarters is in Los Angeles, California.
3. My folks were married on October 12, 1966, in Cheyenne, Wyoming.
4. The population of Zanesville, Ohio, is 28,655.
5. Professor Goodman said, "The final test for this course is next Friday."
6. Blaine, how about going bowling with me?
7. "The choir practices," Mrs. Folsom informed us, "on Tuesdays and Thursdays."
8. Dear Butch,

    Our class will hold its tenth reunion at the Sheraton Hotel in Minneapolis, Minnesota, on June 18, 1993. Rodney said, "I want to see Butch's face at that place!" We've already raised $16,432 (just kidding), so we should have quite a bash. Send your reservation, Butch, to Nora Wilson.

    Yours truly,

    Cappy Patterson

Exercise 5, page 139

1. The business consultant's message can be summarized by these words: provide better service to your customers than your competitors.
2. The heavy snowfall made travel difficult; consequently, we arrived late for the basketball game.
3. Jennifer sang a solo at the concert; I didn't realize she had such a lovely voice.
4. In addition to a tent and sleeping bag, be sure to include these items when you go camping: a compass, matches, and first aid kit.
5. I think Jay looks attractive in glasses; what's your opinion?
6. My closest friends are majoring in the following subjects: Felicia, biology; Allan, elementary education; Scott, philosophy; Terri, psychology.
7. Wayne doesn't know Professor Stillman well; he's had only one course from her.
8. Thelma couldn't remember where she had left her pocketbook; however, she eventually found it on the hall table.
9. I am reading a fascinating book called *A Night to Remember: the Sinking of the Titanic.*
10. Insight into the character of Winston Churchill is provided by the remarks he made, including these: "One ought never to turn one's back on a threatened danger and try to run away from it. If you do that, you will double the danger. But if you meet it promptly and without flinching, you will reduce the danger by half. Never run away from anything. Never!"

Exercise 3, page 156

1. cheerleaders'
2. car's
3. gentlemen's
4. Ross's
5. workers'
6. Marlene's
7. Pamela's and Dino's
8. somebody's
9. friends'
10. Paul's
11. dogs'
12. coach's
13. children's
14. Tyrone and Juanita's
15. horses'
16. Roger Maris's
17. storm's
18. photographers
19. anyone's
20. cities'

Exercise 4, page 156

1. reporters'
2. Evelyn's
3. Don and Anita's
4. men's
5. students'
6. government's
7. parents'
8. sun's
9. Lois's
10. show's

Exercise 5, page 157

(Answers will vary; typical answers are presented.)
1. The clock's battery needs replacing.
2. The police officer listened politely to the woman's explanation.
3. Travis decided to overhaul the motorcycle's engine.
4. Three of the stores' special sales were attracting numerous customers.
5. I would appreciate having someone's opinion about this matter.
6. The ambassador expressed appreciation for the United States's assistance.
7. The players' strike disgusted many fans.
8. Is this anybody's raincoat?
9. My boss's husband is a meteorologist.
10. The students asked for the professors' support.

Exercise 6, page 158

1. '89
2. c's, r's
3. playin'
4. '86
5. a's, e's
6. '61, '65
7. 7's, 2's
8. shinin'
9. '79
10. 3's

Exercise 7, page 158

1. papers, magazines
2. eyes
3. yours
4. correct
5. Our, exams
6. her
7. correct
8. groceries
9. correct
10. books, supplies

Exercise 8, page 159

1. My wife says that it is un-American not to like baseball.
2. I was surprised—no, shocked—to hear that Rosemary and Stuart had eloped.
3. We finished the season undefeated. (By the way, it is rumored that our coach has resigned.)
4. When asked about his future plans, Coach Barker replied, "I'm really not at liberty to—"
5. We lived in California (1984–1990) before moving to Nevada.
6. Stan said that he would arrive by mid-afternoon.
7. Shirley is an excellent student, athlete, and musician—she's a gifted person.
8. Professor Grey, a well-known economist, predicts a drop in the unemployment rate during the next eighteen months.
9. My husband will be thirty-three years old next Monday.
10. Marsha said that I should (1) apologize, (2) buy him a new record, and (3) take him to dinner.

Review Exercise, page 160

Your instructor will check your answers.

C. APPLYING THE FINISHING TOUCH, CHAPTER NINE

(1) Proofreading:
William Henry Harrison: Ninth President, 1841, page 163

(An * indicates where punctuation has been added or corrected; check with your instructor if you have any questions.)

William Henry Harrison *(1773–1841) was born of *well-to-do parents in Berkeley, Virginia. *Harrison's father was one of the signers of the Declaration of Independence, and his mother came from one of *Virginia's most distinguished families.

After attending college in his home state, Harrison went to Philadelphia in 1790 to study medicine; however, after his *father's death in the following year, Harrison quit his medical studies to accept a commission in the army.

Harrison was assigned by the army to the *Ohio-Indiana area, which was then called the Northwest Territory. *Harrison's commander was the *well-known General Anthony "Mad" Wayne. Harrison fought in the Indian campaigns that ended in success*—at least in the white *man's point of view*—in 1794.

The year 1798 was a momentous one for Harrison because he *(1) resigned from the army, *(2) married Judge Symmes's daughter, and *(3) received a federal land grant to homestead in Ohio. Probably due to *his *father-in-law's influence, Harrison was appointed the following year to be the Northwest *Territory's first delegate to Congress.

In the early *1800's, Harrison served as Governor of the Indiana Territory. *Harrison's responsibilities*—this shouldn't surprise you*—were to defend the settlements against the *Indians and to obtain even more title to Indian lands. Under the leadership of Tecumseh, the Indians formed a confederation to halt the *whites' advancement. In 1811, Harrison led a surprise attack on an Indian village at Tippecanoe. *(Incidentally, this is the source of *Harrison's nickname "Tippecanoe.") *Harrison's troops suffered heavy casualties, and the outcome was indecisive; nevertheless, the battle was celebrated as a great victory for *Harrison's troops.

After serving in the War of 1812, Harrison entered politics. In 1840, he became the *Whigs' candidate for president. In the election, Harrison defeated Van Buren, who *wasn't successful in *his bid for a second term.

William Henry Harrison was sworn in as president on March 4, 1841. A month later, however, he died of pneumonia, becoming the first president to die in office.

(2) One of Summers Special Delights, page 165
Your instructor will check your work.

CHAPTER TEN: Capital Letters, pages 167–183

Exercise 1, page 173

1. Has, Atlanta, Georgia
2. My, wife, Honda
3. vacation, Friday, Easter
4. My, husband, I, Saturday
5. religion, American
6. Correct
7. Can, Tuesday
8. Captain
9. east, west
10. Correct
11. national parks, Department, Interior
12. Reverend, Methodist
13. cousin, air force, Italy
14. history, Holocaust
15. states, fall
16. never
17. Correct
18. roommate, economics, *Wall Street Journal*
19. post office, grocery store, cleaners
20. high school, telephone operator

Exercise 2, page 175

1. When, birthday
2. Henry, Louisiana
3. Correct
4. come
5. University
6. High School
7. Correct
8. Web, Feeling
9. south
10. Southeast Paint Company
11. college, Labor Day
12. Lutheran minister
13. captain
14. Bank
15. August
16. but, Dog
17. Correct
18. Correct
19. potato chips, bananas
20. Correct
21. Use, microscope, Professor
22. junior high
23. week, Thursday
24. Down, From
25. Correct
26. Department, Defense
27. tournament, Friday
28. surveying
29. Correct
30. Martha, grandmother

Review Exercise, page 177

Your instructor will check your answers.

C. APPLYING THE FINISHING TOUCH

(1) Proofreading:
John Tyler: Tenth President, 1841–1845, page 179

(Capitalization corrections have been underlined.)

John Tyler was born in Greenway, Virginia, on March 29, 1790. His mother was of English descent; his father was a successful lawyer. After graduating from William and Mary College, Tyler also became a lawyer.

During the War of 1812, Tyler was a militia officer in the Williamsburg-Richmond area. In 1813, he married Letitia Christian, and they became the parents of eight children during their twenty-nine years of marriage.

After the war, Tyler embarked on a successful political career. He was elected to the United States House of Representatives and then to the United States Senate. In addition, Tyler served a term as governor of Virginia, as his father had before him. In 1840, the Whigs selected Tyler to be William Henry Harrison's running mate.

When President Harrison died a month after his inauguration, Tyler became the first vice-president to assume the presidency upon the death of his predecessor. Tyler's political foes, the Democrats, soon referred to him as "His Accidency."

Tyler's political philosophy, particularly his narrow interpretation of the Constitution of the United States and his pro-slavery views, made him extremely unpopular not only with the Democrats but also with the Whigs. The serious illness and eventual death of his wife in 1842 at the White House added to Tyler's problems. In 1844, President Tyler, fifty-four, shocked the nation when he married Julie Gardiner, twenty-four. This marriage produced seven children, so from both of his marriages Tyler was the father of fifteen children.

Because of his extreme unpopularity, Tyler did not run for president in 1844. Years later, at the commencement of the Civil War, Tyler was elected to the Confederate House of Representatives; however, he died on January 18, 1862, at the age of seventy-one before he assumed his duties.

(2) Bad Weather Driving Tips, page 181

Your instructor will check your work.

CHAPTER ELEVEN: Clarity—1, pages 185–195

Exercise 1, page 189

1. ~~The~~ happy players circled ~~around~~ their coach.   (*The* is optional)
2. After ~~the~~ supplies arrived, our troops were able to advance ~~forward~~. (*the* is optional)
3. The stage was round ~~in shape~~.
4. In my hometown ~~where I live~~, there are two popular pizza parlors.
5. Margaret will continue ~~on with~~ her studies.
6. Can you return the book ~~back to me~~ by next week?
7. A ~~huge~~ giant rescued the children.
8. Last night, two ~~armed~~ gunmen robbed the convenience store on McKinley Street.
9. Matt Henderson is attending college in ~~the state of~~ Nebraska.
10. Do you think cars will change much in the ~~coming~~ future?
11. The doctor is attending to ~~an acute~~ crisis in the emergency room.
12. I was twelve ~~in age~~ when we moved to Wyoming.
13. The kitten sank ~~down~~ into the sofa.
14. My grandparents are seldom ~~ever~~ home.
15. All ~~of the~~ morning classes will be switched to ~~the~~ afternoon. (*the* is optional)

Exercise 2, page 189

1. Darrell was ~~very~~ upset not to get the job.
2. We decided to store ~~up~~ wood for the winter.
3. Sondra earned excellent grades in ~~both~~ biology and calculus.
4. Tom almost fell off ~~of~~ the ladder when he heard the ~~very~~ exciting news.
5. The police officer said ~~that~~ my driving was ~~quite~~ satisfactory.
6. Is anyone interested in drinking ~~up~~ the orange juice?
7. Martha was ~~really~~ delighted to hear about your engagement.
8. Although his music fell off ~~of~~ the stand and children were fussing in the audience, the pianist said ~~that~~ he was pleased with his recital.
9. The patient was ~~quite~~ relieved to hear the good news.
10. ~~Both~~ the fans and players were ~~really~~ disappointed when the rain continued ~~on~~.
11. Some rich people ~~with a lot of money~~ are ~~quite~~ generous in giving ~~and donating~~ to charities.
12. ~~In order~~ to reduce the traffic ~~of cars and trucks~~ near campus, ~~I think~~ Central Avenue should be restricted to those walking or ~~to those~~ riding bikes.

13. Blake ~~sort of~~ believes ~~that those~~ people who are angry ~~and mad~~ about the problem should ~~kind of~~ meet this evening to ~~talk over and~~ discuss practical ~~and workable~~ solutions.
14. When Chuck is tired ~~and wornout~~, he ~~really~~ likes to go camping in some isolated ~~and remote~~ place.
15. The fraternities are planning a ~~long~~ marathon carwash over the weekend ~~in order~~ to raise ~~and collect~~ money for ~~the~~ local charities ~~in town~~.

Exercise 3, page 190

1. ~~In my opinion~~, my folks should remodel their kitchen.
2. When I refused to loan Mike my car, he got ~~kind of~~ mad.
3. ~~There are~~ people are waiting to see you.
4. Vincent read the book, ~~which is~~ a mystery, in three hours.
5. Phil needs a course in statistics ~~in order~~ to do his research.
6. ~~I believe~~ my children watch too much television.
7. ~~There is~~ an old car is parked in my neighbor's driveway.
8. Fortunately, Dorothy finds writing ~~to be~~ rewarding as well as frustrating.
9. Teen-agers were ~~sort of~~ wandering throughout the mall.
10. ~~I feel~~ hockey officials should make the penalties for fighting more costly.
11. Sheila's unsure whether ~~or not~~ justice was done.
12. ~~There were~~ a few guests were staying at the old inn.
13. Students ~~who are~~ sitting in the back of the room will have difficulty seeing the slides.
14. Marcie runs five miles every other day ~~in order~~ to stay in shape for basketball.
15. Physical education~~, I believe,~~ should be compulsory.

Review Exercise, page 191

Your instructor will check your answers.

C. APPLYING THE FINISHING TOUCH, CHAPTER ELEVEN

(1) Proofreading:
James K. Polk: Eleventh President, 1845–1849, page 193

(Redundancies and other unnecessary words have been crossed out.)

James K. Polk, the eldest of ten children, was born in ~~the state of~~ North Carolina in 1795. He was raised ~~up~~ there and in Tennessee, where he moved with his family in 1806. Polk returned ~~back~~ to North Carolina in ~~the year of~~ 1815 ~~in order~~ to attend the state university. In the years that followed, Polk became a lawyer, entered politics, and married Sarah Childress.

Polk, ~~who was~~ known as "Young Hickory," served in Congress for fourteen years, and he was elected governor of ~~the state of~~ Tennessee in 1839. ~~The reason~~ Polk was called "Young Hickory" ~~was~~ because he was a ~~personal~~ friend and ~~really~~ an admirer of President Andrew Jackson, ~~who was~~ called "Old Hickory." Whether ~~or not~~ Polk appreciated his nickname is not known.

In the 1844 presidential election, Polk, ~~who was~~ the Democratic candidate, defeated Henry Clay, ~~who was~~ the Whig candidate. Polk expanded ~~and enlarged~~ the territory of the United States more than any other president except Jefferson. ~~The reason the~~ expansion occurred ~~was~~ because of three events: (1) annexation of Texas, (2) settlement of the Oregon Territory dispute with Great Britain, and (3) the Mexican War, resulting in the United States gaining the territory of what is now ~~the states of~~ Arizona, New Mexico, Utah, Colorado, Nevada, California, and part of Wyoming.

Although hardworking and capable throughout his life, Polk was often sick ~~in health,~~ and he decided not to run for reelection in 1848. Three months after leaving office, Polk died at fifty-three ~~years in age~~.

(2) A Special Time, page 194

Your instructor will check your work.

CHAPTER TWELVE: Clarity—2, pages 197–218

Exercise 1, page 207

1. Most senators <u>approved</u> of the President's nominee for the Supreme Court.
2. Charges against the suspect were dropped <u>because</u> of insufficient evidence.
3. The city manager <u>resigned</u> at yesterday's council meeting.

4. The new regulations <u>begin</u> next month.
5. <u>When</u> you go to England, be sure to visit Oxford University.
6. Coach Mannis <u>decided</u> to start Del Greco at quarterback.
7. After her work day <u>ended</u>, Felicia went shopping at the mall.
8. The happy couple will <u>marry</u> in June.
9. My brother plans to save money for college <u>while</u> he's in the navy.
10. The job is yours, <u>if</u> you're still interested.
11. Exams are on everybody's mind when the semester <u>ends</u>.
12. <u>If</u> you hear from Gene, give him my congratulations.
13. Her driving license was suspended <u>because</u> of her previous offenses.
14. During Homecoming Weekend, I was happy to <u>meet</u> my boyfriend's parents.
15. <u>If</u> Harry can't work tonight, can you?

Exercise 2, page 207

1. In the <u>following</u> weeks, the dictator <u>tried</u> to <u>stop (or end)</u> the <u>people's</u> unrest.
2. Unless you can suggest a <u>possible</u> alternative, we will have to <u>use</u> our reserve funds.
3. The engineers are <u>meeting</u> with the construction crew to discuss the <u>dimensions</u> of the project.
4. After <u>ranking</u> his goals, Kirk developed <u>original</u> strategies for <u>completing</u> them.
5. <u>Now</u>, we should <u>find out (or determine)</u> if it's <u>possible</u> to <u>begin (or start)</u> such changes.
6. After the meal <u>ended</u>, Jane's <u>husband showed</u> slides of British Columbia.
7. It is <u>possible</u> seasoning would <u>improve</u> the chowder.
8. After what had <u>occurred (or happened)</u>, it was obvious we had to establish <u>limits</u> to <u>keep</u> control.
9. The young man may be indicted for perjury because his <u>answers (or responses)</u> to the judge's <u>questions</u> contained <u>lies</u>.
10. Although his job requires him to move frequently, Mickey <u>tries</u> to make friends wherever his <u>home</u> happens to be.
11. Judy was <u>helpful</u> in explaining the <u>choices</u> I had.
12. Be sure to <u>examine</u> the contract because its terms would <u>affect</u> not only you but also the <u>people</u> you represent.
13. Are you <u>aware</u> that <u>instead</u> overtime pay workers would get additional vacation time?
14. We hope you will <u>use</u> your influence to have this clause changed before negotiations are <u>completed (or ended)</u>.
15. <u>Now</u>, some workers would have difficulty <u>obeying</u> your orders.

Exercise 3, page 208

A.

1. The <u>hustle and bustle</u> of New York City is <u>a rude awakening</u> to most first-time visitors.

2. <u>In this day and age</u>, it's easy to become <u>green with envy</u> because of the salaries professional athletes make.

3. Due to the members' <u>untiring efforts</u>, the goal was <u>slowly but surely</u> reached.

4. Sheila fell for his excuse <u>hook, line, and sinker</u> because she thought he looked <u>as innocent as a newborn babe</u>.

5. <u>To make a long story short</u>, she became <u>as pale as a ghost</u> when she found out he had been lying.

6. Our business is <u>in full swing</u>, and <u>in a nutshell</u>, we are confident we are <u>on the cutting edge</u> of success.

7. My old dog, <u>who was the apple of my eye</u>, is gone but not forgotten.

8. <u>It goes without saying</u> that if you keep <u>doing your own thing</u>, you are going to have to <u>face the music</u> one of these days.

9. Bucky, who hopes to <u>follow in the footsteps</u> of his two older brothers, is waiting with <u>breathless anticipation</u> to see if he's been accepted at the state university; if so, he'll be <u>as happy as a lark</u>.

10. Although she knows it's <u>easier said than done</u>, Marla has <u>a burning desire</u> to hike the entire length of the Appalachian Trail.

B. (Answers will vary; typical answers are presented.)

1. <u>Remember</u>, good health remains our most important possession.

2. Shelby discovered making straight A's was <u>more difficult than she thought it would be</u>.

3. Although there was a twinkle in her eyes, Amanda <u>maintained an angelic expression</u>.

4. Someone will have to <u>take charge</u> if this project is to be completed.

5. Dexter jumped at the opportunity, believing <u>the risk was worth taking</u>.

Exercise 4, page 210

(Answers will vary; typical answers are presented.)

1. Last Friday, the sunset bathed the valley in striking shades of orange and blue.

2. Mickey's 1991 Oldsmobile has power brakes, power steering, air conditioning, and cruise control.

3. My friend Wayne is considerate, patient, and cheerful.

4. Hometown fans were fighting in the stands, throwing garbage on the ice, and screaming obscenities at the referees.

5. President Franklin Roosevelt reduced unemployment, improved the economy, and inspired the American people.

6. Last Friday evening, Ginny cooked hotdogs stuffed with pineapple chunks and ears of corn coated with maple syrup on a charcoal grill.

7. Dr. Corson's next patient, Mr. Nordyke, complained of pain in his knees, stiffness in his back, and ringing in his ears.
8. When I attended my high school reunion last June, I became nervous and tongue-tied when I talked to my ex-steady, overjoyed when two of my old buddies arrived, and nostalgic when I chatted with Mr. Larson, my former basketball coach.
9. My job as a chef at the Dazzling Grill gives me few opportunities to relax because when I'm not filling orders I'm either busy peeling vegetables, baking desserts, or cleaning the grill.
10. Don is our school's most versatile athlete as he's all-conference in football, undefeated in wrestling, and the leading hitter on the baseball team.

Exercise 5, page 211

(Answers will vary; typical answers are presented.)
1. Human history has always reflected a belief in supernatural powers.
2. Some colleges do not allow first-year students to have cars on campus.
3. Roscoe's wife is a lawyer.
4. Mr. Scrontas, a police officer, and Mrs. Scrontas, a flight attendant, are chairpersons of the planning committee.
5. Men and women over twenty-one are eligible to take the firefighter's test.
6. Any senior interested in interviewing for sales positions should make an appointment with one of the secretaries at the Career Center.
7. Members of our senior class had the time of their lives during Skip Days.
8. Giselle, who works as a camera operator at the campus television station, is studying to be a meteorologist.
9. A student in his or her first semester is ineligible to be chairperson of the committee.
10. This section of the city was settled by the Irish, and their descendants are among the leading citizens of the community, including a prominent judge.

Review Exercise, page 213

Your instructor will check your answers.

C. APPLYING THE FINISHING TOUCH, CHAPTER TWELVE

(1) Proofreading:
Zachary Taylor: Twelfth President, 1849–1850, page 215

*(An * indicates a line containing a correction; corrections can vary, so check with your instructor if you have any questions.)*

Zachary Taylor was the seventh president born in Virginia. However, a few months after his birth in 1784, Taylor and his family moved to Kentucky where he lived until entering the army.

*   Taylor became an excellent officer and <u>was promoted</u> throughout his
* forty years in the army. <u>Unruffled</u> in battle, Taylor participated in the War of 1812, Indian disputes, and the Mexican War (1848–1850). He was called
* "Old Rough and Ready" <u>because</u> he was tough, fearless, and down-to-earth.
*   A few years after entering the army, Taylor <u>met</u> Margaret Smith, and
* they were <u>married</u> in 1810. Although the <u>Taylors</u> were stationed at numerous army bases throughout their marriage, they always considered Louisiana
* their <u>home</u>.

During the Mexican War, Taylor became a national hero after leading his 5,000 troops to a stunning victory over Santa Anna's 20,000 soldiers.
* <u>Because</u> he was so popular, the Whigs nominated Taylor for president in
* 1848. Although <u>lies</u> about his drinking <u>were</u> widely spread, Taylor won the close election. As president, Taylor faced a nation divided over whether slavery should be extended into the territories acquired from Mexico. Taylor, although a slaveowner, strongly opposed the spread of slavery. After some senators indicated the South might secede from the Union over this issue,
* Taylor made it <u>plain</u> he would forcefully deal with any such attempt.

On July 4, 1850, at the laying of the cornerstone of the Washington
* Monument, Taylor became seriously <u>ill</u> from indigestion; he <u>died</u> a few days
* later. Everybody in the nation was shocked when <u>he or she</u> heard the news. Taylor, president for only sixteen months, became the second Chief
* Executive to <u>die</u> in office.

(2) Laptops, page 217

Your instructor will check your work.

CHAPTER THIRTEEN: Spelling—Plurals, pages 219–232

Exercise 1, page 223

1. branches
2. pictures
3. valleys
4. lashes
5. operations
6. buzzes
7. armies
8. porches
9. turkeys
10. rivers
11. Wednesdays
12. boxes
13. misses
14. universities
15. wishes
16. trucks
17. apologies
18. mixes
19. alleys
20. allies
21. ditches
22. chairs
23. companies
24. hushes
25. buildings

Exercise 2, page 224

1. echoes
2. leaves
3. shelves
4. radios
5. chiefs
6. solos
7. beliefs
8. embargoes
9. heroes
10. wolves
11. wives
12. vetoes
13. reefs
14. sopranos
15. volcanoes
16. buffaloes
17. thieves
18. banjos
19. calves
20. studios
21. lives
22. halves
23. potatoes
24. cellos
25. pianos

Exercise 3, page 225

1. sons-in-law
2. criteria
3. geese
4. diagnoses
5. deer
6. crises
7. children
8. women
9. sisters-in-law
10. teeth
11. analyses
12. maids of honor
13. data
14. neuroses
15. attorneys-at-law
16. feet
17. parentheses
18. moose
19. oxen
20. salmon
21. psychoses
22. mice
23. theses
24. sheep
25. media

Review Exercise, page 226

Your instructor will check your answers.

C. APPLYING THE FINISHING TOUCH, CHAPTER THIRTEEN

(1) Proofreading:
Christa McAuliffe, page 229

(Underlined words are corrections of misspellings.)

After President Reagan announced in 1984 that a teacher would be chosen as the first private citizen to travel in space, over 11,000 teachers submitted their names for consideration. Through the following months, NASA officials sifted through piles of data searching for the one teacher who met all of the criteria. Finally, on July 19, 1985, NASA officials announced that Christa McAuliffe, a social studies teacher at Concord High School, Concord, New Hampshire, was their choice.

Christa Corrigan McAuliffe was born in Boston, Massachusetts, in 1948 and raised in nearby Framingham. During her childhood, she joined the Girl Scouts and took dance, voice, and piano lessons. In high school, Christa made the National Honor Society and participated in numerous activities, including basketball, orchestra, and drama. In addition, she loved playing the guitar, piano, and singing solos.

After graduating from high school, Christa attended the state college in Framingham where she majored in American history and secondary education. Despite taking a full load of courses, working nights as a clerk at a trucking firm, and babysitting, Christa found time to captain the debate team, sing in the glee club, and perform in dramas. Christa always lived her philosophy, "To get the most out of life as possible."

In 1970, Christa married Steve McAuliffe, and they moved to Washington, D.C., where Steve attended law school and Christa began her teaching career. In 1978, they moved to Concord, New Hampshire.

As a teacher, Christa was enthusiastic, creative, and committed to her students. As a person, she was energetic, friendly, and devoted to her family, which included her husband and two children.

After undergoing months of training, Christa entered the *Challenger* spacecraft on the morning of January 28, 1986. Seventy-three seconds into the flight, the *Challenger* exploded, killing Christa and her six crew mates. A nation was plunged into mourning.

(2) Millard Fillmore: Thirteenth President, 1850–1853, page 231

Your instructor will check your work.

CHAPTER FOURTEEN: Spelling—Basic Guidelines, pages 233–251

Exercise 1, page 239

1. disapprove	10. preview	19. inconvenient
2. infrequent	11. inadequate	20. mailbox
3. windshield	12. bookkeeper	21. roommate
4. reexamine	13. earring	22. reenter
5. unconscious	14. disappear	23. unpleasant
6. extraordinary	15. nevertheless	24. preeminent
7. disagree	16. fingernail	25. newsstand
8. withhold	17. misuse	
9. misspell	18. knickknack	

Exercise 2, page 240

1. deceive	10. vein	19. achieve
2. mischief	11. shriek	20. conceit
3. grief	12. receipt	21. priest
4. weight	13. sleigh	22. quiet
5. believe	14. neighbor	23. cashier
6. siege	15. brief	24. veil
7. friend	16. receive	25. yield
8. reign	17. niece	
9. field	18. relief	

Exercise 3, page 241

1. hopeful	10. promised	19. excitable
2. examining	11. noticed	20. noiseless
3. careless	12. cuter	21. achievement
4. immediately	13. management	22. sincerity
5. advancement	14. staring	23. peaceful
6. completing	15. having	24. lonely
7. scraped	16. taping	25. removable
8. lovely	17. perspiring	
9. famous	18. timely	

Exercise 4, page 242

1. winning
2. bumped
3. omitted
4. shipped
5. containing
6. regretted
7. traveled
8. benefited
9. wrapped
10. preferred
11. detoured
12. committed
13. developing
14. padded
15. inferred
16. tearing
17. stepping
18. sanding
19. occurred
20. marked
21. reading
22. submitting
23. flooding
24. forgetting
25. regarded

Exercise 5, page 243

1. definite
2. explanation
3. finally
4. doctor
5. committee
6. accommodate
7. absence
8. exercise
9. discipline
10. guarantee
11. cemetery
12. embarrass
13. across
14. eligible
15. a lot
16. forty
17. cousin
18. amateur
19. always
20. description
21. calendar
22. among
23. familiar
24. all right
25. criticize

Exercise 6, page 244

1. professor
2. pronunciation
3. parallel
4. quantity
5. necessary
6. recommend
7. prejudices
8. ridiculous
9. prominent
10. marriage
11. pleasant
12. probably
13. questionnaire
14. license
15. prevalent
16. separate
17. occasion
18. psychology
19. similar
20. nickel
21. succeed
22. peculiar
23. realize
24. restaurant
25. privilege

Review Exercise, page 246

Your instructor will check your answers.